The publisher and the University of California Press
Foundation gratefully acknowledge the generous support of the
Joan Palevsky Imprint in Classical Literature.

Poet, Mystic, Widow, Wife

Poet, Mystic, Widow, Wife

THE EXTRAORDINARY LIVES OF
MEDIEVAL WOMEN

Hetta Howes

UNIVERSITY OF CALIFORNIA PRESS

University of California Press
Oakland, California

© 2025 by Hetta Howes

North American edition published by University of California Press, 2025.

UK edition published by Bloomsbury Publishing Plc, 2024.

Cataloging-in-Publication data is on file at the Library of Congress

ISBN 978-0-520-39658-6 (cloth : alk. paper)
ISBN 978-0-520-39659-3 (ebook)

Manufactured in the United States of America

33 32 31 30 29 28 27 26 25 24
10 9 8 7 6 5 4 3 2 1

For Alana. You are extraordinary.

CONTENTS

Plates follow page 70

Introduction

'a woman lewed, febille, and freylle'*

JULIAN OF NORWICH, *Revelations of Divine Love*

'I am told very bad things about you. I hear it said that you are a very wicked woman.'[1]

The year is 1417, and Margery is in her mid-forties. She came to York to visit the gothic marble shrine of St William, but has caused a stir, as she often did, by travelling without her husband. During the reign of King Edward I, just a hundred years prior to Margery's visit, York had effectively been the capital of England. Wealthy, cosmopolitan and home to a thriving textile trade, it is still a powerhouse city—although, owing to its rising population, it is also crowded, noisy and a bit smelly, or, as one fifteenth-century tourist describes its odour, 'horrible and pernicious'.[2] But even among the hordes of pilgrims and jobseekers flocking to its ancient city walls, Margery stands out.

At this point in her life Margery has already travelled the world, from Jerusalem to Rome—covering over two thousand miles by ship, by donkey and on foot. Although she was denied an education, as many women were, we know her as the author of the first autobiography in the English language.

Margery's knowledge and independence make people suspicious of her. But in York a far more severe accusation is levelled at her—heresy. She is accused of preaching, an act strictly forbidden for women by the medieval Church, and arrested. As she is led to the chapter house for her trial, people come out on to the street to jeer at her, calling her names and saying that she

---

* 'a woman uneducated, feeble and frail'

1

should be put to death. This threat is very real. If the archbishop finds her guilty, she will be burned at the stake.

Margery is in danger, and frightened. She puts her hands under her clothes so no one can see them trembling. And yet, despite the threat, when the archbishop of York calls her a 'wicked woman', she defends herself.

'Sir, I also hear it said that *you* are a wicked man. And if you are as wicked as people say, you will never get to heaven, unless you amend while you are here.'

During the rigorous interrogation that follows, she holds her own. 'I do not go into any pulpit,' she declares. 'I use only conversation and good words, and that I will do while I live.'

Try as he may, the archbishop is unable to wrong-foot her. Eventually, he gives a local man five shillings to escort her out of the city. Uneducated and illiterate, Margery has locked horns with one of the most powerful men in medieval England.

And won.

. . .

This scene from the life of Margery Kempe sheds lights on the expectations and obstacles that medieval women faced. There were some women, like Margery, who could hold their own in the face of male authority, and who found ways to forge their own paths within a patriarchal society. But a woman's place was clearly marked, and those who didn't fit the mould, or who chose to speak out against it, risked putting themselves in real danger.

In this book, we'll journey back to the Middle Ages via the lives of Marie de France, Julian of Norwich, Christine de Pizan and Margery Kempe, four very different women who defied the expectations of their time and wrote back against the misogyny they experienced. We'll compare their own writing with a variety of different sources to help imagine what their lives were like. Medical treatises, encyclopedias, religious treatises, sermons, guidebooks and conduct literature, court records, wills, letters, biographies, historical chronicles, poetry, legend and folklore—all offer a window into their world. From everyday sexism to the pressure society exerts on women to settle down and have children, they reveal how many of the struggles women encounter today are surprisingly analogous to the challenges that medieval women faced—and overcame

We don't need to look far to see how women were viewed. One of the most popular books of medieval natural philosophy, dating to the later thirteenth or early fourteenth century, was *De secretis mulierum*, or '*Women's Secrets*'. It was attributed to Albertus Magnus, an intellectual giant of the thirteenth century who wrote about theology and philosophy as well as science, but is more likely to have been written by one of his disciples. The text was hugely popular—over 80 manuscript versions of it survive, which is a staggering figure for any one text from a period in which copies had to be handwritten. According to this book, a woman was nothing more than 'a failed man' with a 'defective nature'.[3]

At the time when Albertus was writing, Aristotle was still the order of the day in medical knowledge, and his model for understanding is at the heart of much misogynistic rhetoric of this kind. According to the Ancient Greek philosopher, during incubation nature intends to create the perfect animal, which is (naturally) male. But adverse reproductive conditions can result in an unfortunate second-best: girls. In Aristotle's model, when babies are born female it is because they haven't received enough heat during gestation. Women are biologically determined to be wet, cold and weak—whereas men, by contrast, are considered hot, dry and strong. While Aristotle begrudgingly acknowledges that women are necessary for the continuation of humanity, he thinks of them as deficient, half-formed creatures.[4]

As part of this medical interpretation of gender, women were also believed by many to be sex-mad, unable to restrain themselves and practically incapable of remaining faithful to any one partner. Hardwired to seek from men the heat and completion they lacked in their own physiology, they were described as pursuing men with insatiable and frightening desire. And because they were too cold to process their excess moisture, their bodily fluids were believed to be runnier and more likely to escape from them. In the presence of menstrual blood, according to famous encyclopedist Isidore of Seville, crops would wither and plants would die.[5] An old wives' tale even warned that blood might leak through a woman's eyeballs, enabling her to curse those around her with an 'evil eye'.

It wasn't just menstruation. Women were seen as incontinent in other ways too. '*Women's Secrets*' goes on to inform us that women cry more often than men: 'Weeping is indicative of women's ignorance, for dampness coarsens the women's brains and hinders their ability to learn; it points to their excessive wickedness, for it is by way of abundant tears that evil humours leave the body through the eyes.'[6] They also speak too often and move around too much. A popular proverb from the Bible equates women who are 'talkative and wandering' with predatory harlots—'now [she is] abroad', it warns, 'now in the streets, now lying in wait near the corners.'[7] And when Thomas Nesfeld of York attacked and seriously injured his wife, he successfully argued in court that his violence was justified because she had refused to obey his command not to leave the house.[8] A good woman stayed at home, and kept her mouth shut.

Such misogynistic attitudes were built into medical understanding of women's bodies and reinforced by the Church, one of the most powerful institutions in medieval Europe. According to the Bible, Eve caused the 'Fall of Man' when she disobeyed God and was thrown out of the Garden of Eden with Adam, thus exiling all mankind from paradise. The theologian Tertullian never missed an opportunity to remind women that they still bear Eve's sin: 'Woman, you are the gate to hell.'[9] Many medieval sermons expand on this theme, calling women unstable, inconstant, vain, disobedient to their husbands and prone to sexual transgression—whether that be infidelity or excessive desire.

These indictments against women are enough to make even an armchair time traveller wary of returning to the Middle Ages. What is less clear is how these toxic attitudes affected the daily lives of medieval women. Much of the existing literature from the Middle Ages suggests that women were held to impossible standards. When they fell short, authors were quick to label them whores. But although feminism is an anachronistic term which we can't strictly apply to the Middle Ages, there were women who managed to navigate medieval misogyny and make their own way. Women who established careers, negotiated more autonomy in their marriages or who refused to become tied down altogether. Women who became leaders, created networks and battled against the rhetoric that framed them as sinful and deficient.

This book will uncover the lives of four such women—a poet (Marie de France), a mystic (Julian of Norwich), a widow (Christine de Pizan) and a 'no good' wife (Margery Kempe).[10] All four of them were writers, a rare profession for women at the time, and this presents us with a unique opportunity. By reading their words and listening to their voices, we can start to piece together a picture of what life was like for medieval women—especially the challenges they faced, as well as how they managed to overcome them. Crucially, however, we can also learn from them. Over the years these women may have been overlooked or even forgotten, but they still have an astonishing amount to teach us—in their own words—about love, marriage, motherhood, friendship, earning a living and even death.

The enigmatic poet Marie de France (*fl.* 1160–1215) first appears in an Anglo-Norman collection of short poems, known as *lais*, written in octosyllabic couplets and probably set to music to be performed in court.[11] The author, who tells tales of knights, ladies and love affairs, identifies herself simply as 'Marie'. Her *lais* are retellings of stories she would have heard read aloud, and in her retellings she makes a point of foregrounding the female characters. Instead of damsels in distress waiting to be rescued, Marie's women are central protagonists who drive the plot forward, demonstrating bravery and ingenuity. Sometime later—we're not sure of the exact date—her name appears again attached to a translation of Aesop's fables, this time accompanied by 'de France' (of/from France), and it appears for a third and final time in 1190, as the author of a religious tale in which an Irish knight journeys to the underworld.[12] The style of these three texts, together with the fact that they are all attributed to a 'Marie' at a time when authors rarely advertised themselves, means it's reasonable to suggest that Marie de France was responsible for all three.

A first name, a place of origin and three texts, none of which is autobiographical—other than that, we know little about Marie. But it's enough. The first clue as to who Marie may have been is the language in which she wrote. Anglo-Norman came over to England after the Norman Conquest in 1066 and so, although she was originally 'de France', this linguistic choice indicates that she may have spent time in England. The second clue is that her *lais* are dedicated to a 'noble reis' (noble king) which historians agree is most likely Henry II, king of England from 1154 to 1189.[13] This places Marie firmly within court culture during the twelfth-century renaissance, a time during which elite men and women in monasteries, convents and courts in England and France produced an astonishing amount of literary works. Henry II's mother, the empress Matilda, was a royal patron of the arts, and his French wife, Eleanor of Aquitaine, is credited with helping to disseminate the highly popular discourse of 'courtly love', a subject that Marie de France takes up in her *lais*. Eleanor brought her French sophistication to the English court, making it a place of song and creativity—as well as envy and competition— the perfect arena for an ambitious and industrious writer like Marie. The genre of her poetry, her repeated references to court life and her dedication to a king all imply that she spent time rubbing shoulders with the great and the good. Clearly, Marie was a woman with influence.

The final clue her writing gives us regards her education, which is extremely impressive for a woman living in the twelfth century. There were lots of women who couldn't read or write, and women almost always received less schooling than their male counterparts. But the higher up the social ladder you got, the more likely you were to receive something. Noblewomen and nuns were the best educated; they were usually literate and had far more access to books than the average woman. Young gentlewomen would probably have learned enough Latin to read their prayer books and enough instruction in the vernacular (Anglo-Norman or, by the fourteenth century, English) to run their household, manage business affairs and read for pleasure. Their education was less comprehensive and more informal than that of their male siblings, but girls from less wealthy families did sometimes benefit from lessons offered by local nunneries, nurses, chaplains, priests, local charitable institutions or even by mothers.

The breadth of Marie's knowledge, however, is remarkable—so much so that some historians believe that, even if she began her life as a French noblewoman, she must have also spent time in a nunnery. Whoever she was, and whether she was composing at court or from a convent, Marie's stories of werewolves, fairy queens, jealous husbands and adulterous affairs are just as entertaining today as they were in the Middle Ages.

The unassuming mystic Julian of Norwich (c.1343–after 1416) led a very different life from the one we can imagine for Marie de France. Rather than entertaining the courts with poetry, she spent her days enclosed within four walls. Her home was an anchoritic 'cell', a small building attached to a church, with three windows into the outside world—one looking onto the altar of the church, one through which her servant could cater to her needs, and one that looked onto the street. Much of Julian's history has been lost, but we know that she was installed as an anchoress at the church of St Julian's, Norwich, by 1393, and that she was still there 20 years later.

Anchoritism was a religious vocation which became surprisingly popular, especially among women, during the later Middle Ages; two hundred anchoresses are recorded in England between the thirteenth century and the fifteenth. Not just anyone could become an anchoress. An aspirational woman had to petition the Church in writing for one of the coveted spots and pay them enough maintenance money (essentially a dowry) to last her lifetime. If a woman's application was accepted, a priest would read the last rites over her and she would then be sealed—sometimes figuratively, sometimes quite literally, with bricks—into her new home. From this moment on, an anchoress was dead to this world and turned to the next, dedicating her entire existence to God via a punishing regime of fasting, prayer and contemplation. However grim this may sound to us, the status an anchoress held during her internment, and the spiritual rewards she was likely to reap in heaven, made such an existence worth it—at least for some.

Julian became an anchoress later in life. When she was just 30 years old, she caught a terrible sickness—possibly even the plague—and, while suffering in her sickbed, she received a series of visions from God, which she felt compelled to write down. *Revelations of Divine Love* is the earliest work in the English language that we know for certain was authored by a woman. Although Julian makes an apology for being 'a woman lewed [uneducated], febille [feeble] and freylle [frail]', it's clear from her *Revelations* that she was, in fact, highly educated and very intelligent.[14] She was also ahead of her time. Where so many of her contemporaries focused on God's anger, the torments of hell and the shame of sin, she was revolutionarily comforting, concentrating instead on God's love and the rewards of heaven. Her phrase '[a]ll shall be well and all shall be well and all manner of thing shall be well' is still beloved not only by twenty-first-century Christians but also by secular society, as a reminder that things will generally turn out for the best.[15]

Julian's life demonstrates that there were women who refused to be tied down by marriage and motherhood. By choosing a different path, she was able to wield influence and provide spiritual guidance in a world where the official leaders of the Church were exclusively men.

Thanks largely to their own writings, we know far more about the widow Christine de Pizan (1364–c.1430) and the wife Margery Kempe (c.1373–after 1438) than we do about Marie and Julian. Both women, quite remarkable in different ways, achieved far more than just marital status.

Born in the cosmopolitan city of Venice, Christine was from an influential family and academically inclined. Her father, the scholar Thomas de Pizan, moved the family to Paris when she was just four years old. He had been appointed court astrologer to King Charles V, a prestigious position that involved not only the study of the stars but also the meticulous translation and interpretation of ancient texts. Thomas used these arts to advise the king on anything and everything, from healthcare to political alliances, and he quickly became a firm favourite of the royal family. Christine therefore grew up, surrounded by luxury, in the palace—which, at the time, was the Louvre, a majestic castle on the banks of the Seine. She was much sought after as a bride, but was happy to marry Étienne du Castel, her father's choice, when she was 15. Their marriage was a happy one, but it lasted only 11 years. When Étienne caught the plague and died, Christine was heartbroken and astonished at how quickly her finances started to dwindle. Rather than securing another wealthy husband, she wanted to make a name for herself—and so she began to write.

Christine was the definition of a hustler. She became one of the most prolific and well-respected writers of her lifetime, with a career that spanned almost four decades and included 30 major works, as well as an array of shorter poems. A veritable entrepreneur, Christine became an expert in book production too, taking charge of the manufacture of many of her own manuscripts. Her reputation preceded her, and she attracted patronage from various high-profile members of the nobility, including Philip, duke of Burgundy (the influential brother of Charles V), and Isabeau of Bavaria, the queen of France, herself.

Her most famous work, *The Book of the City of Ladies* (*c*.1405) is the first proto-feminist tract to come out of Europe.[16] In it, Christine systematically works through the accusations levelled against women in literature—that they are gateways to hell (Tertullian) or faulty and defective (Albertus Magnus)—and uses examples of historical and contemporary women to counter them, proving them to be nothing but lies. Christine didn't believe in the equality of the sexes—that would have been too far, even for a progressive noblewoman. But her *City of Ladies* shows us that women weren't just passive recipients of sexist ideology. They were actively pushing back against it, in their own words.

According to one online review of a recent edition of *The Book of Margery Kempe*, '[t]he only bad thing about the book was Margery. If I had travelled with her, I probably would have thrown her overboard.' Throughout her life, Margery always was quick to find enemies (although she was equally adept at making friends in high places). Her account of her life dates to the fifteenth century and is the first extant autobiography written in English. Ever since her *Book*'s accidental rediscovery in 1934, Margery has become one of the most divisive figures in medieval history. Thanks to fits of loud and disruptive crying, which she claimed were sent from heaven, and her holier-than-thou attitude, many have deemed Margery infuriating, deceitful or even mad. Others (like myself) have admired her, finding her resistance to prescribed roles a breath of fresh air.

Margery was born in East Anglia around 1373. She was not from a noble family but part of the emerging, and increasingly wealthy, middle class. Her father was well heeled and well respected. He was mayor five times for Bishop's Lynn (now King's Lynn), and an MP, representing the harbour town's population of around 6,000 people—an impressive number at the time. Sending out wool and bringing in herring, timber, iron and wax, Bishop's Lynn was such a significant hub for trade that King John awarded the town its own charter in 1204, granting it the powers of self-governance in recognition of its contribution to the economy. Margery would therefore have grown up well known in her town and with a sense of importance. She tells us that she was used to finery, and that she wanted to be the envy of her neighbours. She was also quick to remind her husband, John—they tied the knot when she was 20—that she had married beneath her. Still, their relationship seemed to be a happy one (at first), and Margery was knocked up at least 14 times. This didn't stop her setting up enterprises in brewing and milling. There is a pervading belief that women were all housewives in the Middle Ages and didn't work at all. But, in fact, while the more elite, well-paid industries were restricted to men, women could and did pursue professional work, especially after the Black Death created a labour shortage in the fourteenth century. Women were frequently active partners in family businesses, helping to run small farms, urban workshops or even great estates; there were female apprentices learning trades, and it wouldn't have been unusual for an artisan to train their daughter or their wife. Perhaps to give the impression that she was putting her wifely duties first, Margery refers to her businesses as 'a newe huswyfre', but it's clear that her aim was to make money.[17]

After the birth of her first child, however, something happened to Margery. She experienced a crisis—an illness that sounds remarkably like post-natal depression—which sparked a newfound religious devotion accompanied by visions of God, much like those of Julian of Norwich. As a result, Margery decided to do everything in her power to live more spiritually, including trying to negotiate a vow of chastity with her frustrated husband. Rather than offering herself to a convent, or enclosing herself in an anchorhold, Margery insisted on living her newly devotional life out in the world, giving in to her wanderlust and travelling to major holy sites across the known world. She drew attention to herself by wearing white (a colour usually reserved for virgins), told people off for swearing wherever she went and refused to talk about anything other than God. One weary monk in Canterbury, sick of her disruptive outbursts, told her that he wished she were enclosed in a house of stone. But Margery actively resisted living a life behind closed doors, and teaches us to do the same, to follow the path that feels right, however uncomfortable it might make those in power.

Margery, unlike Marie, Julian and Christine, was not well educated—she could neither read nor write and had to dictate her *Book* to two different priests. However, her extensive knowledge of the Bible and of the writings of other holy women across Europe (many of whom she tried to emulate), shows that she had absorbed an impressive amount of spiritual information during her lifetime through listening to sermons, having discussions with learned clergy and asking for devotional works be read aloud to her. This knowledge sometimes got Margery into (and then out of) serious trouble, as did her refusal to tread the prescribed routes outlined for her. Through her, we will come to discover how women attempted to 'have it all' in the medieval period.

· · ·

I have been fascinated by the writings of medieval women ever since I first came across them at university, more than 15 years ago. I have read the poetry of Marie and Christine, and the visions of Julian and Margery, countless times. Their compositions never fail to delight and astonish me (and, in the case of Margery, to make me laugh). I have spent all my working life teaching their lives and their words, winning students round to the literature of a time that can feel, at least at first, distant and strange. But in the past two years I have felt closer to these women than ever. When I first started working on this book, I was planning a wedding. And, while writing the first chapter on medieval childbirth, I discovered I was pregnant. In the time since, I have swung between gratitude at the progress we have made—pain medication during labour! maternity leave! a husband who does night feeds!—and frustration at how little has changed. In my first perinatal appointment, I asked my (male) GP what to expect. 'I'm afraid I don't usually deal with women's stuff,' he replied, and then suggested I try asking the female receptionist instead. Finishing a book with a newborn baby has given me renewed respect for working mothers like Margery and Christine and, in my weariest moments, I have understood why a woman like Julian might have shut herself away to get some work done.

It can be challenging—and frustrating—to research the lives of medieval women. Few wrote and, even when they did, it was never in the confessional vein we find today. Marie tells old stories in a new language, but reveals nothing of herself. In a text that she kept secret during her lifetime, Julian removes almost every trace of self. Margery's *Book* was dictated to male scribes who may well have added their own flourishes and interventions. And Christine, overseeing the production of all her manuscripts, was creating a brand. She only ever tells us what she wanted us to know. Of the four women this book follows, only two (Christine and Margery) venture into autobiography, and there are still many gaps to fill between their lines. We can flesh out the picture with other sources, from court records to religious iconography and folklore, but there are some things we'll just never know.

However, there is still much that these four women can tell us—and teach us—if we take the time to listen. My expertise is in literature, and so I have put the writing and the voices of Marie, Julian, Christine and Margery front and centre of *Poet, Mystic, Widow, Wife*. By reading their words alongside those of other writers of the time, this book hopes to challenge what we think we know about medieval women. Their society may have been a restrictive one, and the obstacles they faced must have sometimes been insurmountable. But their words show us that there were women who fell in love, had children, worked, travelled, made enemies and relied on friends—all while making history. Their world may have looked very different, but these extraordinary women were, in many ways, just like us.

ONE

Knocked Up

> 'and than, what for labowr sche had in chyldyng and for seke-
> nesse goyng beforn, sche dyspered of hyr lyfe, wenyng sche mygth
> not levyn'*
>
> **MARGERY KEMPE**, *The Book of Margery Kempe*

At just 20 years old, Margery Kempe lay on a bed in indescribable agony surrounded by women from her family. She was in the throes of an extremely challenging birth, and the medieval birthing room was no place for men. Since conceiving her first child, shortly after getting married, Margery had suffered relentless waves of fever and sickness. Now, these symptoms were all coming to a head. She was in so much pain she wondered if she would survive it.

After several gruelling hours, each of which stretched out for an eternity, Margery's child was delivered safe and well. But her torment was far from over. For half a year, eight weeks and odd days afterwards, Margery remained traumatized by the birth, plagued by visions of demons, their mouths open and full of vicious flames, ready to swallow her up. They grabbed at her night and day without relief. In her agony, Margery threatened and attacked her family, her friends, herself. She tore at her skin so viciously that her husband was forced to restrain her. She bit herself on the hand so savagely that she would bear the scar for the rest of her life. Her suffering was so great, Margery tells us, that it drove her 'out of her mind'.[1]

Margery was one of the first women in England to describe her experience of childbirth. It is, perhaps more remarkably, the story with which she opens her autobiography, even though for the rest of her *Book* she is much more interested in her religious endeavours, rather than day-to-day family life. It might be that Margery saw resonances between the birth of her first child and the lives of key figures in the Christian story: the Virgin Mary (a mother) and Jesus Christ, whose pains during the Crucifixion were comparable with the labours of childbirth. It was the first of 14 such labours that she would

---

* 'and then, because of the difficulty of her labour and the sickness she had experienced during her pregnancy, she feared for her life, believing she might not live'

endure over the course of her life. As far as we can tell, none of the subsequent births was quite so difficult, but this number is still high, especially bearing in the mind the stress and physical demands that pregnancy can put on the female body, not to mention what we know about childbirth in the Middle Ages. No painkillers, save natural ones—St John's Wort, an amulet, alcohol—would have been available to a woman like Margery, and there was no real knowledge of mental illness or of conditions such as post-natal psychosis, to help her cope with the trauma that continued after her baby had been delivered.

It's hard to know how representative Margery's experience was, as evidence surrounding medieval childbirth remains scarce. Births were not regularly or systematically recorded during the Middle Ages, and other factors also contribute to a maddeningly fragmentary picture. Childbirth was an experience so common and ordinary that, unless it heralded the arrival of a long-awaited heir or something went wrong, it didn't invite much discourse. The enclosed, even secretive, nature of the medieval birthing room makes it difficult for us to peer inside, and the fact that this was an experience that affected women rather than men means that it rarely attracted the notice of the predominantly male writers of the time. However, it is possible to uncover a better idea of medieval childbirth if we pay attention to the glimpses offered by legal documents, letters, medical treatises and the rare first-hand accounts by women writers such as Margery Kempe.

We know that it was profoundly dangerous. European women in the 1300s had more children, owing to societal pressures, religion and a lack of robust contraception, and less access to the kind of medical care and understanding of the female body many of us enjoy today. Tragically, they died more often during labour and lost more of their children. But there are some experiences that endure, despite the intervening years. The agony and trauma that can attend a birth; the frustrations and complexities of bringing a child into the world; the devastation of the loss of a child—certainly. But, also, and as importantly, the joy of holding a newborn baby for the first time—and watching them grow up—is something that resonates across time.

.   .   .

According to the Church, having children was one of the primary goals of marriage. But even though it was prescribed by God, childbirth was also associated with women's sin. It was taught that labour would have been painless for women if it weren't for Eve. As punishment for eating the fruit of the Tree of Knowledge, God had bestowed upon both Adam and Eve a unique, gendered punishment. A life of hard, back-breaking work now lay before Adam and his sons, whereas Eve and her daughters would now give birth to their children in pain. The Bible places equal blame on Adam and Eve, and God punishes them both for what is often referred to as the Fall of Man. But it was not unusual for theologians to save their most furious ire for Eve.

Tertullian, an early Christian author whose books were highly influential in the Middle Ages, writes to all women:

> Do you not realize that Eve is you? The curse that God pronounced on your sex weighs still on the world. Guilty, you must bear its hardships. You are the devil's gateway, you desecrated the fatal tree, you first betrayed the law of God, you softened up with your cajoling words the man against whom the devil could not prevail by force.[2]

Eve and therefore all women were thought to act as agents of the devil himself, using their arts of persuasion to do his dirty work. Because blame for the Fall was so often placed on Eve's shoulders, any pain that a woman felt in childbirth was considered well deserved, something she should submit to as a justified punishment from God.

But, according to the same theology, childbirth was also associated with the most perfect of all women: the mother of God, the immaculate Mary, whose son would undo the damage done by Adam and Eve and allow, through his sacrifice, the re-entry of humanity into paradise. Medieval images of her, which still grace churches and Christmas cards today, usually present a pale, serene, chaste-looking woman, dressed in blue, either holding the baby Jesus in her arms or grieving his death at the Crucifixion. In the former, she may be wearing a slight smile as she gazes out at the viewer, or down at her infant son. She may even be breastfeeding. In the latter, she weeps, or reaches towards her dying boy.

While Mary was a popular figurehead throughout much of the medieval era, the fifteenth century witnessed an unprecedented explosion of Marian devotion. She became synonymous with compassion, a kindly and maternal intercessor who could act as a go-between on behalf of anxious Christian souls to a fearsome God. Three-dimensional statues called 'cupboard Madonnas' or 'Shrine Madonnas', which opened up to reveal the Trinity inside her womb, could be found in houses and churches across Europe. John Lydgate, a Benedictine monk and contemporary of Chaucer, wrote countless meditations on the life of the Blessed Virgin. In his poem 'A Ballad in Commendation of Our Lady' he describes her as the 'well and spring' of mercy, the starriest of all stars, a fountain yielding pure, 'clear streams', the 'original beginning of all grace and goodness'.[3] Mary was the perfect mother. But, as if this wasn't miraculous enough, she was also the perfect virgin.

This contradiction wasn't lost on medieval theologians. While they accepted the premise (it was in the Bible, and so the word of God), they fiercely debated the nitty gritty details of the virgin birth. Anselm of Canterbury believed that Mary had been born with the stain of original sin, but that God cleansed her of that taint as soon as Jesus was conceived since it would not have been appropriate for the son of God to be incubated in a vessel of sin.[4] Exempt from the curse of Eve, Mary was able to give birth painlessly. Most theologians agreed with Anselm, but there was some discord over Mary's involvement in the conception of Christ. While some insisted that Mary had been a passive and insensible recipient of this miracle, others suggested that she had, in accordance with Galenic reproductive theory, orgasmed.[5]

To explain this suggestion, we need to take a brief detour into the medieval understanding of conception. There were two leading figures who dominated medieval Western medicine: Galen and Aristotle, both Ancient Greek physicians whose writings made their way to Britain via Arabic translations in the early Middle Ages. Both agreed that, during conception, the woman provided the *materia*—the matter, or flesh—to the embryo, while the man provided something far more important: the embryo's form.[6] This is how '*Women's Secrets*' describes conception:

> When a woman is having sexual intercourse with a man she releases her menses at the same time that the man releases sperm, and both seeds enter the vulva (vagina) simultaneously and are mixed together, and then the woman conceives. [And after these seeds are received in the womb] the womb closes up like a purse on every side, so that nothing can fall out of it.[7]

We should take '*Women's Secrets*' with a pinch of salt. It is so full of misogynistic rhetoric that in later years it was quoted authoritatively at witch trials as evidence of women's nefarious natures, and Christine de Pizan includes it in her list of books that spread libel about women, because 'it states that the female body is inherently flawed and defective in many of its functions'.[8] However, its description of conception is standard for the time. Male sperm provided shape, motion and life to raw matter. The (feminine) *materia* was therefore characterized by its nurturing properties—the *materia* that feeds the developing embryo—but also by its passivity, while the (male) form was marked by its active nature and its strength. Think of the woman as wax, and the man as a wax seal, imprinting and forming her raw *materia*. Women, who carry the baby in their own body for nine months, and who suffer the pains of giving birth, are nothing more than a vessel in this model. Men and their sperm are doing all the hard work.

While Galen and Aristotle agreed on how the embryo was formed, they differed in their explanations of how the embryo originated. According to Aristotle, the woman did not submit any sperm to conception; her only contribution was *materia*. Galen, however, argued that, for a baby to be conceived, women had to submit sperm (or 'menses') as well as *materia*. This sperm might be colder, wetter and scantier than the man's, unable to impress a form all on its own. But it was a contributing factor nonetheless and essential for success, which meant that, in order to conceive, a woman needed to orgasm. Galen's version of events, which by the later Middle Ages had won consensus among natural philosophers, therefore places a real and surprising emphasis on female pleasure. Despite the misogyny that underscored medieval medical understanding of women's health, Galen's theory still gained traction within scientific discourse around conception. And this discussion made its way into discourse about the Virgin Mother, one of the most venerated figures in Christendom.

It's hard to imagine medieval Christian theologians arguing about whether or not God had made her come. But argue they did. Hugh of St Victor, a contemporary of Anselm, argued for the Galenic model in all cases of reproduction, including the conception of Christ.[9] The idea that Mary must have orgasmed for Christ to have been conceived clearly made its way into the mainstream. In pageant plays, which tell the story of Christian history from creation to Judgement Day and were performed all over England as part of religious festivals, the Virgin Mother experiences what sounds suspiciously like orgasmic ecstasy during the Annunciation: 'I cannot tell what joy, what bliss/Now I feel in my body.' And the angel who delivers the news tells the audience that 'Her body shall be so fulfilled with bliss/That she shall soon believe my story.'[10] The Virgin Mother's augmented orgasmic experience served to elevate her experience of conception above all others; hers was an exceptionally powerful orgasm, because it was, quite literally, heaven-sent.

. . .

So went the theology. Beyond the binaries of curse (Eve) and miracle (Mary), many medieval women, regardless of their status, spent a huge span of their adult lives pregnant. And while medieval women could look to Mary as a model of motherhood, in terms of childbirth (the pains of which Mary herself mercifully escaped), they were in it alone. But not all women who wanted to have children were easily able to conceive—many struggled. IVF may have been hundreds of years away from invention, but that's not to say that authors of medieval medical texts didn't offer their own fertility treatments.

Medieval medical and scientific writers viewed women's menstruation either with ambivalence (a necessary evil required for a woman to purge her excess moisture) or outright hostility. '*Women's Secrets*' labels menstruation as 'impure', and John Trevisa, the author of a popular encyclopedia, calls the blood 'vile and unstable'.[11] However, despite this rhetoric, periods were widely understood as being instrumental in conception, and medicines such as water of plaintain were prescribed if a woman needed to regulate her cycle in order to get pregnant. If the issue laid elsewhere and not with menstruation, then there were various things a couple could try. The biggest authority on this matter by far was a collection of three texts dedicated to the health and well-being of women, which became known as the *Trotula*.[12] All three were composed in the twelfth century in the Italian town of Salerno, and in the earliest manuscripts one of them is attributed to a woman, a healer from the area named Trota; because of this, it was assumed in the Middle Ages that all three texts came from Trota's quill.

Sadly, we know next to nothing about Trota, except that she lived in Salerno and, based on the knowledge gathered together in the *Trotula*, it is likely that she was a general practitioner of medicine. Her texts, which give substantial space to fertility treatments, became the equivalent of best-sellers throughout Europe. One of the books suggests that women could test the hospitality of their womb by soaking a small cloth attached to a string in pennyroyal, laurel or another hot oil, inserting it into their vagina, tying the string around their leg and then going to sleep. If the patient woke up to find that the cloth had fallen out, it meant that her body was too hot for conception. If it was still inside her, it meant she was too cold. She could then improve her chance of conception by fumigating herself with herbs of the opposite temperature and rebalancing her humours. If this failed, she should turn her attention to her sex life. Too much sex or, even worse, sex outside of marriage, could make a woman infertile, because the more sexual partners she enjoyed, it was believed, the more slippery her womb became. And if she cut back on sex and was still not getting pregnant, then both the husband and wife were instructed to look to their weight, which, medieval medicine believed, could affect fertility. Sweating off any excess fat with hot baths or the application of hot sand might just do the trick for a struggling couple.[13] For those who did manage to conceive, new anxieties quickly took the place of fertility worries. According to 'Women's Secrets', women who had sex while on their period could give birth to babies who suffered from leprosy or epilepsy—devastatingly, such children were often considered by medieval society to be monstrous.[14] And in the Middle Ages, just as today, not all women managed to carry their children to term. Until she held the baby in her arms, there was a lot for an expectant mother to worry about.

There is evidence to suggest that male infertility was at least recognized. The *Trotula*, for example, prescribes a urine test to determine whether the husband or wife (or both) was the source of a couple's fertility troubles. In two separate pots each partner should mix their urine with wheat bran. If, after ten days had passed, one of the pots was smelly and full of worms, then something might be awry for whoever that urine belonged to. However, most medical advice, when it came to fertility, was targeted towards the woman. She was to blame for being sexually promiscuous, for being the wrong temperature or for having sex while menstruating. Even the works of the female-authored *Trotula* devote far more space to the infertility of women than they do to the infertility of men. Women who never managed to conceive had to deal not only with their own grief and loss but also with the stigma of having failed their husbands.

Medical books such as the *Trotula* and 'Women's Secrets' are weighty tomes and, while their advice is applicable to the general public, it's difficult to know how much the average medieval woman would have been aware of them. However, the apothecary bills of Anne of Bohemia, queen of England and wife of Richard II, from the last year of her life, suggest that wealthier women may well have kept abreast of medical information about their fertility. *Trifera magna*, which Anne purchased for the expensive sum of two shillings and sixpence, was prescribed in the *Trotula* on a number of occasions to aid conception. Because herbs and medicines often had multiple usages, we cannot say for sure that Anne was buying these products to aid conception. However, bearing in mind she was a childless queen, it seems likely.[15]

Sadly for Anne, these treatments never worked. But for those women who did manage to get positive results, whether through home remedies, pilgrimages to the shrines of saints devoted to fertility or sheer luck, the experience of pregnancy could feel more of a trial than a blessing. The *Hali Meidhad*—which translates into modern English as *Holy Virginity*—is a thirteenth-century Christian treatise which encourages young women to turn to a life of religion. It survives, alongside several other religious texts, in two manuscripts, the earliest of which was simple, unadorned and small enough to be held in the hand. It was probably put together as a private book of devotion, designed to be used rather than admired, and wear and tear on the folios suggests that readers did indeed pore over its contents. In its mission to persuade readers into a life of celibacy, the treatise paints an especially off-putting picture of pregnancy:

> your rosy face will grow thin, and turn green as grass, your eyes will grow dulled, and shadowed underneath, and because of your dizziness your head will ache cruelly. Inside, in your belly, a swelling in your womb which bulges you out like a water-skin, discomfort in your bowels and stitches in your side, and often painful backache; heaviness in every limb, the dragging weight of your two breasts, and the streams of milk that run from them. Your beauty is all destroyed by pallor; there is a bitter taste in your mouth, and everything that you eat makes you feel sick; and whatever food your stomach disdainfully receives it throws it up again [. . .] Worry about your labour pains keeps you awake at night.[16]

It's worth remembering that this treatise is actively trying to encourage its female readers to pursue a holy life of sexual abstinence. However, despite the ulterior motives of its anonymous author, at least some of the symptoms described—the constant morning sickness, the aching back, the middle-of-the-night panics about impending labour—are likely to sound familiar to anyone who has experienced pregnancy.

While some poor women would have given birth in a hospital, most expectant medieval parents prepared a room, known as a birthing chamber, for labour in their own home. This could be any room in the house but was ideally positioned upstairs, where it was warmer. In preparation for the birth, the chosen room would be transformed, decorated with images of saints, darkened and lit by candlelight. On a woman's entry into her birthing chamber the room was closed, the curtains were drawn and the keyholes stopped up. Pregnant women in the Middle Ages would inhabit this chamber during their labour, but also for a longer period that encompassed the weeks before and after the birth, called a 'lying-in'. For most of her 'lying-in', a woman would be confined to her room; for the final stretch she might be allowed to move around the house, if there were no concerns for her health, but she wasn't allowed to go outside at any time. In her *Treasure of the City of Ladies*, Christine de Pizan describes it as a time of festivity, an open house for female family and friends in which visitors were treated to sumptuous food and drink as the mother-to-be, often dressed in a white gown, would receive her guests propped up in bed.[17]

In Italy, husbands were in charge of preparing the birthing chamber, choosing and purchasing their wife's outfits for 'lying-in' and decorating the trays that carried food to the new mother after labour. In Britain, however, both 'lying-in' and labour were very much the mother's remit. For the wealthy, the preparations for this room were nothing short of lavish; the more elaborate the birthing chamber, the greater the status of the woman who inhabited it. When Elizabeth of York gave birth to Margaret Tudor (the future queen of Scotland) in 1489, the room was covered with rich, expensive tapestries, decorated with gold fleur-de-lis. Her bed was 'made up of a wool-stuffed mattress, a featherbed, a down-filled bolster, and four down pillows, the finest linen sheets and pillow cases, a linen quilt, and a coverlet of ermine and cloth of gold'.[18] The expenditure on birthing chambers was clearly common enough for the author of the *Knight of the Tower*, a book of advice addressed from a knight to his daughters, to feel it necessary to warn against incurring God's wrath through excessive extravagance.[19]

Christine de Pizan is also quick to cast judgement on those women who went too far in their preparation of the birthing chamber. She describes one expectant mother in particular, the wife of a grocer, who had 'two very fine chambers', decorated with vessels and dishes of silver and gold, and who put up exquisite hangings around her bed, 'of such fine linen of Rheims that they were worth three hundred francs'. Far from being impressed by this display, Christine is critical: 'God knows what money was wasted on amusements, bathing and various social gatherings, according to the customs in Paris for women in childbed [. . .] Although there are many examples of great prodigality, this extravagance exceeds all the others, and so is worth putting in a book!'[20] It is important to note the social status of this woman as part of the emerging middle class. Christine, a noblewoman, is not just expressing disdain at luxurious birthing chambers but also at the idea that a grocer's wife could dare to aspire to the nobility through the excesses of her birthing chamber.

There is not much evidence to reveal how women felt during their 'lying in', or how they experienced their labour. Was the darkness and confinement soothing and therapeutic? Or claustrophobic and boring? Were expectant and new mothers pleased to receive an endless troop of visitors or did they wish they could just be left alone? It is likely, regrettably, that we'll never know. However, what we do know is that the birthing room was very much a female space. In medieval Europe, a woman who realized that she was going into labour would call on her 'godsibs' ('sisters in God') to come to her aid. These might be female friends, family members or neighbours, with usually at least one midwife among them.

When the godsibs arrived, they came armed with food, drink, herbal tisanes to ease the mother's pain, charms and amulets, oils and fats to massage the perineum and their prayers for a safe delivery for both mum and baby. Not only was this all very intimate (it's hard to imagine many women today wanting their female friends or family members to massage their perineum); it was also crowded, noisy and festive. Forget the image of the mother and birth partner with their pre-made soothing playlist and essential oils; this was very much a family affair. Moreover, it was a feminine one. Margaret of Anjou, queen of England in the thirteenth century, issued a royal decree ahead of her 'lying-in' that a curtain be drawn across her inner chamber until a few weeks after she had given birth.[21] No men were allowed closer than her outer chamber. While most women didn't gender their birthing chambers via royal decree, this sort of segregation was the norm. In the case of an emergency, a male surgeon or physician might be called to the birthing room, but in the majority of cases midwives were as capable of dealing with common birth problems as physicians. There was rarely any need for men to invade this intimate space. Not that most men seemed to mind this state of affairs. Simon de Seyles of Spaldynton 'dared not enter the house for the cries [of his son's mother] in childbirth', and a number of other expectant fathers recollect keeping out of the way, dining out while their wife endured the throes of labour.[22]

It's very hard to know whether this separation of the sexes was designed to preserve the dignity and privacy of the woman in labour or whether it had its roots in the medieval Christian idea of childbirth as intrinsically shameful, its pains and struggles encoded as a punishment from God. The manuscript for a thirteenth-century French poem entitled *Le Roman de Silence* (*The Romance of Silence*) was discovered in 1911, tucked away in a manor house in England, in a box labelled 'old papers—no value'. But the light this poem sheds on attitudes to childbirth in medieval Europe, not to mention the fact that it offers an early account of queer experience, proves its worth. It tells the story of a count who is worried that his wife may have given birth to a daughter instead of a son, which would entail the loss of their family inheritance. Unable to wait, he runs to the chamber where his wife is giving birth to find out the sex of his baby. Closing the door behind him, 'his desire to know the truth takes away any shame that might prevent him from approaching the bed of the woman in childbirth. He touches her with his right hand and she feels great shame.'[23] There is something degrading in the man's presence in the chamber, both for himself and for the new mother.

Such stories suggest that men's absence from the birthing chamber may have had more to do with shame and propriety than with the woman's wishes or her comfort. While we have no real evidence to suggest how women *or* men felt about the childbirth status quo, the likelihood is that everyone was so used to it that they didn't question it much.

We get some lurid descriptions of birth, from texts like *Hali Meidhad*, which aim to put women off having any children as a 'cruel distressing anguish', an 'incessant misery', a 'torment upon torment'.[24] But, beyond such scaremongering, there is silence surrounding the actual experience of childbirth in the Middle Ages. For hints and clues we must therefore look to material culture—the items kept in birthing rooms, beyond their sometimes lavish decorations, which can tell us about the birth itself.

There would be sweet-smelling herbs scattered on the floor, designed to soothe the mother with their scent, and a well-stoked fire to keep the baby warm when it came. On the side the midwife might place a gem called eaglestone, which could be attached to the mother's thigh to help alleviate her pain, and vinegar, which would be rubbed on the baby's tongue to ensure that one day the child would speak. There might be a birthing stool, which in some areas of Europe were believed to help position the mother for optimum labour; these would usually be made of wood with a semicircle cut out on the seat, designed to support the mother in an upright position and allow the midwives access underneath to help ease out the baby. Books were also a popular choice; manuscripts telling the tale of Margaret of Antioch, the patron saint of childbirth because she leapt out of the stomach of a dragon unscathed, were an especially common feature of the birthing chamber; in many of the manuscripts that tell her story the scribe will recommend gifting the object to expectant mothers, to help them achieve a painless birth. One was also likely to find talismans and amulets, which were specifically designed to keep mother and baby safe, and which tread a fine line between religion and magic.

Such charms were not simply old wives' tales but were frequently prescribed by learned doctors too. The *Trotula* prescribes that snakeskin should be laid over the woman in labour, to speed her delivery and ease her pain.[25] *The Sickness of Women*, an English medical handbook of women's health, recommends the use of silk, iron or deerskin and the *Tomida Femina* (a tenth-century poem, which also serves as a charm, from the south of France and whose title translates as 'a swollen woman') encourages the birthing woman and her godsibs to chant magical language during the labour.[26] The fourteenth-century surgeon John Arderne, whose medical books were some of the most widely read in England, includes a charm which he insists will hasten the birth of a child—an inscribed amulet that should be bound below the knee of the women in labour while holy words are spoken.[27] To us these may sound bizarre and, we now know, snakeskin and iron would be very little help in medical terms. However, they may well have had something of a placebo effect on the labouring mother, just as the incantations and chants from their godsibs may have acted as a kind of medieval hypnobirthing.

The talismans that involved strips of parchment and magic words anticipate the use and popularity in the later Middle Ages of something we now call the birthing girdle. These girdles were inscribed with holy prayers and invocations and were designed to be wrapped around the stomach of the woman in labour. They could be made from silk but were more likely to consist of parchment or paper. Various Christian institutions kept birthing girdles which they would lend out to well-to-do expectant mothers; several noblewomen borrowed the Virgin Mary's Girdle from Westminster Abbey, for example, to assist their labour. According to legend, this girdle was dropped down from heaven by the Virgin Mary, to convince the doubting disciple Thomas that she had ascended to the celestial realm. In the Middle Ages there were a couple of these girdles that laid claim to being 'original'; one was the girdle at Westminster, of which no descriptions endure, but the other is still in Prato Cathedral in Italy. It is 87cm long, made of a strip of green sheep's wool and decorated with golden brocade.

Few of these girdles have survived in Britain; they were identified as heretical items during the Reformation and were destroyed. But there is one rare survival. The Wellcome Trust in London harbours a very fragile but beautiful and legible birthing girdle, dated to around 1500. It is thin, narrow and very long—a full 11 feet, which equates to three golf clubs or two leaf rakes. Its parchment is decorated with both images and words, illustrations of Christ's suffering during the Crucifixion sit alongside prayers in Latin for the health of the baby and the mother. It contains a handy how-to guide, '[a]nd if a woman is in labour with a child, gird this length around her womb and she shall deliver without peril and the child shall have Christendom and the mother purification', as well as exercises to distract the birthing mother. She should focus her mind on something other than pain by counting the drops of Christ's blood shed on the cross.[28]

The popularity and prevalence of talismans such as birthing girdles can tell us much about women's experience of childbirth in the Middle Ages. They remind us that religion was as integral to the childbirth room as it was to all aspects of medieval society. They evoke the thin line between the medical and the spiritual—or even between the medical and the superstitious. Most of all, however, they make clear the very real perils involved in childbirth in the Middle Ages. The need for so many rituals of protection, both for the mother and her baby, suggest that, tragically, many didn't survive.

While it's difficult to get exact figures on the mortality rates of mothers and babies during this time, some scholars have suggested that as many as one in three infants died during or shortly after childbirth. Estimates for mothers range from one in ten to one in 40, and many believe that childbirth was the main cause of death for women in early medieval England. This is unsurprising when we remember the paucity of medical knowledge about women's bodies. The Book of Common Prayer, written in 1549, emphasized the perils women faced, praising God for safely delivering women from 'the great danger of childbirth', and the Sarum Rite, a set of liturgical rites developed in medieval Salisbury, urges pregnant women to go to confession as soon as they feel labour coming on, so they do not die with any unabsolved sins.[29]

The dangers were many. Common complications included infection, eclampsia, prolapsed wombs, retained placenta or haemorrhaging. In one particularly grisly example from the *Trotula* there is a graphic description of the extreme tearing of the perineum: 'there are some women in whom the vagina and the anus become one opening and the same pathway. Whence in these women the womb comes out and hardens.'[30] Some of these complications, such as excessive bleeding, could be dealt with relatively successfully by midwives or, in more extreme cases, by doctors. But other problems could sound the death knell for the mother, the baby or both.

A common, devastating complication was stillbirth. Even today, stillbirths are far more dangerous for the mother than live births, and, while it is again impossible to glean exact figures from the evidence available, some studies suggest that one in five medieval children was stillborn. We know from both religious items and medical texts that stillbirth was a worry that preoccupied pregnant women. The medieval birthing girdle at the Wellcome Trust contains a prayer that addresses the unborn baby: 'O child, be you living or dead, come from the womb like Lazarus's, an incantation that not only seeks delivery of the child but also hints that a miracle revival might be possible—Lazarus rose from the dead, so perhaps the baby can too.[31]

Stillborn babies in the Middle Ages couldn't be baptized or buried in consecrated ground, according to common law in Europe, and so were often buried either on the edges of the churchyard or completely outside of them, metaphorically shut out from society. Some have theorized that, owing to the higher probability of stillborn births, parents may have become more hardened to such loss. But there is ample evidence that the grief from a stillborn birth could hit just as hard in the Middle Ages as it does today. Midwives, for example, did sometimes relent and offer baptism for stillborn children, even though such an act was technically illegal; and it wasn't unusual for clandestine burials of stillborn and unbaptized babies within the borders of the churchyard to take place, or for stillborn children to be commemorated by their parents or other family members.

. . .

One or two first-hand accounts do draw us into the birthing chamber, allowing us to discover new details about an event that usually happened behind closed doors.

Isabel de la Cavallería was a widow. Her husband had died while she was still pregnant with their first child, and Isabel knew that, owing to Spanish law at the time, the posthumous birth of an heir could empower her with property and administration rights that she would otherwise not be entitled to. It was therefore essential that she proved the birth to be legitimate, to avoid legal trouble further down the line. In cases like Isabel's, when money was on the line, elite women often came under an excess amount of scrutiny. There were sometimes attempts from the husband's family to prove that such women might try and trick the authorities through the production of a fake heir to retain property that would otherwise be bequeathed to them.

Clearly a savvy woman who wanted to take no chances, Isabel invited a male notary, Domengo de Cuerlo, to witness the birth of her child and prove its legitimacy.[32] For Isabel, providing evidence that she had a child, and that the child was her own, was more important than maintaining the status quo of the medieval birthing chamber. Rather than keeping the windows closed and the curtains drawn, Isabel flung hers wide, so that any passer-by could see inside; in doing so, she transformed the usual private affair of labour into a public one, proof that no deception was occurring within the chamber. Domengo describes how she encouraged him to substantiate his report by getting up close and personal. He checked under the clothes of Isabel and the midwives, to ensure they were not hiding another baby for a swap if required. And, at the time of the baby's birth, he was close enough to proceedings to hear and see 'the blood and the water which were coming out from the body of the aforesaid Isabel'. He sees the baby being born, 'completely wet and with his eyes closed' and observes as the midwife, Salina, takes out the placenta and cuts the umbilical cord.

The fact that Isabel felt it necessary to make her labour so public, and to invite men into a space usually reserved for women, is telling. Everything happened at Isabel's invitation, and with her consent, but her actions make clear the distrust that male authorities placed on women and their bodies, and the suspicions that could arise from the private space of the birthing chamber.

As well as showing us what was unusual, and therefore worthy of note, in medieval childbirth (the presence of men, the legal witness, the oath sworn by the midwives), Domengo's account of Isabel's birthing also gives us a unique insight into the more routine aspects of labour. The 'great pains' that Isabel suffered, the 'relics on her belly and many blessed candles lit around', the midwives situated between her legs with a clean vessel of water, the blood and water that gush out of Isabel's body along with the baby, the cutting of the umbilical cord and the image of Isabel, 'sleepy and almost out of herself' afterwards: such details not only give us a rare insight into the mother's experience of medieval childbirth but also remind us that, in terms of the essentials, the process of giving birth has changed surprisingly little.

Isabel's story makes clear the anxieties around legitimacy where children were concerned, especially among the nobility when inheritance was on the line. This is a subject that Marie de France takes up in several of her *lais*. Her stories may be fictional, but they draw on contemporary concerns about what it meant for a woman to have a child out of wedlock, or for the paternity of an heir to be called into question.

Le Fresne begins with two valiant knights who both get married around the same time.[33] When one of the knights receives word that his friend's wife has given birth to twins, his own wife is quick to offer her opinion. With a smile, she announces in front of the entire household: 'So help me God, I am astonished that this worthy man decided to inform my husband of his shame and dishonour, that his wife has had two sons. They have both incurred shame because of it.' According to this 'deceitful and arrogant' woman, it was impossible for a woman to give birth to two sons at once, unless they were the progeny of two different fathers. Marie tells us that the woman's foolish words spread like wildfire throughout Brittany, making all women who heard them furious. And for good reason; they understood that by parroting this old wife's tale, this lady was unfairly calling into question the honour of any mother of twins.

Of course, she gets her comeuppance. Not long after the dinner, she becomes pregnant and, nine months later, she also gives birth to twins—two little girls. She is devastated, realizing what she has done and breaks down in tears. Unable to see another way out, her thoughts turn to infanticide: 'To ward off shame, I will have to murder one of the children: I would rather make amends with God than shame and dishonour myself.' The other women in the birthing chamber immediately come up with a plan to put a stop to these dark thoughts. Her maid offers to take one of the children and abandon her outside a monastery, wrapped in a sumptuous blanket to indicate that she is a child of noble birth.

This tale warns women not to slander one another, or to repeat misogynistic rhetoric. However, it also shows how fraught issues of legitimacy were among the wealthy. However foolish, slanderous and envious the protagonist might be, she must have been terrified about the potential consequences of her supposed 'dishonour' to contemplate murdering one of her children.

. . .

While many women were happy to become mothers in the Middle Ages, there were of course others who did not want to have children. There is little documentation to help us here—this was a taboo subject, not one that women would have felt comfortable openly committing to paper. The only path available for them was the life of religion, and its accompanying abstinence. There was no way of reconciling sex and childlessness. According to the Church Fathers, and especially St Augustine, sex was only acceptable within marriage and only with the express purpose of producing offspring. But in reality there will have been plenty of married couples who had enough children but wanted to continue enjoying sex with one another—as well as plenty of unmarried couples who wanted to have sex without bearing children. Moreover, there is an underlying current of thought in medieval medicine that not having sex could be bad for your health. The *Trotula* warns women that they can become gravely ill if they don't have sex often enough.[34]

Even St Augustine himself acknowledges the dangers of abstinence, claiming that a couple who forgo sex grow in religious purity but decline in health, becoming almost corpse-like.[35]

While contraception wasn't as widely accepted as it is today, that's not to say that there weren't some tried and tested methods used by sexually active women to avoid getting pregnant. The only good reason for not having a child that the *Trotula* and other medical texts acknowledge is the physical inability to give birth safely, but they do list tricks and tips for having sex without getting pregnant. These range from the more familiar—quick withdrawal (the 'pull out' method)—to the more bizarre: urinating or hopping backwards while sneezing after sex, inserting tar, cabbage seeds or elephant dung into the vagina, anointing the penis with balsam, tar and ceruse lead before sex, making an amulet of boiled ass's milk and honey and tying it around the stomach or, my personal favourite, castrating a male weasel and wearing the testicles around the neck during intercourse.

None of these methods would have had a high success rate. But there is evidence to suggest that other, more chemical, solutions would have been more likely to work. Modern science has proved the efficacy of herbs and plants such as artemisia (mugwort), pennyroyal, rue and cedar, all of which were prescribed as contraceptives in the Middle Ages, in ending an early pregnancy. In the *Canterbury Tales*, Chaucer's Parson refers to women who drink venomous herbs, or women who put certain objects into their secret places, in order to 'slay their child', and in the records of various sermons women who are worried about the economic burden of a child are warned against employing such methods.[36] References such as these, in sermons and literature, suggest that the use of such chemicals was not uncommon, despite awareness of the dangers attendant on them—medical texts that recommend these substances are careful to advise caution. In too great a quantity, many of these herbs could end up being deadly for the mother.

Early medieval penitentials identify the use of contraception as a sin but prescribe much harsher courses of penance for the use of herbs like artemisia and rue than they do for the use of preventative talismans and amulets. Where chemicals are involved, the line between abortion and contraception becomes blurry. Medieval people had a different understanding of pregnancy from ours today: as a general rule, women weren't considered properly pregnant until they declared it themselves or were so visibly pregnant that it was apparent to everyone. Because of this, practices that we would likely classify as abortion often came under the umbrella of contraception in medieval

Europe. This was a grey area that even the Church recognized; any interference with the foetus before the 'quickening' (when the child was believed to acquire a soul, roughly around the fourth month) was considered to be a form of contraception, not abortion, and carried a much more lenient penalty both legally and in the eyes of the Christian church.

There is the suggestion too that many medical texts were subtly trying to assist women with contraceptive methods, flying under the radar of the Church and the law. For example, we find abortive remedies coming under the guise of remedies for bad menstrual cramps or the removal of a dead foetus. The *Trotula* series includes a recipe recommended for the 'retention and suppression of menstruation' that was likely to bring about a miscarriage.[37] Take a handful each of calamint, catmint, fennel, pellitory, savory, hyssop, artemisia, rue, wormwood, anise, cumin, rosemary, thyme, pennyroyal and mountain organum, mix with wine and water, boil and ingest. While advertised as a relief for period pains, many of the ingredients (fennel, anise, cumin, sage, artemisia, and rue) are substances with proven abortive qualities, while the pennyroyal, mint and wine would act as sedatives to ease the pain of ingesting such a tincture while pregnant.

Beyond this literature, we have very little evidence of women who put them to use. And, despite a vast array of legislation against abortion, there were almost no prosecutions during the Middle Ages for women using abortive methods—to date, historians have found only seven such prosecutions from the entire medieval period. However, the existence of the remedies and the frequent references made to them in sermons and other religious literature suggest that they were common knowledge, and it's not hard to imagine various scenarios in which a woman might have risked her own life by turning to such measures. Moreover, the grey line between contraception and abortion that we find in the Middle Ages, and the scarcity of prosecutions against women who practised either, suggest that, in some ways, medieval society had a progressive attitude towards abortion. Prior to four months, any termination of a pregnancy was considered preventative rather than abortive, which is more in line with modern thinking than we might expect.

No matter how severely medieval society frowned on the act of extramarital sex, of course it still happened—probably quite regularly—and, as a result, unmarried women did sometimes fall pregnant, regardless of whether or not they had made use of the contraceptive methods available to them. The same *Hali Meidhad* that advises its readers to eschew marriage and children saves its harshest insults for women who allow themselves to indulge in sex outside of marriage. According to this polemical text, such women are the devil's playthings and consorts, the absolute filth of the earth.[38]

And it wasn't just *Hali Meidhad* that espoused this opinion. There are numerous medieval lyrics that tell the tales of unfortunate, fallen women and which implicitly criticize their anti-heroines for being foolish enough to get knocked up outside the commitment of marriage. With their origins in oral culture, these poems are impossible to attribute to a particular author, and while they were probably performed by young maidens at local feasts and festivals, they have made their way down to us thanks to male scribes, who presumably saw them as useful cautionary tales. In 'The Single Women's Lament', dated to approximately 1200 and either German or French in origin, the poetic voice is a pregnant, unmarried mum who sits at home alone because she is afraid to go outside and face the scorn of the public. 'When I do go outside', she tells us, 'I am stared at/As if I were some monster/When they see this belly [...] I am in the stories and mouths of everyone.'[39]

While medieval Italy and other European countries had many foundling hospitals, which catered to unmarried women, England had no such provisions. King Edward III tasked the hospital of St Mary without Bishopsgate in London with receiving poor pregnant women and giving them a place to give birth, but the hospital would only offer ongoing support for a child if the mother died in labour. The odds were very much stacked against women who either became pregnant by accident, were abandoned by the father of the child or were raped. Remember that, according to Galenic theory, a woman could conceive *only* if she orgasmed—which made it almost impossible for a woman who became pregnant by rape to seek justice. If a woman couldn't get pregnant without orgasm, then any intercourse that resulted in a child must have been pleasurable and consensual according to medieval medicine.

That's not to say that no one questioned the premise of this idea. In a text on reproduction by William of Conches, a French Christian philosopher, he imagines a conversation between a Duke and a Philosopher. The Duke deems the theory that women can only conceive if they orgasm implausible. 'We have met women who were raped, who have suffered violence despite their wailing, and still have conceived,' he argues. 'It seems that they never experienced delight in the act. But without delight they cannot produce sperm.' The Philosopher is quick to dismiss this argument with one of his own, however: 'Although the act of rape displeases at the start,' he says, 'in the end as a result of carnal weakness, it pleases.' According to the Philosopher, who gets the last word on this topic, a woman's natural lust will take over, whether or not she consented.[40] This argument is an incredibly damaging one. But, alas, it is not one that is completely out of currency, even in the twenty-first century. Its legacy lives on in the words of Todd Akin, a Missouri Republican Senate candidate in 2012, who claimed that legitimate rape rarely ends in pregnancy because 'the female body has ways to try and shut that whole thing down'.

· · ·

Medieval childbirth wasn't all doom and gloom. While it's certainly true that having a baby *was* more dangerous in the Middle Ages (as Margery Kempe's experience attests), there are still things that the time period has to teach us about giving birth: the importance of midwifery, how meditative techniques can act as a natural form of pain relief, the crucial role that other women can play in supporting an expectant mother through labour. That's not to say that medieval childbirth was preferable to labour in the twenty-first century, with its epidurals, the inclusion of male partners in the birthing room and a more general openness about the process. Nor is it to say that the pressure on women to have children wasn't far more extreme then than it is now. But exploring medieval childbirth through letters, first-hand accounts, medical texts and legal documents can remind us that the basic premise of pregnancy and childbirth has remained the same, and that there were some surprisingly positive aspects to the experience which, as a society, we are now incorporating back into our own, twenty-first-century approach.

TWO

Tied Down

'Ye arn no good wyfe'

MARGERY KEMPE, *The Book of Margery Kempe*

Christine de Pizan sat in her study, surrounded by her beloved books, and rubbed her eyes. More time than she thought had passed, as often happened when she was lost in her work and freed from the domestic duties that made up the lives of most women her age. Ever since she was a child, Christine had always preferred writing and learning to almost any other activity. It was a love that had never left her.

Weary from her intellectual endeavours, she searched idly for some lighter reading material and stumbled by chance upon a book by Matheolus, a French cleric and poet, that she could not remember coming across before. She started to read—and grew quickly, and increasingly, frustrated. It wasn't that Matheolus was saying anything new. There was nothing she hadn't heard before. But she was tired of picking up books, whatever their purported intention or genre, and finding them filled with a seemingly endless stream of libel against women.

'Why on earth is it that so many men have said and continue to say such awful, damning things about women?' she wondered. Exhausted by the injustice of it all, she slumped against the arm of her chair, arguing with all these stupid men in her mind. And just like that, her most well-known work, *The Book of the City of Ladies*, was born.[1]

The Book of the City of Ladies (1405) is the first proto-feminist tract to come out of Europe. Anyone in the West who has written or engaged with feminist theory and literature, or who has written back to misogyny in any form, has Christine de Pizan to thank. *The Book of the City of Ladies* begins with Christine in her study, so infuriated by the sexism in her male-authored books that she flings one of them across the room. After falling into a disturbed sleep, she is visited in a dream by Lady Reason, Lady Rectitude and Lady Justice, who help her to build an allegorical city, populated by famous women throughout history. Christine built her City of Ladies to combat the various claims made against women's character with examples to the contrary, exposing typical attacks on women—that they can't keep a secret, are serially unfaithful, unintelligent and, ultimately, a bunch of hen-pecking nags—as nothing more than 'an outrageous pack of lies'.[2]

Writing when she was around 40 years old, at the court of the French king Charles VI, Christine aimed high in terms of her readership. She presented a copy to Charles's wife, Isabeau of France, as part of a lavishly illustrated manuscript known as 'The Book of the Queen'.[3] Christine not only supervised the production of this manuscript herself but may even have been responsible for copying some of the passages in her own hand. In its frontispiece she is portrayed presenting the large, red, leather-bound book to Isabeau in the queen's bedchamber. While the manuscript includes other of Christine's works, the miniatures accompanying *City of Ladies* are the most numerous and the most beautiful, and she even gives Isabeau herself, an example of a kind and benevolent queen, a home within the allegorical city.

A recurring theme of the *City of Ladies* is marriage. Women, Christine argues, are frequently depicted as terrible wives, bringing misery to their husbands. Their 'shrewish, vengeful nagging' makes marriage a constant hell for their spouses, they 'cause trouble, lack affection, and gossip incessantly', and they are incapable of being faithful, or so men say. But this is nothing but slander, Christine argues. Not only are there countless caring and loyal wives but it's more likely that they will be the ones who have to put up with their husbands' bad behaviour, not the other way around. She reminds us that '[t]here are some married couples who love each other, and live together in peace'. If both spouses are 'sensible, kind and gentle', then a married life can be a contented one.[4]

Many of our least flattering stereotypes about wives—the gold-digger, the nag, the unfaithful flirt—emerge from medieval precedents. But the stories of women like Christine de Pizan make clear that such stereotypes do not reflect reality. And while it is true that many women experienced a lack of freedom and liberation in marriage, others found ways to make the institution work for them, on their own terms.

· · ·

Getting married in the Middle Ages was surprisingly simple. All that was required for a legally binding union was an exchange of vows, in the present tense, and the free consent of both parties. This exchange was usually something along the lines of 'I [name] take you [name] to be my wedded wife/husband', but as long as the words expressed intention and consent, the exact formula didn't matter. Nor did the setting—it could be a church, but it might also be a bedroom—and nor, technically, did the couple need the consent of their parents. Marriages that happened without the involvement of the Church (so called 'clandestine' marriages) were considered sinful, but they were still legal. Being able to get married so easily was a boon for those who wanted to wed without the blessing or interference of their families, but it also led to a great deal of confusion over whether or not a man and woman were truly married. The medieval court was full of cases trying to determine the legitimacy of marriages, from parents hoping to annul the clandestine marriages of their children to spouses (and especially husbands) who refused to acknowledge that the promises they made were binding.

Typically, a wedding would be preceded by a public, formal betrothal, often at the house of the bride's parents, in which the couple made promises to one another. Bearing in mind that the only apparent legal requirement of a marriage was a promise made in the present tense, the couple might become married at the point of betrothal. Couples today may still get engaged, but we don't count such promises as *marriage*. In the Middle Ages, however, the seriousness of betrothal led to a real grey area. Even if the promises weren't made in the present tense, medieval couples were still considered 'married before God' after their engagement.[5] Sex during this interim stage was frowned on by the Church, but there is evidence that couples did often have sexual contact post-betrothal and pre-wedding. During this time, just as with a church wedding today, banns were read three times in the local parishes of the couple to publicize the match, and these would be followed by a wedding, which might be at a church or at the house of the groom. The two families, with the bride and groom leading the procession, would make their celebratory way through the streets to wherever the wedding was taking place, accompanied by friends, well-wishers and even musicians.

While wealthy women might have a special dress commissioned, most women simply wore their 'best', and this could be of any colour, but was rarely white. There are surviving illustrations of brides wearing pink and green (which was associated with love), but by far the most popular choice was Marian blue. If the service took place at a church, the priest would welcome the couple on the steps outside and carry out a brief ceremony there. Transaction was at the heart of these proceedings. The father of the bride would ceremoniously hand over his daughter to the groom, and the dowry would be paid then and there, or a written document outlining the financial agreement would be passed over. The groom would then give his bride a present (known as a 'wed'), which was usually a brooch or, more likely, a ring. Only women wore a wedding band, on their right hand.

Family and friends—and perhaps even the couple—would have been far less interested in the service than in the celebrations afterwards. There would be a big feast, with plenty of wine, dancing and general merriment, and the wealthier the groom (whose family usually footed the bill), the more extravagant this would be. In one popular medieval romance the wedding of the eponymous protagonist Melusine to her husband is unbelievably grand. The bride was 'so beautiful and sumptuously attired that the ladies, marvelling, said they'd never seen her equal', and the festivities afterwards became the talk of the town.[6] The rich variety of foods, the spiced wine and delicate pastries, the opulent tents where the guests could stay the night, the meticulous service, the spectacular jousting—all these little details were designed to make clear that this young couple was going places.

For the elite, marriage had very little to do with love and much more with social advancement. It was a vehicle by which families could forge alliances, gain political advantage or simply increase their wealth through strategic matches. The more money there was at stake, the more pressure medieval parents exerted on their children. Arranged marriages were the norm for most upper-class couples, with parents overseeing protracted negotiations and meetings to ensure the economic advancement of future generations. While the free consent of a couple was required to make a marriage legal, there was a big difference between free consent and free *choice*. It seems that, most of the time, children accepted that they needed to 'honour [their] father and mother' and respect the authority of their parents when it came to choosing a spouse. However, there is evidence in marriage negotiation documents, as well as in wills (in which provisions for dowries were made for daughters), that some parents did seek to find a balance between individual preference and family interest. 'Liking' between a prospective pair was considered an important stipulation. Relative parity in terms of age and social class was also thought to be important—although large age gaps were tolerated if the price was right.

The poorer her parents were, the more freedom in choosing a husband their daughter was likely to have. Couples might meet at taverns, fairs, dances or in service at royal households. They would then share a meal or a drink, swap gifts, kiss (or more) and talk of marriage. In essence, they dated. Parents might intervene, either to take over marriage negotiations or to end the match, but many couples married without consulting their families at all. Doing so could be risky: without witnesses or economic protections, those safeguards built into the formal processes of arranged marriages, there was more potential for broken promises and broken hearts. In 1292 Alicia le Mareschal took Elias of Suffolk to court, claiming that he was sleeping with other women despite being married to her.[7] He had been seen having sex with another woman in one of London's common mixed baths. Rather than denying the allegations, Elias defended himself by claiming that he and Alicia had never actually been married so it didn't matter who he had been sleeping with.

According to the medieval marriage vows, wifely obedience to a husband was expected. A popular version in England had women promising to be 'bonour and buxom' (good and obedient) at bed and board, while men made no such promise. But this didn't mean that all women were under the thumb of their husbands. Not all wives upheld their vow of obedience and nor did all men keep their end of the bargain—to treat their wife with love and tenderness, to look after and provide for her. While expectations were clearly laid out by parents, the Church, advice literature and even the law, these expectations didn't always match reality.

The idea that women should stay in the background as silent, hidden support systems, has shown a remarkable staying power throughout the ages. There are still many who would agree with Tammy Wynette that a woman should stand by her man. Christine de Pizan may have hailed from the 1380s rather than the 1980s, but she offered remarkably similar advice.

To find an exemplary wife by medieval standards, one needn't look much further than Christine. We know that she was much sought after. She tells us that

> the time arrived when I was approaching the age when young girls are customarily assigned husbands. Yet I was still unmarried even though several men—knights, other gentlemen, and wealthy scholars—had asked for me; and this truth should not be credited to vanity, for the authority of the honour and affection that the King showed my father was responsible for it, not my own worth.[8]

Christine's husband was chosen for her when the time was right, by her father, Thomas de Pizan. Happily for Christine, she and her father were close, and she tells us in her own words that she couldn't have picked better herself. Christine married Étienne du Castel, a handsome royal secretary ten years her senior, in 1379, when she was 15 years old. This might feel like a large age gap to us, but the two were far closer in age than many medieval couples, and Christine was pleased. She describes him lovingly as 'a young scholar and graduate, well-born, of a noble Parisian family, whose virtues surpassed his wealth'.[9]

There are no surviving records of Christine and Étienne's betrothal and wedding, but we can piece together a picture. Both families were wealthy and favoured by the king, and so the meetings to iron out the marriage contract, as well as the wedding itself, would all have been accompanied by feasting, music, dancing and the exchanging of gifts, with friends and family of the couple invited to join in the festivities. Such negotiations could take a long time, especially among the rich. For one particular couple, John Paston III and Margery Brews, it took eight months, various family meetings, 21 letters and a contract to hammer out the marriage term.

John Paston was from one of the most wealthy and powerful families in medieval England. Originally peasants from Norfolk, the Pastons moved swiftly through the ranks to become an influential landowning family in just two generations. John's great-grandfather Clement Paston had been a peasant bondsman, but had taken advantage of the higher wages following the Black Death to buy up land and engineer a profitable marriage to a well-connected woman called Beatrice. They saved enough money to send their son, William, off to study law. Like his father, William used a strategic marriage to climb further up the ladder—his wife, Agnes, was the heiress of a knight and just as ambitious as he was. Their sons and grandsons (including John) made it their mission to accrue as much money and status as possible through education, networking and some canny side-swapping during the Wars of the Roses. Not only are they a rare example of social mobility, but they left behind a remarkable archive of more than a thousand private letters which they wrote to one another and to their friends. It is through these letters that we find out more about the lengthy—and almost disastrous—engagement of Margery Brews and John Paston III.

Margery was in her late teens or early twenties when she first became engaged to John and, as far as we know, he was her first love. John, on the other hand, was in his thirties and had already been involved in at least ten failed attempts at marriage. As the second son, he wanted to secure an affluent wife but Margery's father, an esteemed knight but not the wealthiest of men, did not want to pay a large dowry. For a while, it looked as though the engagement was going to fall through. A resolution was only reached thanks to Margery and her mother. Margery sent John the earliest Valentine's letter written in English, a sweet missive in which she calls him her 'right well beloved Valentine' and confesses that she loves him more than any earthly thing. This letter is not just an outpouring of affection; it is part of a strategy to take their relationship over the finish line while negotiations remained tense. Margery tells John not to forsake her even if her father can't pay the desired dowry: 'if you love me, as I trust verily that you do, you will not leave me. For even if you had not half the livelihood that you have [...] I would not forsake you.'[10] Her mother also wrote to John with a plan of her own: 'Friday is St Valentine's day, and every bird chooseth him a mate; and if it like you to come on Thursday at night and so purvey you that you may abide there til Monday, I trust to God that you shall so speak to my husband, and I pray that we shall bring the matter to a conclusion.'[11] This two-pronged attack from mother and daughter worked. Two months after the Valentine's weekend there was a wedding, and not long after that Margery fell pregnant.

It's unlikely the negotiations for Christine and Étienne were so lengthy. Their apparently happy relationship is an example of how arranged marriage could blossom into mutual affection, especially when parents took their children's preferences into account. Christine tells us that Étienne was 'so faithful' that she 'could not praise highly enough the good things that [she] received from him'. In particular, she frequently expresses respect for his education and learning. Men often looked for beauty and virtue in their prospective wives, but for Christine intellect was far more important. We know from her writings that she excelled in her studies from a young age and was incredibly well read for a woman in the fifteenth century. Her mother prevented her from studying any science (she believed that too much knowledge would devalue Christine's worth on the marriage market) but she did allow her to be educated in the arts, and it seems that the university-educated Étienne and Christine enjoyed a marriage of true minds.

After 11 happy years together tragedy struck when Étienne caught the plague on a royal mission to Beauvais and died. Christine was devastated. She never stopped grieving Étienne, nor did she remarry. The fact that she preferred to make her own living instead of finding another husband may be a testament to the enduring candle she held for her husband. Or perhaps she felt it just wasn't worth the risk. For, while Christine enjoyed marriage, she was painfully aware that many women were not so lucky. 'There are so many wives', she complains in *The City of Ladies*, 'who lead a wretched existence, bound in marriage to a brutish husband', wives who are 'viciously beaten' and who are the victim of constant 'insults, obscenities, and curses', wives who are 'laden down with lots of tiny mouths to feed' while their husbands are out gallivanting, 'visiting places of depravity' or 'living it up in town or in taverns'. Christine may well have wanted to avoid falling prey to a marriage of this kind, after being so lucky the first time around.

By the late Middle Ages wedding vows tended to include 'till death us depart' as an expression of lifelong commitment. Medieval marriage was for life, and it could only be completely dissolved under extreme circumstances— if there was evidence of incest or impotence, or if a marriage contract was deemed illegal in the first place. Separation was only legally sanctioned if evidence of excessive cruelty (and the courts had a high tolerance for domestic violence), infidelity or heresy could be proved, and the process was lengthy and expensive. Even in those cases where separation was permitted, remarriage was not, unless the previous spouse died.

Marie de France explores how one woman finds a way out of this conundrum through the story of a man named Bisclavret, from Brittany.[12] Bisclavret is a 'good and handsome knight' who marries an attractive woman, and they are happy for a while, until one day it dawns on this lady that, three nights a month, her husband vanishes. Convinced that he must be cheating, she begs him to tell her the truth. After much coaxing, he confesses: 'Lady, I become a werewolf: I enter the vast forest and live in the deepest part of the wood where I feed off the prey I can capture.' His wife is (understandably) alarmed. She begins 'to consider various means of parting from him, as she no longer wished to lie with him'. But she doesn't let her husband know. Instead, she convinces him to tell her where he leaves his clothes when he is transformed into a wolf, because without them he will be stuck in his animal form for ever and she'll be rid of him. Wasting no time at all, she promises a knight who has long harboured a great love for her that she will marry him if he steals Bisclavret's clothes. To sever herself from a man she considers an unsuitable husband, she is prepared to condemn him to a life as a wolf.

Christine de Pizan was more of a pragmatist than Marie. Aware of how unlikely, even impossible, separation was, she advised her readers on how to survive unhappy relationships rather than how to leave them. This means her writing on marriage can be difficult for a twenty-first-century reader to stomach. She encourages wives to be grateful for the security marriage offers, to do their best to moderate their husbands' behaviour and strive for a peaceful coexistence, regardless of their treatment. Where *City of Ladies* envisages a fantastical city populated by great women, her sequel, *The Treasure of the City of Ladies* (1405), is more a practical handbook. Although it purports to be for women from all walks of life, it dedicates most of its attention to royalty and nobility. Christine instructs her readers to obey their husbands without complaint and to ignore their infidelity and 'perverse and rude behaviour' because 'you must live and die with him whatever he is like'.[13]

Courts punished women who deserted their husbands, as well as any family members who aided and abetted them, regardless of how badly they had been treated. When Robert Bull was caught 'misbehaving with other women', his wife, Isabel, left him to move back home. Soon after, her father found himself at court on charges of abduction—she may have gone there of her own free will but, in the eyes of the law, she was her husband's stolen 'property'.[14] And when Katherine, wife of John atte Mulle, used her husband's money to bankroll her escape from him, the court forced her to return, threatening her with a public beating in the marketplace if she refused.[15] Christine acknowledged that husbands like Robert and John were in the wrong, but she placed the onus firmly on wives to try and change the behaviour of the men they were stuck with or to bear the abuse patiently if they failed.

. . .

'It seems a thousand years since I spoke with you. I would rather be with you than have all the goods in the world.'[16] These ardent words are from a letter that Richard Calle, a grocer's son from Framlingham, sent to Margery Paston, the younger sister of John Paston. Richard was a servant to the Paston family, and in no way a suitable match. But that didn't stop them falling in love. In 1469 Margery rejected all that her family stood for to marry Richard without their permission. As soon as they found out, they separated the lovers, hoping that the marriage could be annulled or declared nonexistent.

The bishop of Norfolk was called in to intervene. He interviewed Richard and Margery, trying to determine what words had actually been said in order to understood whether or not they were truly married in the eyes of the Church. Margery declared that 'she thought in conscience she was bound, whatsoever her words were', and the bishop must have agreed, because Richard and Margery were allowed to stay together.[17] Her brother warned her that in marrying Richard she had consigned herself to a life of selling candles and mustard and, when Margery refused to listen, he and his parents cast her out.[18] Clearly, all the goods in the world didn't matter to Margery— she'd make do with candles and mustard if it meant she got to keep her man.

We don't know anything about Margery's life after the marriage, or the state of her relationship with her family, but we do know that Richard continued to work for them as their bailiff. Either the couple had been forgiven or the Pastons realized they couldn't manage without their long-standing member of staff and reluctantly kept him on.

The romance between Margery and Richard sounds like the kind of 'passionate love' that Christine de Pizan warns her readers against. In a section of *The City of Ladies* which considers whether women can be faithful in relationships, Christine makes clear that both men and women are susceptible to excessive desire, which will cloud their judgement and lead them to make bad decisions. She describes such emotion as a kind of 'natural attraction', a carnal 'instinct of the flesh', and warns her readers so energetically against this 'wild and ardent love' that we might wonder if the lady doth protest too much. It's telling that a woman who apparently found contentment in her arranged marriage should warn others to 'fly, fly from the passionate love with which they try to tempt you!'[19] Had she experienced this kind of unbridled passion prior to her marriage and been burned by it? Or was she trying to convince herself that she hadn't been missing out on anything?

. . .

One of the most famous wives from the Middle Ages is not a real historical figure at all, but a work of fiction. Alyson—or, as she's more commonly known, 'The Wife of Bath'—is the invention of Geoffrey Chaucer, one of the giants of medieval literature. She is arguably the most memorable character from his *Canterbury Tales*, a collection of poems that follows a group of pilgrims on the long journey from Southwark in London to the shrine of St Thomas Becket in Canterbury. To pass the time, the pilgrims embark on a storytelling competition—the winner will get supper and ale at the tavern on their return. We never find out who seized this coveted prize (the *Canterbury Tales* is unfinished), but many readers have favoured the crass, loud-mouthed, eminently entertaining Wife of Bath. She is a reminder that not all medieval wives were docile housekeepers—they could be loud and in charge, matching and even surpassing the bawdy jokes of their husbands.[20]

Alyson tells us that she first married when she was 12 years old, which is horrifyingly young to us but was considered an eligible age at the time. More surprisingly, Alyson tells us that she has been widowed four times and married five. One of her reasons for marrying so often, even though the Church recommended that widows took a vow of chastity, is her enjoyment of sex. Advice literature from the time, often written by men of the Church, is fairly obsessed with sex (or rather, with not having it). The Church understood the primary function of marriage to be procreation and was alarmed by anything it considered to be excessive sexual desire, even within marriage. As far as St Jerome was concerned, a man who was 'too passionately in love with his wife' was 'an adulterer', and Thomas Aquinas cautioned that a man who slept with his wife purely for pleasure was treating her like a prostitute.[21] The very existence of such warnings suggests that enough people were enjoying a healthy sex life to warrant them. Alyson is very open about how much she likes sex. She frequently references the 'marital debt', the medieval idea that husbands and wives owed each other sex as part of their marriage vows—and asks God to send her sorrow should she ever be ungenerous with her 'instrument'. She crows at the memory of how hard she made her older husbands work to satisfy her in the bedroom and says that she doesn't mind how much money a man has, so long as he can please her sexually.

Alyson also systematically refutes many of the prevailing ideas about wives when she relays the arguments she used to have with her husbands. Men are fond of saying that 'leaky houses, and also smoke/And scolding wives' force them to 'flee' out of their own homes; they complain that wives hide their vices until they are 'securely tied in marriage' and their husbands can't escape them. They say that women are vain and that they need constant attention and flattery, and they compare the love of wives to 'a barren land where no water may remain'. Such criticisms, according to Alyson, are nothing but the 'proverb[s] of a scoundrel' and an 'old barrelful of lies'—and she tells her husbands so. However, let's not forget that Alyson was the creation of a male author. Despite such protestations, she doesn't reflect well on medieval wives, because she doesn't practise what she preaches. She may defend the virtue of wives in one breath, but in the other she brags about how she manipulated her husbands; she cheated on them, lied to them, tricked them and nagged them constantly. 'Of wenches would I falsely accuse them,' she confesses, and she would always start an argument with them before they could start one with her, wearing them out with relentless false allegations to distract them from her own misdemeanours. Part of Chaucer's joke is that she inadvertently emulates most of the traits whose existence she denies.

A darker strand of Alyson's story relates to her fifth husband, Jankyn, whom she married for love (or lust) rather than for money. From the 1100s onwards, a concept called *coverture* was inscribed into medieval law. It meant that a husband and wife were considered, legally speaking, to be one financial entity, giving a husband control of his wife's capital while he was alive. A husband couldn't sell off his wife's dowry without her consent, but he was at liberty to sell or give away any of her personal effects, and any money she earned came under his control. A common trope in medieval literature is of men marrying their wives for money. 'Some had rather marry an old widow, although she is ugly and unable to bear children,' a priest warns in his sermon. 'And once he's got the money he married her for, and he feels her stinking breath and sees her bleary, scabbed eyes, he goes off and spends all his money on strumpets and ill-gotten goods.'

In most of her marriages, Alyson ignores *coverture*. 'Why hidest thou . . . the keys of your strongbox away from me?' she chides one of her husbands, when 'it is my property as well as thine'. However, things are different with her last husband, Jankyn, who convinces her to hand over everything to him and then beats her badly. Alyson's plight here is not unusual. Canonical authorities gave husbands the right of 'correction', which meant that, if their wives weren't behaving themselves, their husbands could punish them, which might involve tying them up, depriving them of food or assaulting them. A fourteenth-century handbook, *The Book of the Knight of the Tower*, tells a frightening anecdote about a wife who answered back to her husband 'vexatiously' and 'shamefully' in public.[22] In retaliation, the knight tells us, her husband struck her so hard that she fell to the ground, where he then kicked her in the face, disfiguring her nose.

The moral of this story? Wives should suffer silently and hold their peace; if they are quarrelsome or troublesome, then they deserve whatever punishment their husband decides to mete out. This story was written by a French knight for his daughters after their mother died, because he wanted to make sure they were educated properly in her absence. We know it proved popular. Nearly a dozen copies survive, translated into both English and German, and it was given to its first readers, the knight's daughters, at a young age—the knight tells us that he wrote the advice in prose, not poetry, so that it could be used by his children to 'lerne to rede'.[23] Knowing the youth of the readers makes the violence of the knight's story—and the message at its heart—especially grim.

Evidence from ecclesiastical courts suggests there was legal tolerance for an astonishingly high level of violence. Women may also have been afraid to speak up about their suffering in case the court didn't take their side. One Margaret Nesfeld, living in England in 1395, gave witness in court that her husband had attacked her with a knife, cut her arm and broken her knee.[24] After giving her testimony, she was sent back home. It may be an urban myth that the phrase 'rule of thumb' derives from the maximum width of stick with which a medieval husband could, by law, beat his wife—but it's easy to see how the false etymology came about.

. . .

There were women who, whether put off by stories like Alyson's or just for lack of interest, didn't want to get married at all. *Hali Meidhad* paints a harrowing portrait of marriage. Its author, probably a monk from the Welsh marches, asks the female reader to imagine herself married and to envisage in vivid detail how her husband would treat her. 'He rails at you and scolds you and abuses you shamefully', the author warns, 'treats you disgracefully as a lecher does his whore, beats you and thrashes you like his bought slave and born servant. Your bones ache and your flesh smarts, your heart within you swells with violent rage.'[25] He cautions the reader not to be tricked into marriage by the stirrings of sexual desire, that 'burning itch of physical desire' which leads to a 'sinful act', a 'shameless coupling', a 'stinking and wanton deed, full of filthiness'. And he dismisses the idea of happy marriages as a rare commodity: 'You say that a wife has much happiness from her husband when they are well matched, and each is pleased with the other in every way. Yes— but it is seldom seen in this world. And even supposing they do have such happiness and such delight, what does the greatest part consist in but carnal filthiness or worldly vanity.'

It seems that the anonymous author tailored his treatise either for women who had only recently taken religious vows or who were considering doing so—and might be getting cold feet. While we don't know if one such woman, Theodora, read *Hali Meidhad* or not, she certainly seemed to agree that there were options for women that were preferable to marriage—such as a life dedicated to religion.

When she was a little girl, Theodora visited a monastery in St Albans, on a pilgrimage that would change the trajectory of her life. Theodora had been a little different from a young age. Every night as she lay in her bed, she spoke to God as if he were in the room with her. Given such early signs of sanctity, Theodora was understandably delighted to visit St Albans. She was shown the sacred bones of the town's namesake, the blessed martyr St Alban, and met the monks in grey habits who had dedicated their lives to worship. She was so delighted, in fact, that, after her family left, she stayed behind to secretly scratch one of her fingernails on the door, marking the place where she had realized her heart's desire: to join a holy fellowship herself one day. The next night, as her family gossiped in the tavern, Theodora was struck by a vivid vision. She saw her future, and an image of herself on her deathbed. She realized in that instant that, were she to live a good life and devote herself to God, her spirit would be freed after death and ascend to heaven.

The next morning, Theodora approached the altar of the church near where she and her family were staying. She bent to her knees, offered a penny and made a vow of chastity. Keeping her vow would not be easy; she would endure countless cruelties from those who wanted her to break her word. But, despite the odds, she managed to remain a virgin all her life and, not long after she made her promise to God, she changed her name to honour it. She became Christina.

It was common for aristocratic families to offer at least one child to a religious life. There were social, political and spiritual advantages to having a member of the family lodged in the most powerful institutions of the West, and for the parents such an offering was a good way to help secure a path to salvation, or to offer penance for wrongdoing. Technically children needed to consent, but the letters written by various holy men to interred women suggest that many of them acquiesced under pressure. Some women, however, didn't need any persuading and had to battle furiously to win their families around—especially if there weren't many other siblings who could be pawned off into advantageous marriages.

Christina is a particularly extreme example of what could happen to a daughter who wanted to enter the religious life against the will of her parents. Her story is documented by an unknown biographer, probably a monk at St Albans monastery and certainly someone who knew Christina well, owing to the intimate knowledge he has of her life. The biography is written in Latin, as was most usual for holy matters, and survives in only one manuscript. We find it tucked away at the end of a fourteenth-century collection of saints' lives, owned by an abbot of St Albans, where it breaks off mid-sentence. Whether the scribe died before he could complete it or simply forgot to go back and finish it we'll never know. What we do have of Christina's story, however, makes for unpleasant and distressing reading, outlining the abuse she suffered at the hands of her own family.

According to her biographer, Christina was a woman of extraordinary beauty and holiness, so it's hardly surprising that she received a lot of male attention. However, not only was this attention unwanted, but it came from those she should have been able to trust. Not long after her trip to St Albans, she caught the eye of a supposed man of God. Ranulf, the bishop of Durham, invited her family to his home and, while they were distracted drinking wine downstairs, he arranged to have Christina brought to his bedchamber. Once he gave a signal his companions left him alone with her, where he attempted to rape her. She was terrified. She didn't dare call out for her parents; they had already gone to bed, and she didn't want to anger her attacker by shouting for help. Nor did she want to openly resist him or fight back, afraid that he would overpower her and take her by force. Thinking on her feet, she played along and told Ranulf that she was going to bolt the door, so that no one would walk in on them as they had sex. As soon as she reached the door, she made her escape, slipping out and locking him inside. Any relief Christina felt must have been short-lived, because, as she would soon discover, this was only the beginning of Ranulf's viciousness. Humiliated at having been rejected and tricked, the bishop made it his life's mission to ruin Christina's. Knowing how dearly she prized her vow of chastity, the best revenge he could think of was to find someone who could succeed where he had failed.

He approached a young nobleman named Beorhtred and urged him to ask for Christina's hand in marriage. Beorhtred and Christina's family were delighted—this was a good match. But Christina was devastated and resisted every attempt they made to persuade her to marry, re-declaring her vow to God. Her parents tried everything. They gave her presents, cajoled her, threatened her, punished her, all to no avail. But one day Christina's family gathered at church and accosted her. 'What more is there to say?' laments her biographer. 'I do not know how, all I know is that with God's consent Christina gave into this chorus of haranguing voices. And in the same hour Beorhtred was betrothed to her.'[26]

Christina's situation reflects the broader theological and legal context surrounding marriage. Her parents considered her married—she had made an oath, in a church, in front of witnesses—but she refused to acknowledge Beorhtred as her husband, claiming that whatever had happened between them couldn't preclude her preexisting vow to God. In the twelfth century an exchange of marriage vows was binding, but it still had to be cemented with sex. It seems that Christina's parents were well aware of this. After the incident in the church, they repeatedly let Beorhtred into her chamber at night, in the hope that he would find her sleeping and be able to violate her before she could wake up and resist.

The first night, luckily, Beorhtred found Christina awake and dressed. Rather than yielding, she stayed up all night talking to him about God. She offered to play along at marriage for a few years, while secretly remaining chaste so that his friends wouldn't think she'd jilted him, after which time they could both offer themselves up to a religious house. She must have been persuasive, because at first Beorhtred agreed. Christina's family were furious that he gave in so easily, calling him spineless and unmanly, and sent him in to try again twice more. Christina only managed to evade his unwanted advances by hiding the second night and fleeing the house altogether on the third.

Alongside these nightly attacks, Christina's parents doubled their efforts to beat and humiliate their daughter into submission. One evening her father forced her to strip into just her underskirt and ordered her to leave the house; her exile was prevented only by a guest of the family who interceded on her behalf. Another night Christina's mother beat her so badly that she bore the scars for the rest of her life.

Eventually Christina made a daring escape by dressing as a boy and riding away on horseback. After years spent in hiding she finally got her happy ending. Her marriage was annulled on the basis of parental duress and a pre-existing vow of chastity to God, and she was allowed to realize her dream of entering religious life. But why were her parents so hell-bent on forcing their daughter into a marriage she clearly didn't want, when many other families would have applauded her decision as a sign of sanctity?

It all comes back to the idea that it was the duty of the child to advance their family through marriage. According to Christina's biographer, 'such integrity, such beauty, such graciousness shone forth in Christina that all who knew her esteemed her to be above all other women.'[27] She could therefore attract the kind of economically beneficial match that a wealthy nobleman like Beorhtred offered. Put simply, Christina was worth more to her parents on the marriage market than enclosed within the walls of a nunnery.

Moreover, parents who could not keep their children to agreed promises of marriage would often become an object of shame and scandal, and would often find it difficult to arrange marriages for their other children as a consequence. When Christina's father petitioned the reverend prior and various canons of their local monastery for help, he acknowledged that both he and Christina's mother had forced their unwilling daughter into the marriage pact, but he also argued that the family would become a laughingstock if she was allowed to break it. 'I know and bear witness before my daughter that her mother and I forced her when she was unwilling into this marriage pact,' he admitted, according to her biographer. 'Yet no matter how she was led into it, if she resists our authority and rejects it, we shall be [...] a source of mockery and derision to those round about.'[28] He begged the prior, therefore, to spare them such shame by forcing Christina to honour the vow she made. Bearing in mind the abuse to which Christina had been subjected by this point, her father's admission gave her a surprising amount of power. The fate of their family, he seemed to suggest, rested in her hands.

The opposition of Christina's parents to her vow of chastity may, at first, have revolved around the idea of investment and return; but the longer Christina held out, the more it transformed into something else—a power struggle that threatened the patriarchal hierarchy of medieval society itself. If the Church allowed Christina to reject her parents' wishes, then she would become the mistress *over* her father, the head of the family and household. More than that she would become, in effect, a man—able to come and go as she pleased, to do as she liked. What was really at stake was power. It may have taken years, and at times her suffering may have been almost impossible to bear, but power is exactly what Christina eventually achieved.

• • •

'You are no good wife, Margery.'[29]

These are the words of John Kempe to his wife. She has been married to him for long enough to give him 14 children, but now, she tells him, she's had enough. She doesn't want to have sex with him ever again. After eight weeks of abstinence, a sexually frustrated John asks her what she would do if a man appeared and threatened to cut off his head unless she agreed to resume having sex with him? Margery, beer in hand, thinks for a moment and replies: 'Truly, I would rather see you murdered than have sex with you again.'

What might explain this sudden change of heart in Margery, who at this point had been married for many years? Perhaps the clue lies in the astonishing number of children she bore. In the fifteenth century contraception was far less effective. Anaesthetics wouldn't be invented for another four hundred years, and nor would painkillers—Margery would have relied on amulets and gemstones to ease her agony in the birth chamber. Or perhaps she simply considered her sexual duties fulfilled, having given her husband so many children already. Margery insinuates at various points in her autobiography that, at the beginning of her marriage, she enjoyed having sex with John. However, she also says that their unbridled lust and 'inordinate love' disappointed God. Whatever the reason, denying your spouse sex in the Middle Ages was a serious business. According to the Church, sex was something owed, both legally and morally, to your partner; and the promises you made in your wedding vows were not open to renegotiation. A legal treatise written in 1736, long after Margery's death, tells us that 'the husband of a woman cannot himself be guilty of an actual rape upon his wife, on account of the matrimonial consent which she has given, and which she cannot retract'—this fact was even more true in the medieval period.[30]

It may be that Margery sought to avoid pregnancy, that the desire had left the relationship, or that she felt her feelings for her husband had been too 'inordinate'.[31] However, there is another reason that she gives us for her refusal, one that is both simpler and much more complex. Margery didn't want to have sex with her husband any more because there was another man in her life. Like Christina's, her head had been turned by God.

. . .

The first time Margery noticed God she was in bed with her husband. Until then, Margery hadn't paid him too much attention. She was a Christian woman who went to church, but neither God nor religion had played an especially big part in her life. This was about to change. On the night in question, Margery heard music so sweet and delectable that she thought she might be in paradise. She jumped up and declared, 'Alas that ever I sinned, it is full merry in heaven!'[32]

This experience had a transformative effect on Margery. For ever after, when she heard music of any kind, she was reminded of her heavenly vision and burst into noisy tears of devotion. Often, when she was in company, she was possessed with an uncontrollable urge to shout 'It is full merry in heaven!'—which often startled and infuriated whoever she happened to be talking to. This musical epiphany was just the beginning. Not long afterwards, God started to appear to Margery: she could see him, touch him, speak to him, hear him speak back. By the time God urged Margery to take him into bed as if he were her wedded husband, John had been well and truly displaced. Margery might have become a 'no good wife' to her earthly spouse, but she was desperate to be the best possible wife to her spiritual one. We know from her autobiography that on pilgrimage in Rome, on 9 November 1414, a wedding between God and Margery took place 'in her soul', for which she borrowed the language of a late medieval English ceremony: 'I take you, Margery,' God said to her, 'to be my wedded wife, for better, for worse, for richer, for poorer.' She even purchased a wedding ring, inscribed with the words 'Jesus is my love', as a token of their marriage.[33]

Getting married to God wasn't an idea unique to Margery. When nuns took their vows at convents, they did so in the form of a wedding ceremony. Often wearing white to represent their virginity, they would don a headdress and veil, and receive a ring which symbolically 'tied' them to their new husband. Margery, however, was not a nun, and her wedding ceremony took place in her vision, far from the prying eyes—and control—of the Church. Moreover, unlike a nun, Margery already had a husband. Her new, self-imposed status as bride of Christ meant that she couldn't have sex with John any more; by this point she would have considered doing so to be adultery—against God. But he certainly didn't give in easily. When he eventually did concede and swore chastity alongside Margery in Lincoln, in front of Bishop Repingdon, he only did so because Margery had agreed to pay off his debts.

Margery is an exceptional example of a medieval wife. But her story reminds us that people changed their minds as much in the Middle Ages as they do now. It seems that the first years of Margery and John's marriage were relatively happy ones, and that they may even have been wildly in love. But, as Margery grew older, her dreams and her ambitions grew with her—and the marriage had to follow suit.

. . .

The lives and writings of Christine de Pizan, Christina and Margery Kempe make clear the harsh realities of medieval marriage, especially when it comes to wives. They highlight the lack of choice women had in romantic partnerships, the expectations placed on them by their families and by society, the misbehaviour, even violence, that they were expected to endure from their husbands. For women, marriage meant handing over their money and property, not to mention their body, to a man they might know very little about, who may well have been chosen for them and from whom only death, impotence or excessive cruelty could separate them.

However, their stories also remind us that there were medieval women who did manage to find love and happiness in marriage—or who, failing that, found creative ways to resist or rework it. Christine de Pizan may have been frustrated by the stereotypes of marriage in her books but, rather than advocating against the institution itself (a step too far for a medieval noble-woman, albeit a progressive one), she chose to platform examples of when it had worked for both men and women. She knew such a thing was possible because she herself had experienced it. When Margery Kempe decided to take up a religious life, she didn't abandon her relationship. Rather, she worked hard to reshape it. Her savvy negotiations with her husband are an example of how, even in the Middle Ages, there were women who believed they had a right to say no, or to change their mind, regardless of what promises they might have once made. And then, of course, there were women like Christina, who successfully managed to resist the institution altogether. A young girl with everything to lose, she stood up to her family and refused a wedding, convinced that marriage was not for her. All these women approached marriage on their own terms, deciding what being a 'good' wife meant for them, regardless of what society might say—and even if it meant not becoming a wife at all.

THREE

Bit on the Side

'Des que sis sires s'en depart,/E nuit e jur e tost e tart/Ele l'ad
tut a sun pleisir./Or l'en duinst Deus lunges joïr!'*

MARIE DE FRANCE, *Lais*

Who are the most famous lovers of all time? The star-crossed Romeo and
Juliet from feuding families. The grumpy, eccentric Mr Rochester and his
fiercely independent governess in Charlotte Bronte's *Jane Eyre*. The intelligent, vivacious Elizabeth Bennett who gives Mr Darcy a run for his money
in *Pride and Prejudice*. Not to mention Beauty and the Beast, Harry and
Sally, Mary and Joseph, Cinderella and Prince Charming, Angel and Buffy,
Robin and Marian. While all these relationships have their hiccups, none of
them involves sexual infidelity—*Jane Eyre* does get close, but the heroine
flees before becoming an accidental mistress. The most famous lovers of the
Middle Ages, however, were often adulterous.

Even those who don't know much about the medieval era are likely to have
heard of King Arthur of Camelot, who presided over a Round Table of illustri-
ous knights. Arthur occupies a shady space between reality and fiction. Evidence
for a historical King Arthur is scant. Two early Latin chronicles, the *Annales
Cambriae* and the *Historia Brittonum,* briefly reference a leader named Arthur,
or Arturus, who led a band of warriors in bloody resistance against invading
forces around the fifth and sixth centuries—but both sources are significantly
earlier than most medieval legends.[1] By the later Middle Ages, however, there
were countless stories about Arthur and his adventures, and, despite their many
fantastical elements, Arthur is always presented as a real historical figure.
Arthur was married to a beautiful noblewoman named Guinevere. About her
we know very little—she remains a shadowy figure throughout most of the
legends. In some of the earliest versions she is a prize won by a warrior king, in
others she is a Roman lady, but she is always described as being very beautiful.

---

* 'as soon as her husband went away/early and late, night and day/she had her pleasure
with the knight;/God grant these two long delight!'

She can be kind and loving but also jealous, quarrelsome and inconstant; and in terms of her actions, she is usually being abducted and then rescued, or precipitating the downfall of the Round Table through her infidelity.

Interestingly, in the first ever reference to Guinevere she is unfaithful—a cursory aside in Geoffrey of Monmouth's *History of the Kings of Britain* reveals that she is cheating on her husband with his nephew Mordred.[2] But her character remained largely undeveloped until one particularly prolific and popular French writer, Chrétien de Troyes, came along to flesh out her story in 1177.[3] In his Arthurian legends he introduced a compelling and enduring affair between the queen and Lancelot, one of Arthur's best and most loyal knights, which captured the hearts of readers and writers alike. Many other authors followed suit, and by the later Middle Ages the love story between Guinevere and Lancelot had far outstripped that of the queen and her king. This was the real love story of Camelot.

The many different accounts culminate in Thomas Malory's fifteenth-century English compilation *Le Morte d'Arthur* (The Death of Arthur).[4] In his version the affair between Lancelot and Guinevere is unproblematic while it remains a secret, but when some of the knights begin to suspect what's happening and report their concerns to King Arthur, events take a darker turn. Because Arthur is a king, Guinevere's actions are treasonous, and although he doesn't want to punish the lovers, he must. In a high-stakes scene where Lancelot and Guinevere are in bed together and various knights are attempting to break down their door, Lancelot escapes just in time, but Guinevere is not so lucky. She is arrested and condemned to the grisly death of being burned at the stake. While it breaks Arthur's heart to mete out this punishment, he is certain that Lancelot will save her before she comes to harm. And he's right. Just as the flames begin to lick her feet, Lancelot swoops in to throw her over his horse and charge away to safety.

It's not long before she returns, wracked with guilt, to beg her husband's forgiveness. Arthur takes her back but mobilizes an army against Lancelot, leaving his kingdom in the care of his illegitimate son Mordred. With Camelot left unprotected, Mordred betrays Arthur and attempts to abduct Guinevere. When Arthur returns to fight him, both father and son are fatally wounded and Camelot crumbles. The adulterous love between Guinevere and Lancelot, so the story goes, brings about the fall of the most celebrated kingdom in medieval British history.

What is especially interesting about this popular medieval love story is the lack of criticism directed at Lancelot or Guinevere for their infidelity. The kingdom of Camelot was a desperately nostalgic one for many English writers. Arthur was the best king, his knights were the best knights and his rule was a golden age that would never be seen again. Guinevere and Lancelot, and their illicit love, are largely to blame for this loss, according to so many Arthurian legends. And yet most authors still extol Guinevere as the noblest of queens and lavish praise on Lancelot. The love triangle is presented as a tragedy that cannot be prevented, in which all three parties are full of mutual admiration and love for one another, despite the betrayal that has occurred. The grief when their delicate threesome is disbanded is very real, and the underlying moral seems to be that their affair wasn't hurting anyone while it was kept secret. Things only start to go awry when the affair is brought to light and the king is forced to act.

Suffice to say, the treatment of Lancelot and Guinevere subverts any expectation that all affairs were treated as scandalous and wicked in the Middle Ages. It's difficult to know what to make of this leniency. Adultery was a sin, even a crime, in the Middle Ages. But while medieval Europe was a heteronormative and religious society, clearly there was an interest in stories of both men and women who strayed. The sympathy shown towards characters such as Guinevere and Lancelot hints at the reality that, despite the best efforts of the Church and legal system to deter adultery, there were men and women who felt trapped, miserable or just a bit bored in their marriages— and did something about it.

• • •

The word 'adultery' originally comes from Middle English, when it had the quite general meaning of 'voluntary violation of the marriage bed' and therefore covered all kinds of sexual misdemeanours, from excessive desire within marriage to sex with a priest.[5] But in the twelfth century canon lawyers began to define the term more narrowly and it came to mean much the same as it does today: sex between a single or married person and someone else's spouse of the opposite sex. There were some exceptions. Sex between two men was deemed sodomy, not adultery—still a crime, but a different one. Moreover, because of their biological makeup, women were believed to be more sexually voracious, so when they committed adultery their husbands were thought to be at least partly to blame for not controlling them. 'Women's Secrets' puts it this way: 'Woman is less suited to morals than man, for the humidity in her complexion is easily mobile, and thus she is inconstant and always seeking something new.' Because of this belief, 'there is no faith in woman', and husbands who allowed their wives to work in jobs with high temptation rates (an alehouse, for example) were not allowed to press charges, the idea being they should know better than to let their lustful wives stray into the path of temptation.[6]

The sin of adultery was something that the Church took very seriously. It was an offence that was actionable in Church courts and equated with the mortal sin of 'blasphemy' because it was a sin against the body and the body was the temple of the lord. In fact, adultery was established during the Middle Ages as one of the three capital sins, alongside idolatry (observing a religion other than Christianity) and murder. Male authors of penitentials waxed lyrical on the sin of adultery and suggested appropriate reparation. A married man caught cheating with a neighbour's wife or daughter, for example, would have to do penance, be it fasting, extra prayers or self-flagellation for a year, and abstain from having sex with his wife for the same length of time. Such punishments were almost impossible to enforce and were very much precautionary, designed to put people off committing the crime in the first place. In the most severe cases of extramarital activities, the adulterous perpetrators could be excommunicated, which meant being exiled from most social activities in the community and treated like a pariah. While technically the sin of adultery was grave for both men and women, and should be punished equally according to the Church, canonists were far more interested in the adultery of women.

The Middle Ages were kinder to adulterous parties than their Roman predecessors, who allowed a betrayed husband to murder the man who had slept with his wife. There is evidence of medieval jurors putting a certain spin on events to exonerate men who had committed murder in just these circumstances, but most cases of adultery were settled with either a punishment or a fine. In July 1347 Isabel, the wife of Robert atte Kyrk, was found guilty of deserting her husband and sleeping with the local chaplain. She was required to return to her husband and 'to treat him peacefully and quietly and to humbly obey him and not provoke his anger'.[7] If she didn't comply, then she would suffer the pain of six beatings around the church of Skelinton, dressed only in her nightshirt. This was designed not only to cause physical pain to an adulterer but also, more importantly, to humiliate them. Being forced out onto the streets in just a nightshirt was almost as bad as being naked in public. Everyone who saw the unhappy criminal would know what they had done and could add to their degradation by jeering or throwing things. All the while, the adulterer was expected to bear their pain and embarrassment humbly, a visual reminder of what could befall anyone who broke their marriage vows. The threat of such a shameful experience was probably enough to keep Isabel obedient, and it looks as though she returned to her husband to avoid it. As for the chaplain, who would probably have preached against adultery in his Sunday sermons, no penalty is ascribed to him in the court records.

Straightforward cases of adultery were left to the Church courts, but if there were financial or patrimonial consequences, then the secular law courts might get involved. Financial repercussions could include an adulterous wife's dowry, property or other means; from 1285 onwards, if a wife abandoned her husband for a lover, even if she left consensually, her desertion was framed as abduction or kidnap, a crime for which the lover could be prosecuted and the wayward wife could lose her inheritance. Such measures were clearly intended to protect not only the sanctity of marriage but also the property rights of men. There were variations and nuances in adultery laws across Europe. Adulterers in France were far more likely to pay a fine than to enact public penance, for example, whereas in London the reverse was true. But in general, the principles remained the same. Adultery was a sin and a crime, and it should be punished, but the ideal outcome was reconciliation of the married couple.

. . .

Bearing in mind most marriages in the medieval European courts were arranged, and not everyone would have been enamoured of their new spouse, a concept called 'courtly love' was devised among the nobility. This was a code of conduct that allowed the youth at court to 'play' at adultery, without taking it too far. Originating in the French-speaking courts of Aquitaine, Provence, Burgundy, Champagne, Sicily and Normandy, it quickly grew in popularity as members of those courts were married off across Europe. Rather than committing any sin, or breaking the law, the lovelorn would write poems and songs for the objects of their desire, bring them secret gifts and letters and shower them with compliments. Usually, lovers were single men who had their eye on married women.

Courtly love was a game with its own set of rules, penned by a man named Andreas Capellanus. All we know of Capellanus's life is that he describes himself as a chaplain of the French court, an unlikely candidate for a love manual perhaps but someone who, sworn to celibacy, would have experienced unfulfilled desire. He apparently wrote *De Amore* ('On Love') at the request of Countess Marie of Troyes, a princess of the royal French court and an energetic patron of the arts. His book enjoyed considerable popularity— various manuscripts survive, translated into several different languages—and provides insight into attitudes towards extramarital romance in the courts. 'When made public, love rarely endures', Capellanus warns, condoning instead the hidden messages and secret glances that we find in the *lais* of Marie de France. 'The easy attainment of love makes it of little value; difficulty of attainment makes it prized' and 'A true lover is constantly and without intermission possessed by the thought of his beloved.' Love means suffering, obsession, and it also means suspicion, for 'real jealousy always increases the feeling of love'. There is an element of snobbery embedded in these rules too. According to Capellanus, only rich people could truly experience love. Peasants, too unintelligent to comprehend the ennobling force that drove knights to chivalric acts, simply copulated like animals.[8]

It is hard to determine to what extent courtly love really played out in the courts. Was *De Amore* satirical, a wry comment on the adultery that went on among the nobility, and the excuses they used to justify it? Or was it genuinely used as a practical handbook for young lovers? Christine de Pizan's *Treasure of the City of Ladies* suggests that men at court did model themselves on the behaviour prescribed by Capellanus, but she is quick to warn her readers against entertaining such conduct. According to Christine, 'knights and squires and all men (especially certain men)' will 'plead for love tokens' from women and 'try to seduce them', only to brag about their conquests as soon as their lady's back is turned.[9]

The precepts of courtly love leaked into literature too, where it is often presented as a problem to be solved. Capellanus makes clear that an adulterous affair doesn't necessarily undermine the relationship between a husband and wife ('nothing forbids one woman being loved by two men or one man by two women'), and he suggests that a woman 'owes' it to a faithful lover to ease his suffering by reciprocation. If a vassal pursues the wife of his lord, then he is paying him the highest kind of compliment. Marie de France reasons out another scenario in one of her adulterous tales.

In *Equitan* a king falls in love with the wife of his seneschal, a man who governed his territory and meted out justice on the king's behalf and who, more importantly, was a loyal friend to his king.[10] At first, the king is wracked with guilt: 'I think I have no option but to love her. Yet, if I did love her, I should be acting wrongly, as she is the seneschal's wife. I ought to keep faith with him and love him as I want him to do with me.' After some soul-search-ing, however, he uses the ideals of courtly love to justify his actions: 'How could she be a true courtly lady, if she had no true love?' Convincing himself that the seneschal has no right to be upset—'he cannot keep her entirely for himself. I am certainly willing to share her with him'—he reveals his love to the seneschal's wife, who reciprocates. But the tale ends in tragedy: the king kills himself when the affair is discovered, out of shame, and the seneschal kills his wife. The moral of the story, as Marie gives it, is that 'evil can easily rebound on him who seeks another's misfortune'. Her story serves to play out the logic of courtly love to expose how easily it crumbles when two clandes-tine lovers are found in bed together.

It's unlikely that adulterous behaviour was condoned in noble or royal circles. If anything, the murderous ending to Marie de France's *Equitan* feels more realistic than the king's internal reasoning about how the seneschal should react. Perhaps these stories and games of courtly love were a kind of wish fulfilment—a playing out of fantasy in a strict and regimented world, especially for women. In real medieval royal life affairs *did* happen, but kings and princes rarely turned a blind eye, and they could have disastrous, even deadly, consequences.

In 1313 Queen Isabella of England, known as the 'she-wolf', was visiting her family in France and enjoying herself at a tournament when something caught her eye. Two knights, the handsome d'Aulnay brothers, were carrying expensively embroidered silk purses as they charged about on their horses. Isabella had seen those purses before. She'd given them as gifts to her sisters-in-law—one to Blanche, wife of Prince Charles, the youngest son of King Philip IV of France, and one to Marguerite, wife of Prince Louis of Navarre, the heir to the French throne. So what were these knights doing with Isabella's gifts?

It was common knowledge that Marguerite and Louis had an unhappy marriage—Louis was known in France as 'The Quarreller'—and Blanche was a naïve young woman, easily led astray. Suspecting foul play, Isabella bit her tongue. But in 1314, on her next visit, she went to her father the king to express her deepest fear: the two princesses were having an affair with the d'Aulnay knights and had given them the purses as a token of their love. The brothers were put under immediate surveillance and, not long after, impris-oned and tortured, eventually confessing to a three-year affair with Marguerite and Blanche. The princesses were also arrested and interrogated. Marguerite confessed. One contemporary chronicle describes how she 'continually wept and cried, not for her trouble, but her sin, and particularly because, on account of what she'd done, other noblewomen would be subjected to suspicion'.[11] Blanche, on the other hand, never admitted any wrongdoing, and according to some sources she was led astray by the 'slut and concubine' Marguerite.[12] Whether Blanche was innocent or simply did a better job at holding out against interrogation, we'll never know—but both princesses were found guilty.

We don't know the truth behind the scandalous happenings of the spring of 1314. It was a sensitive topic—why had the king and his sons not done a better job of keeping these women in check?—and contemporary commentators shied away from risking the king's wrath by writing about it. Nearly everything we know about the affair comes from a small handful of historical chronicles, a genre that was known for intermingling fact and fiction. There are discrepancies, for example, as to the severity of the punishments. The *Grandes Chroniques de France* tells us that 'Marguerite and Blanche were exiled and locked up in prison for ever [. . .] condemned to die there', but other sources add in more detail—that their hair was shorn, they were stripped of their fine robes and forced to wear sackcloths and that, most horrifyingly of all, they were ordered to witness the ghastly, drawn-out execution of their lovers.[13]

The unfortunate knights, according to all the chronicles, were 'skinned and castrated' before being dragged to the gallows and hanged, drawn and quartered.[14] After that, accounts differ, but they are all lurid. Some say that the private parts of the brothers were thrown to the dogs while they watched. Others say that molten lead was poured onto their exposed and vulnerable flesh after they'd been flayed. And some describe their bleeding bodies being strapped to a wheel while their bones were broken with iron bars before they were finally decapitated.[15] We don't know how many of these depictions are accurate, or at which point during their lengthy torture and execution the knights finally died, but it's not hard to imagine what the princesses must have felt watching the bodies of these young men being broken.

Blanche and Marguerite avoided execution themselves, but more punishment lay in store for them. Marguerite, as the wife of the dauphin, had the harsher retribution. She was imprisoned in a high tower, where, according to one source, she was exposed to the wind and the rain, shivering in her sackcloth, provided with no other clothing or bedding and very little food.[16] If this is true, then her death in prison, when it came, must have been something of a relief. Blanche was separated from her sister-in-law and imprisoned underground in primitive conditions until her husband paid the pope to annul their marriage and she was ushered off to a convent. In that convent she gave birth to a child. The father? Her jailer. The most likely assumption to make here, however harrowing, is that he raped her.

This so-called 'Tour de Nesle' affair is one of the most infamous, and one of the most gruesome, examples of adultery. While royal wives were often accused of being unfaithful, and sometimes executed for it, the protracted nature of the suffering of everyone involved is unusual. But the events in France make clear how high the stakes were when the infidelity of women whose children might be heir to the throne was suspected. We don't know if Isabella was really responsible for blowing the whistle on her sisters-in-law—it could have just been a rumour. We don't even know if the princesses were guilty of their crime. Chronicles express amazement that it could have gone unnoticed for so long, especially given the number of watchful eyes always trained on the royal family. 'Some commonly said that they arranged things through enchantment', one reports, but then coyly reminds us not to believe everything that we hear.[17] Duress may have been a factor. The knights confessed under torture, and Marguerite herself may well have been pressured into confessing. Or perhaps she hoped she might avoid execution if she owned up to wrongdoing and repented. It's also possible, as some historians have speculated, that the husbands of these princesses were looking for a way out of their marriage contracts because neither wife had produced a male heir.

Regardless, the allegations were clearly taken with a deadly seriousness by the king, and the ripple effect was expansive. Marguerite and Louis had one child, Jeanne, but her mother's apparent infidelity called her legitimacy as an heir into question. When his father died, Louis knew he had to produce an heir quickly to secure his position on the throne, and in August 1315 Marguerite died in prison. Just five days later, Louis married another woman. Rumour had it that Marguerite had been strangled, on the orders of the king. The timing does seem convenient. The issues with succession that followed the affair may even have contributed, albeit indirectly, to the Hundred Years of War between England and France. Because the French throne had been left without a watertight male heir, it created an opportunity. Some years later King Edward III of England, the son of Queen Isabella, declared himself king of France and invaded the country to claim his birthright.

The most common accusations of adultery were directed at the mother of whoever was king at the time, as this was a sure-fire way to cast doubt on the legitimacy of their son's noble blood. We see this happen time and again during the infamous Wars of the Roses. This conflict took place at the tail end of the Middle Ages, by which time the four women this book follows had passed away—and they were lucky to have missed it. It is impossible to know precise figures, but some estimate that the Wars of the Roses killed 50,000 people. While ordinary people laid down their lives in continual battles, the nobility argued over who had the right to claim the throne, with each side using allegations of adultery to undermine the legitimacy of the other. When Henry IV deposed Richard II in 1399, a rumour spread that Richard was the product of an affair between his mother and a clerk of Bordeaux, not a prince at all. Three years later, when an attempt to extract Henry IV was made, more rumours circulated, this time claiming that Henry himself was not of noble blood but the son of a lowly butcher in Ghent. And in 1469, when George, the duke of Clarence, challenged his brother Edward IV for the throne, he justified his actions by claiming that Edward was a bastard. George's rebellion failed, and he met a grisly end, executed by his brother. But even with George out of the way, the rumours persisted and would crop up with renewed vigour whenever Edward's decisions proved unpopular.

Most of these accusations were simply rumours, with no real evidence to support them. But they reveal a culture of looking to women's sexual behaviour to explain the misfortune of a king. Is he ruling badly? Maybe his mother had an affair. Or his wife. Of course, there were plenty of rumours about kings sleeping with other people, both women and men. But their infidelities didn't throw the royal bloodline into question—queens made a far better scapegoat when things were going south. Perhaps Guinevere got off lightly in medieval opinion because there were never any children involved—no heirs whose legitimacy could be called into question because of their mother's infidelity.

The Church preached that adultery was a sin, regardless of whether you were a husband or a wife, and there is no evidence to suggest that women were treated more harshly for adultery than their husbands in the medieval courts. However, the stakes were far higher for women. Medieval writers moaned that, ever since Eve ate the apple, good men had been led astray by wicked women. Some were even accused of using witchcraft to entice men away from their wives. The infamous witch trials of the early modern period may have been a hundred or so years away, but the foundations for the craze had already been laid in medieval attitudes towards women, sex and magic.

The *Malleus Maleficarum* (The Hammer of Witches) was a Latin text used by the authorities during the trials to identify witches, and much of its rhetoric has its roots in misogynistic medieval ideas about women's bodies and their predilection to sin and to sex. '*Women's Secrets*' tells readers that 'the more women have sexual intercourse, the stronger they become, because they are made hot from the motion that the man makes during coitus' and that 'woman has a greater desire for coitus than a man, for something foul is drawn to the good'.[18] The *Malleus* could easily be quoting from this earlier text when it claims that 'all witchcraft comes from carnal lust, which in women is insatiable'.[19] Women are obsessed with sex and determined to obtain it at any cost. And while most magic was condemned during the Middle Ages as superstition, European courts do cite cases in which women were suspected of enchantment, usually in relation to adultery.

In 1359 a widow called Bartholomea from San Lorenzo a Vaccoli, in Tuscany, was accused of enchanting a married man named Ciucchino. According to the court records, 'she performed harmful magic and other enchantments, on account of which Ciucchino, like one accursed, did not and does not wish to remain with his wife, but has expelled her from his bed and home, and lives with Bartholomea. And he has often visited harsh and intolerable beatings on his innocent wife Bella.'[20] Rather than accept that Ciucchino was a bit of a rat, his friends preferred to believe that his lover was a witch. The charges of witchcraft were eventually dropped, but Bartholomea was still punished for adultery, ordered to spend the rest of her life at least five miles away from the commune of Vaccoli at all times, on pain of excommunication and perpetual imprisonment. For Ciucchino there were no such repercussions, either for his adultery or for his physical violence towards his wife.

· · ·

Medieval art and literature often revolved around the fear of hell and damnation, so one might assume people were too scared of the spiritual consequences to act on their secret desires. But hundreds of years ago men and woman felt the same yearnings as we do today, and there were some medieval women who did seek solace outside of marriage, for many different reasons and with varying degrees of risk. Even the most religious and devout women were susceptible to temptation.

Since her conversion, Margery Kempe had been unshakeable in her faith. 'She could well endure fasting—it did not trouble her', her *Book* tells us. She no longer cared about the latest fashion or gossiping with her friends, and 'she felt not rebellion in her flesh'—by which she means that she no longer had any interest in sex, either with her husband or anyone else. 'She was so strong—as she thought—that she feared no devil in hell.'[21] Unfortunately for Margery, she thought wrong. In congratulating herself so readily, she had unknowingly succumbed to the deadly sin of pride. And so, to punish her, Jesus put Margery through a gruelling period of temptation. For three years she felt an intense and constant desire, but not for her husband. Her local priest, her neighbour, the butcher, the baker, the candlestick maker—they all got her feeling hot under the collar, which was 'very painful and horrible to her' because she knew such desires were a sin.[22] In the second year of her affliction, when she was attending evensong at her local church, a man 'whom she liked' approached her before the service. He said that he would do anything to 'sleep with her and enjoy the lust of his body' and that, even if she resisted him, 'she should not withstand him.' If he couldn't 'have his desire' this time, then he would take it another time by force.

This man was threatening to rape Margery. She assumed that his words were 'in earnest' and said very little in reply. But rather than being terrified or angry, as you might expect, Margery was interested. For the rest of the service, 'she could not listen to evensong or say prayers, or think any good thought', but was more troubled with lustful feelings than she had ever been before. By the time it was over, her mind was made up. She walked up to the man, intending to let him have his way with her, but he acted as if he had no idea what she was talking about and left her standing there, confused. Lying next to her husband that night, burning up with desire for anyone but him, Margery decided she had to give things another try. The next morning she marched straight up to the man and asked him if he was willing to have sex with her. Despite all his declarations of desire the day before, he rejected her. 'Not for all the wealth in the world', he replied. 'I'd rather be chopped up as small as meat for the pot.'

It's hard to read Margery's account of these events without feeling sorry for her. The desire she feels is not organic; it's a spiritual test which leads her to pursue an adulterous relationship with a would-be rapist. Moreover, she's left feeling ashamed when her suitor turns the tables on her. The anecdote reminds us that, despite having dedicated her life to God, Margery was only human. She felt love and desire just like anyone else, and she didn't always make the right choices when her feelings got in the way.

My students are always surprised to hear that people in the Middle Ages had sex at all, let alone outside of marriage. They imagine this to be a prudish period, controlled as it was by the Church and the threat of what capital sins such as adultery, or any kind of sex that the Church deemed to be 'improper', could do to one's soul. But evidence suggests that medieval people often had a much healthier attitude to sex than we've imagined.

For a start, medieval people found sex funny. One of the most popular poems was the thirteenth-century French dream poem the *Roman de la Rose* ('Romance of the Rose').[23] Following a man's romantic pursuit of a rose-maiden, it claims to reveal to readers the secrets of courtship. It is hard to overstate how venerated, influential and controversial this poem was in medieval Europe. It survives in over three hundred manuscripts, and was translated into multiple languages, including English thanks to Geoffrey Chaucer, and was particularly popular among the nobility. While purporting to explore the high ideals of courtly love, it often treated women as nothing more than sex objects. The male protagonist, an allegorical figure called Genius, compares writing with sexual penetration. Those who do not write with their 'tools' on the precious 'tablets' (women) that nature has made for them 'should be buried alive'.[24] Here the Old French word for 'tool' doubles as both pen and penis, and Genius uses the pun to describe women as passively awaiting the imprint of men. Any man who either neglects to use his penis to penetrate women—or who uses it to penetrate other men instead—deserves to be castrated.

While many readers loved the poem, some were less impressed. Christine de Pizan, responding to the poet's claim that 'all of you women are, will be and have been whores', entered into a fiery and contentious debate about the *Roman* with a number of men, including influential scholars and intellectuals.[25] 'If only [the poet] had blamed the dishonest women and advised avoiding them, he would have provided a good and just lesson', she laments. 'But no! Without exception, he accuses them all.'[26] She takes up this theme again in *The City of Ladies*, in which she aims to have the last word. Her examples of historical and legendary women are designed to prove that 'the female sex is in fact extremely steadfast in matters of the heart'.[27] She tells of the ancient Roman queen, Hypsicratea, wife of King Mithridates, who 'bore her husband such a deep love' that she always remained with him, despite his 'several concubines', even when he marched into battle.[28] And of Cornelia, the wife of Pompey, who 'loved her husband so dearly that she refused to leave him, no matter what misfortune befell him', and who 'faced every danger at his side'.[29]

What does all of this have to do with humour? At least a dozen copies of the *Roman de la Rose* were illuminated by a woman, Jeanne de Montbaston, who managed a famous bookshop in Paris with her husband. In the margins of one copy of the book made in Paris around 1325, we find some surprising images in her hand. A monk with fiery red hair offers a demure-looking nun a comically large penis, which she opens her hands wide to receive. The same monk, in a different vignette, lies on top of the nun with his trousers down, on a bale of hay—her facial expression one of resignation, or perhaps incredulity, rather than enjoyment. And in a third image she picks fruit from a tree made entirely of big, red-tipped penises which she pops into her basket for safe-keeping. These illuminations have become iconic (especially the penis tree), despite having absolutely nothing to do with the events of the poem, because they reveal a playful side to medieval people that hasn't always been acknowledged. While some have suggested that Jeanne was illiterate and couldn't read the poem she was illustrating, I think her plethora of penises befits a poem obsessed with a man's 'tool' and how he should use it.

Imagery of genitalia found its way to religious spaces too. The illustrations in medieval prayer books showing the wound in Christ's side at the crucifixion look suspiciously like blood-soaked, menstruating vulvas. Pilgrim badges boast male genitalia, and we also find 'Sheela Na Gigs', the name given to quasi-erotic stone carvings, on Norman churches all over Britain, Ireland and even France and Spain. In these carvings an old woman squats and pulls apart her vulva while either smiling or leering at passers-by. Some believe that the Sheela Na Gigs are a warning against the sins of lust, or a talisman guarding against evil. Others think that they represent a pre-Christian folk goddess, and that their exaggerated vulvas are a sign of fertility and life-giving powers. Whatever their meaning, these carvings may be grotesque but are also undeniably comical.

Medieval literature about adultery wasn't all the high stakes, tortured glances and agonized soul-searching that we find in the writing of Marie de France and Arthurian legend either. One of the most famous of Chaucer's *Canterbury Tales* is told by a drunken miller; in it a carpenter named John marries a beautiful teenager called Alison.[30] He loved her 'more than his life' but he was also jealous—he was old, she was young and 'wild', with a 'wanton eye'. Fearing she might make a cuckold out of him, he tried to keep her as confined as possible, but she quickly caught the attention of two local men. One was Nicholas, an astrology student renting a room from John, and the other was Absolon, a parish clerk. Absolon mounted a determined campaign to win Alison over, 'dressing himself elegantly', combing his 'flowing locks' of hair, 'trilling like a nightingale' under her window, sending her gifts of 'sweetened wine, mead, and spiced ale', even offering her money—but she remained uninterested. Nicholas's first attempt to woo Alison was equally unsuccessful. He grabbed her by the 'queynte' (her private parts) and told her he would die if he couldn't have sex with her. She 'sprang as a colt does when restrained' at this sexual harassment, and furiously told him to take his hands off her or she would cry for help.

However, Nicholas refused to give up. He begged for her mercy, and he 'spoke so fair' and 'pressed his suit' so well that Alison finally agreed to have sex with him. Together, they hatched a plan. When Nicholas told the carpenter that there was going to be a massive flood the following Monday night, which was expected to be even more destructive than the one in Noah's time, the gullible carpenter believed him. Nicholas suggested that to save themselves, he, Alison and John should hang three large tubs from the ceiling of the barn, each loaded up with provisions and an axe. When the flood waters rose, they would be able to use the axe to cut the ropes and drift off to safety. Dutifully, John engineered the three tubs and when, exhausted from his labours, he fell asleep, Alison and Nicholas slipped away to the bedroom. While John snored and the two young lovers turned his marital bed into a place of 'mirth and pleasure,' the lovelorn Absolon made another visit to Alison's window, seeking a kiss. By now, Alison was fed up with her stalker. Seeing an opportunity to humiliate him, she promised to give him what he asked for. Absolon 'wiped his mouth very dry' and chewed on some cardamon and liquorice to sweeten his breath in preparation. Alison, barely able to stifle her giggles, put her bare bum out the window ('out the window she put her hole') and Absolon, unable to see in the dark of the night, 'kissed her naked arse'. With the laughter of Nicholas and Alison ringing in his ears, Absolon went home and returned to the window with a red-hot poker concealed behind his back. This time, he asked Alison for another real kiss in exchange for a ring. Nicholas, who had just 'risen to piss', put his own bare bum out the window to 'let fly a fart, as great as if it had been a thunderbolt'. Furious, Absolon retaliated with a blow from his poker, 'right in the middle of [Nicholas's] arse'. In agony, Nicholas cried out 'Water!', and John, thinking the flood had come, instantly woke up. Quick as a flash, he cut the ropes of his boat and crashed to the ground, breaking his arm. After all this commotion, the people of the town came running and, hearing what had happened, all fell about laughing. John had a broken arm, Absolon had kissed a naked arse and Nicholas had been struck up the bum with a red-hot poker. Alison is the only one who emerges unscathed.

The joke is not on the adulterous lovers but on John—for being stupid enough to believe their story and for marrying a wife far younger and more attractive than himself. While this is a fictional tale, it suggests that, when adultery occurred among the lower classes, it was perceived as humorous rather than tragic or ennobling. Clearly, medieval readers were able to sympathize with young women who were stuck with jealous, older husbands and to laugh along with them when they came out on top.

· · ·

There are lots of reasons why women, be they princesses or carpenter's wives, might have had an affair. Whether they were badly treated, had fallen out of love, were in a mismatched arranged marriage or bored, the reasons are not so different from those unfaithful partners might give today. But what about those women who committed adultery because they couldn't find sexual satisfaction in a heterosexual marriage? Sex between two men was condemned during the medieval period, a time rife with homophobia. According to one English legal document, men guilty of sodomy should be buried alive; another recommends burning. There is no evidence to suggest that these capital punishments were ever carried out, but their existence is testament to the attitude of the time. And from 1200 onwards, in much of Italy, France and Spain, those found guilty of sodomy could be tortured, castrated and executed. Relationships between two women, however, barely even get a mention. This was not because they were deemed acceptable but, rather, because medieval writers and legislators had a hard time imagining they existed at all.

A French Royal Register from 1405 contains the appeal documents from a young woman sentenced for engaging in lesbian activity, who attempted to blame it all on her ex-lover. Two years earlier, in the provincial French town of Bleury, a woman called Laurence confessed that she was seduced by another woman, Jehanne, the wife of Perrin Goula. The two had set out for a walk together in the nearby fields one sunny August morning when Jehanne propositioned Laurence, promising that 'if you will be my sweetheart, I will do you much good.' Laurence, who suspected nothing untoward (in her own words, she 'thought there was nothing evil in it'), agreed and was astonished when Jehanne threw here onto a haystack and mounted her 'as a man does a woman'.[31] Reading between the lines, Laurence's claims that she was taken by surprise may well be a fabrication because she had sex with Jehanne multiple more times—in Laurence's home, in the vineyards outside their town, even near the communal public fountain. When Laurence eventually did try to end things with Jehanne, her lover attacked her with a knife. We don't know what happened to Jehanne, or how badly Laurence was hurt, but we do know that Laurence ended up in prison. In her plea for release, she cast herself as a good woman, naïve, regretful of her sin, the victim of an aggressor. The story is plausible, and it clearly convinced the right people, because she was allowed to return home to her husband after six months. However, it is equally possible that the love affair between Laurence and Jehanne was genuine, even if it ended badly, and that Laurence was just saying what she had to in order to free herself from prison.

While sex between women was technically a crime, subsumed under the general umbrella term of 'sodomy' (along with bestiality, masturbation and sex in 'unnatural positions', such as doggy style and anal), there is very little evidence of convictions against women. It's tempting to think that this was because medieval people didn't think lesbianism was too terrible a crime, but it seems more likely that the absence of prosecution was rooted in men (and straight women) struggling to wrap their heads around the idea, and the mechanics, of sex between women.

What we do know about attitudes towards same-sex female relationships doesn't suggest tolerance. In the fourteenth century the French scholar and poet Jean Gerson counted sexual acts between women among other crimes against nature. Anything else was a violation of the natural order of things.[32] As chancellor of the University of Paris and a prolific writer, Gerson had plenty of opportunity to spread his thoughts on same-sex intercourse to the masses. The famous German mystic Hildegard of Bingen seemed disgusted by the idea. '[A] woman who takes up devilish ways and plays a male role in coupling with another woman is most vile', she declares, 'and so is she who subjects herself to such a one in this evil deed.'[33] Some medical writers suggested 'cures'; others describe a disease called *ragadia* of the womb, in which fleshly growths appeared outside the vagina, forming a penis-like protuberance which some women used to have sex with other women.[34]

Such writers were clearly aware that women had sex with one other, and found the idea threatening. The poet Étienne de Fougères, who was composing at the same court as Marie de France, contrasts the 'beautiful' sex between men and women with the 'vile' sin against nature that is homosexuality. His images of women sleeping together are all marked, revealingly, by the lack of a penis. Sex between two women is like two coffins banging together, two shields clumsily joining, or a fire being stirred without a poker.[35] For men like Étienne, sex wasn't really sex if it didn't involve a penis.

It seems, then, that women who had sex with each other were particularly dangerous because they disrupted the demarcations of gender and seemed to usurp the need for a man's penis. Katherina Hetzeldorfer from Nuremberg was charged with having sex with several women and drowned as a punishment.[36] When she was first arrested, Katherina claimed that the woman she was living with was her sister. After further questioning she admitted that she was not related to the woman but denied any physical relationship. Finally, the pressures of the trial proved too much, and she confessed that 'she had [had] her ways' with the woman and that she had sexually propositioned at least two others, both of whom were called as witnesses against her. Interestingly, the trial was focused on Katherina's masculine dress and behaviour, rather than on same-sex desire. One of the witnesses, Else Muter, described Katherina as being like a man in physique and demeanour, as well as sexually aggressive, sporting a fake phallus. The others went further, claiming that they thought Katherina *was* a man. While the manner of Katherina's execution is recorded, her 'crime' is never actually named in the trial notes. Was it sex with a woman? Or, bearing in mind that very few women went to trial for sodomy in Europe, was Katherina's real crime that she dared to infiltrate the world of men—with, it seems, some measure of success?

It goes without saying that gay women existed in the Middle Ages. But, owing to intolerant attitudes towards homosexuality in general, and the deliberate silence surrounding same-sex female desire in particular, evidence of lesbian relationships is extremely rare. Where it can be found, historians have been slow to catch on. Letters between two twelfth-century nuns who had clearly spent time together but were now separated, are unquestionably romantic.[37] In the first letter the author describes her recipient as 'unique and special' and 'sweeter than honeycomb'. She refers to herself as 'a hungry little bird' who sighs for her love at every hour, then lets out a stream of unabashed affection: 'In you is all gentleness, all perfection, so my spirit languished perpetually by your absence [...] you are sweeter than milk and honey, you are peerless among thousands, I love you more than any. You alone are my love and longing, you the sweet cooling of my mind, no joy for me anywhere without you.' Her ardour is reciprocated; her lover complains that she aches night and day from longing, remembering 'with what words of joy' her lover caressed her 'little breasts' and claiming she will be in 'endless pain' until the two are reunited.

Until very recently, historians failed to describe this correspondence as what it so clearly is: an exchange of love letters between two women. We know nothing about them beyond their gender, their occupation, the century in which they lived and the fact that they were in love with each other. There were undoubtedly more Laurences, more Jehannes, more Katherinas, more lovesick nuns—but with records dominated by the heteronormative, we are left to imagine their stories.

PLATE 1. Marie de France writes with a quill and stylus in a manuscript containing her *lais*.

PLATE 2. Jeanne de Montbaston's penis tree in *Roman de la Rose*.

PLATE 3. Lancelot and Guinevere embrace in a gathering of Arthurian tales.

PLATES 4 AND 5. Two scenes of women in their birthing chambers at different stages of their lying-in

PLATE 6. The Wife of Bath from Caxton's second edition of *The Canterbury Tales*.

PLATE 7. On a satirical plate, a wife beats her husband with a foxtail.

PLATE 8. Christine de Pizan writes in her study.

PLATE 9. Christine de Pizan presents a bound copy of her work to Isabeau of Bavaria, the queen of France. This manuscript, likely overseen by Christine herself and held at the British Library, is known as *The Book of the Queen*.

PLATE 10. The disembodied wound of Christ from a prayer book.

PLATE 11. A bishop blesses an anchoress.

PLATE 12. An early fourteenth-century depiction of Trota of Salerno, a twelfth-century physician and writer whose work was included in the *Trotula*, an ensemble of texts dedicated to women's health.

PLATE 13. A vulval pilgrim badge.

PLATE 14. Monsters from the travels of the fictitious Sir John Mandeville.

PLATE 15. The *arma Christi*.

PLATE 16. Sinners pushed into a hellmouth by devils.

PLATE 17. An illumination of the Annunciation by Jean Bourdichon.

PLATE 18. Margaret of Antioch.

PLATE 19. Joan of Arc.

PLATE 20. Fortuna turning the Wheel of Fortune.

FOUR

Wanderlust

'Man shal nat suffre his wyf go roule aboute.'*
GEOFFREY CHAUCER, *The Wife of Bath*

Margery Kempe was far from home. She had travelled over a thousand miles, on foot and by galley ship, from Bishop's Lynn to Yarmouth, from Yarmouth to the Flemish port of Zierikzee, from Zierikzee to Constance (now Konstanz in Germany). Many long months had gone by, but her final destination of Jerusalem still felt like a lifetime away. The journey was punishing, not just physically but also emotionally. Ever since she'd set out, her fellow pilgrims had ostracized her. They hated Margery. She was a woman who had abandoned her husband to see the world. They were annoyed 'because she wept so much and spoke all the time about the love and goodness of our Lord' while they just tried to enjoy their supper. In Constance, when she refused to restrain her holy talk, they decided to humiliate her by cutting her gown short and making her wear a white sack-cloth so that, wherever she went, she would be 'taken for a fool'. They 'rebuked her shamefully and chided her harshly' and made her sit at the end of the table as if she was a common servant, so that 'she scarcely dared speak a word'.[1]

Margery put up with all these injustices as meekly as she could. She knew that the more she suffered, the more reward she would accrue in heaven. But when they arrived in Constance, things reached breaking point. This time her fellow pilgrims didn't just mock and tease her. They stole her money and, even worse, convinced her maidservant to abandon her. It was hopeless. For the first time since she left home, Margery didn't know what to do. She was painfully aware of the dangers that could befall a woman travelling unprotected. It was too risky for her to go to the Holy Land alone, but she couldn't bear the idea that she'd never make it. She'd already come so far.

With nowhere else to turn, Margery did what she did best—she prayed. 'Lord, drive away my enemies, and guard well my chastity that I vowed to

---

* 'A husband should not let his wife go wandering about.'

you, and never let me be defiled. And if I am, Lord, I will make a vow that I will never come back to England as long as I live.'[2]

Travel in the Middle Ages was not easy. Journeys of any significant distance were expensive, laborious and could take an incredibly long time. Various parts of the world were home to military conflict, and there were pirates, thieves and robbers all along the common travel routes, preying on the vulnerable. Margery Kempe's fears for her chastity were well founded, and the road to Constance was particularly notorious. She and her fellow pilgrims were warned that 'they should be harmed and have great trouble' on their journey unless God bestowed his grace and protection upon them.[3] Because of the risks and challenges, as well as prevailing attitudes that the best place for women was at home, historians assumed for many years that women rarely travelled during the Middle Ages. But the life of Margery Kempe (as well as the lives of many other women whose journeys we can glimpse in travel guides, historical chronicles and conduct literature) tells a different story. While they may have been less likely or able to do so than men, women did travel, and often. They braved the bandits, the heat and the exhaustion, the expense and uncertainty (not to mention the wagging tongues of their neighbours), packed up their bags and took to the road.

. . .

The word 'wanderlust' originated as recently as the twentieth century, and it describes a concept that would have been unrecognizable to those living in the Middle Ages: 'an eager desire or fondness for wandering or travelling'. Bearing in mind the effort, planning and money involved in getting from A to B, travel was rarely (if ever) undertaken for the sheer pleasure of it. Rather, people would venture abroad for a specific purpose, with pilgrimage at the very top of the list. The destinations of these sacred journeys might be as close as a neighbouring town or as far as a different continent altogether; despite their solemn purpose, they were usually sociable, even raucous, affairs and responsible for a roaring tourist trade. The second most likely reason for travel was commerce. Thousands of ships sailed in and out of Britain each year from almost two hundred harbour towns, bringing in Spanish silks, Indian spices, Norwegian furs and Gascony wine and carrying out tin, herring and wool. Third would be warfare, diplomacy or a combination of the two; noblemen could be called away from home to accompany their king on royal missions, or to act as his envoy (it was on such an assignment that

Christine de Pizan's husband died), and men from the full social spectrum were often called to arms in the relentless battles punctuating the period. And it was not unheard of for women to accompany them.

The medieval court, in a time before capital cities had developed, was itinerant in nature. Kings and queens, noblemen and noblewomen, would all pack up their belongings and accompany the royal household as it travelled around the country. Even armies would be accompanied by women, wives, girlfriends or sex workers whose job it was to wash the soldiers' clothes, tend to their wounds and keep their spirits up. Or, in some cases, the women might even fight. If a king was absent, perhaps imprisoned or embroiled in another battle elsewhere, then it could fall to his queen to don her armour and command the troops. The Greek historian Nicetas describes queens and noblewomen in the Crusades in 1174 dressed as men, riding on horseback and carrying a lance and a battleaxe, led by a stately Eleanor of Aquitaine in her golden spurs. And then, of course, there was a whole host of personal reasons for travel for both men and women, such as visiting family or friends, seeking employment or attending big events like weddings and funerals.

Medieval travel wasn't the spontaneous affair it so often is today. If you were a peasant, then you would need the permission of your lord (the owner of your house and land); if you were the member of a religious order, you would need permission from an abbot, abbess, prioress or even a bishop. And a married woman would need the consent of her husband. When Margery Kempe sought her husband's permission to go on pilgrimage, he said he would allow her to go if she resumed sexual relations with him, paid off all his debts and, instead of fasting as had long been her habit, started eating and drinking with him on Fridays again.[4] Ever the shrewd negotiator, Margery wouldn't budge on the sex, but she did compromise by clearing her husband's debts and agreeing to sup with him on a Friday once more. This must have been good enough for John because, not long afterwards, off she went.

It was also expensive. Felix Fabri was a fifteenth-century German monk who made two pilgrimages to the Holy Land and wrote down a record of both journeys to fulfil a promise to his monastic brethren in Ulm. His *Evagatorium* ('Book of Wanderings') is one of the most endearing and entertaining works of travel writing to survive the medieval period. In it, he is explicit about the challenges facing a would-be traveller: 'It was a serious matter for me to ask leave for so long,' he informs us, 'nor could I form any idea of how I should raise the money for such an expensive journey.'[5] Travellers needed money—to pay for food, board, guides and safe passage—

and they needed equipment, all of which Fabri was lucky enough to be gifted by his monastery.

Two absolute essentials were a staff (called a 'bourdon'), for both support and self-defence, and a bag (called a 'scrip'), in which the right money for the regions and countries they were going to pass through could be kept. The bag would be worn over the shoulder, close to the body to make it more difficult to steal, and on a return journey a pilgrim might adorn it with little talismans from the holy places they had visited. The wealthiest of travellers would be accompanied by large trunks packed, managed and carted around by a slew of servants. Whether rich or poor, many travellers might also carry with them itineraries for key destinations and advice on the best shrines to visit.

Even more essential was a guide to local vocabulary. Margery often describes her difficulty in communicating with the locals—after seeing her weep in devotion, a group of women in Rome use 'signs and tokens' to cheer her up, 'for she did not understand their language'.[6] And Fabri gets into difficulty in the Alps when 'there was no one [. . .] who could talk German' at the inn he is staying. '[I]gnorant of Italian', he 'had to ask for everything by signs'.[7] Some portable, handwritten phrase books covering the major European languages, as well as Greek and Hebrew, do survive the Middle Ages, and it's likely that many more existed but have been lost to us because of their flimsy nature. The French pilgrim Bertrandon de La Broquière finds himself without one on his pilgrimage to the Holy Land but, thankfully, he is helped out by a kind Jewish man who makes a list for him in Italian, Tartar and Turkish of 'everything that I might need on the road, for myself and for my horse'.[8]

Travellers were at the mercy of the elements, from pouring rain to blazing sun. In the earlier Middle Ages men and women wore remarkably similar clothes—simple tunics with social status flagged by the quality of the fabric or the colour of its dye rather than by the style or cut. But by the end of the fourteenth century, thanks in large part to advances in technology and tailoring, fashion and style became more important, and more gendered. Men sported doublets, with their legs covered only in hose; women were more modest, in dresses that usually covered both arms and legs, but they did start to show off the lines of the body far more than in previous centuries. To mark out an honest pilgrim, a simple broad-brimmed hat and a unisex cloak were required, and it was important to be clued up on the sumptuary laws (rules that dictated what people of different social standing were allowed to wear) of the countries and towns that would be passed through. In France, only members of the royal household were allowed to wear grey fur or ermine, and there were restrictions on how long the pointed toes on shoes could be (the longer the toe, the richer their owner.) One should be careful not to wear flat shoes or slippers in Siena, or risk being mistaken as a prostitute. A noble-woman like Christine de Pizan, visiting Germany, would have been allowed to wear one brooch of silver or gold, but Margery Kempe would have been forbidden from wearing any gold, silver, jewels or pearls.

On saying goodbye to his spiritual father at the monastery, Fabri suffered from such anxiety about the dangers and stress of travelling that he almost called off his trip altogether: 'the delightful eagerness to see Jerusalem and the holy places with which I had until that time been glowing, altogether died within me, and I felt a loathing for travel.'[9] And, while he did eventually return home safe and sound, he had been right to be cautious. Aside from the physical dangers, tourists were also an easy mark for swindlers and con men. One of the earliest identifiable travel guides from Europe, the *Codex Calixtinus* (*c.*1138–45), offers advice for those travelling to Santiago de Compostela. The *Codex* warns of monks and shrine managers who tricked naïve pilgrims into parting with their money by falsely claiming to possess relics, and of nefarious boatmen in the village of St-Jean de Sorde who were quick to extort those seeking to cross the river: 'The boatmen are trouble— big trouble', it cautions. '[They] have been known to collect the fares and pile the boat full of pilgrims, so that the boat capsizes and the pilgrims are drowned. Then the evil scoundrels delight in stealing the possessions of the dead.'[10]

In light of such risks, many took steps to protect themselves before setting off. It was prudent to dictate a last will and testament, to make sure one's affairs were in order if disaster struck. Pilgrims might also carry charms, inscribed on coins, rings, travel chests, books or ribbons, designed to keep them safe (travellers were particularly fond of Luke 4:30, 'But Jesus passing through their midst went on His way'). Physicians also gave advice for how to stay healthy. *The Rose of Medicine*, a text composed around 1314 by the London-based physician John of Gaddesden, recommends the all-purpose treatment of bloodletting to purge the body before departure.[11] Also on Gaddesden's list was absinthe, prescribed to help combat the physical exhaus-tion of travel, dried rhubarb root or violet syrup to combat nausea, as well as a whole host of different laxatives. Travellers shouldn't drink water unless they absolutely had to, as it was known to harbour disease and cause fevers, abscesses and constipation. And, if at all possible, journeys should not start in springtime, because those taking them would be more prone to melancholy or even madness.

Travel maps were rare in the Middle Ages, so getting around was not easy. European *mappae mundi* ('maps of the world') were not intended to help people find their way; rather, they were huge, decorative, educational works of art, usually housed in cathedrals or churches, and designed to attract visitors and demonstrate the dominance of Christianity across the globe. Drawn on cloths, animal skins or the walls, these beautiful objects were a dizzying blend of fact and fiction, where the names of real places jostled alongside legendary sites and mythical beasts. They were Eurocentric and Christocentric; where European, Christian kings sat on stately thrones, with crowns and sumptuous clothes, the leaders of Africa were portrayed ruling from their tents, marked out as heathens and worshippers of idols. We find East at the top of these maps rather than the North, because it was believed that Christ would come from this direction on Judgement Day. And Jerusalem takes pride of place in the middle, the symbolic centre of the Christian world. The largest surviving example of these *mappae mundi* is the Hereford Map, which visitors can still see in the town's cathedral today. Created around 1290 by a team of artisans, scribes, scholars and clergymen, it is an impressive five feet tall. Safe to say, such an artefact was not something that could be lugged around on a long journey—and it would have proved no use to travellers, even if it could, because its dimensions adhere to no geographical scale but rather prioritize and make prominent places considered important to the faith.

Some travellers did try and give others a helping hand with directions. William Wey was a Devon-born English author who recorded his travels to the Holy Land in a book called *The Matter of Jerusalem*.[12] A graduate of Oxford, William was one of the first fellows of Eton College, but he wasn't a terribly gifted writer. Nevertheless, he loved putting quill to parchment, and his recollections of his journey to Jerusalem give us an insight into the practicalities of travel. He provided a kind of 'literary map' for his readers, in which he listed the main towns along his route to the Holy Land and estimated the distances between them. And in 1250 the monk Matthew Paris included a map at the start of his *Chronica Majora*, an account of the world's history from beginning to end. Stretching over seven pages, this map, drawn in Paris's own hand, shows the pilgrim route from London to Jerusalem.[13] While these two examples were more portable than *mappae mundi*, they are still not quite travel-size, and it's unlikely that either was used for actual travel. Rather, *The Matter of Jerusalem* and the *Chronica Majora*, both written for a literate, Latinate, clerical audience, were designed to help cloistered readers visualize the journeys being described to them, which they might never be permitted to take themselves.

In the absence of portable maps, those who did venture abroad had to rely on word-of-mouth, the knowledge of their companions and helpful locals and guides to find their way. The main form of inland transport in the Middle Ages was by road, but the exact mode depended on how much money you had. While some people (usually the very poor, or pilgrims) went on foot, travel on horseback was far more common. Carts and wagons were reserved for the movement of produce, not people; you might be able to persuade the driver to let you hitch a lift on the back, but you had to put up with feeling every bump in the road. For the wealthy, something called a 'litter' was more usual, a seat suspended between two long poles, with one horse supporting it in front and another in the back, to which a handy cover could be attached to ensure those being carried were protected from rain. The medieval coach was reserved for the richest (usually royalty, or aristocratic women).

Peppered along the highways and byways throughout Europe were inns where weary travellers could rest their heads. How comfortable that rest would be, however, depended on the inn. Each would have several rooms, designed for sharing, as well as a common hall where patrons could gather by the fire to get warm, drink ale, have some supper (most likely simple bread and cheese) and swap stories. A decent inn would change the rushes on the floor of all the rooms regularly, and intersperse them with lavender, rose petals and other herbs to keep them fresh. Less respectable hostelries wouldn't bother, and visitors would be welcomed upon entering by the smell of horse dung, mud and mouldy food. All inns would provide their guests with a straw mattress, and some might even throw in a pitcher of water and a chest for their belongings. If there was no inn near by, or a room was too expensive, then another accommodation option was a monastery. Monks were duty-bound to provide their guests with food and shelter, and monasteries were usually more sanitary than inns, thanks to their clean water and flushing privies (such advanced plumbing was something that only the royal household and religious institutions of this period could enjoy, owing to its significant expense). Some who had run out of money had to rely on the charity and kindness of ordinary people. Margery Kempe, as we shall see, often found herself taken in by friendly locals and given a bed for the night.

Of course, going abroad for anyone living in Britain meant spending a significant time at sea. Travel by ship could take months, even years, and struck fear into the hearts of many. Most people didn't know how to swim, and many had heard horror stories of drowning in storms, being attacked by pirates or being blown off course. Fabri recalls the terror of being marooned, when everything on board becomes 'putrid, foul and mouldy', the wine becomes 'undrinkable', the meat, 'even when dried and smoked' becomes maggot-ridden and even the water 'begins to stink'. Out of nowhere, 'there spring into life innumerable flies, gnats, fleas, lice, worms, mice and rats' and, as if that wasn't bad enough, 'all men on board become lazy, sleepy and untidy from the heat, fretful from the evil passions of melancholy, anger, and envy'.[14]

Even if they escaped such trials, almost everyone was likely to fall victim to seasickness. A fifteenth-century medieval poem, penned by a knight from Metz, in Lorraine, called Sir Nicole Louve, gives us a gruesome insight into how this may have felt. The food is 'putrid', the biscuits are 'rotten', and there is no shade to be found anywhere on deck. Passengers make a habit of emptying their stomachs less than six feet away from the common dinner table. Good sleep is a forlorn hope thanks to the smell of farts and belches, not to mention the fleas and the lice. If you want to go on pilgrimage to the Holy Land, Louve concludes, then you need a strong stomach, a stoic endurance and hopefully a short memory so you can forget how awful it was.[15] William Wey urged passengers to avoid the 'smouldering hot and stinking' lower quarters by schmoozing with the ship's captain and thus securing one of the coveted and eye-wateringly expensive cabins on the upper deck.[16] Due to the rampant anti-Semitism throughout Europe, Jewish travellers were advised to pay for one of these expensive cabins to avoid harassment; this meant that, for Jewish people, travel was reserved for the wealthiest or for those willing to take their chances down below.

One can only imagine the wretchedness of day-in, day-out nausea on one of these ships. Gilbert the Englishman, a physician who had studied at the leading medical school in Europe at Salerno, put together an overview of what he considered to be the best advice in his *Compendium of Medicine*.[17] He recommended eating bitter fruit such as quinces, pomegranates and oranges, drinking aniseed, sucking sweets, eating seeds to produce burps, which eased the symptoms, or avoiding food and drink altogether. Passengers were advised to sit upright and hold on tight to the beams of the ship, keeping as still as possible and only turning their head with the motion of the ship. They might also try and distract one another by singing songs and telling stories.

If none of this worked, having God on your side was a foolproof solution. Sailing between Gdansk and Stralsund on the Baltic Sea, Margery Kempe felt frightened and ill when the boat was rocked relentlessly by large waves. God appeared in a vision and gave her some helpful advice; she should lie down and avoid looking at the waves altogether.[18] On another journey not long afterwards, a rough passage from Calais to Dover, Margery prayed to God once more, asking that he 'give her the grace to hold her head up and preserve her from bringing up vomit'. He kept her free from sickness, but she makes sure to tell us that he did not extend the same courtesy to her fellow passengers, who all ended up 'vomiting and throwing up very violently and foully'.[19]

It's hard to imagine anyone having wanderlust in the Middle Ages. However, that's not to say that no one longed for travel. The genre of 'travel writing' that survives the medieval period proves that people were interested in the outside world, even if they didn't always manage to visit much of it themselves. Modern-day travel writers tend to pride themselves on accuracy, but medieval authors of this genre (almost always men) were happy to work from hearsay. It didn't matter to them if they'd been to a certain place themselves or not; they still felt able to write about it based on the stories and tales they'd heard from those who had—merchants, shipmen and pilgrims who had returned from distant lands. Even Felix Fabri, who was so careful to make an accurate record of his journeys, admitted that he wasn't an eyewitness to everything he describes.

Accounts of faraway places are often closer to fiction than to fact. One of the most famous surviving texts from this genre, *The Book of Marvels and Travels*, is supposedly written by a knight called John Mandeville.[20] We have no idea if John Mandeville even existed or if he was a fictional creation by some other author. Regardless, it is almost certain that whoever penned the *Book* hadn't visited most of the places they describe. There are stories of women from Turkey, Syria, Arabia, Egypt and India who sound weird and wonderful to both medieval European ears and our own. Women who have jewels in their eyes and the power to kill with one murderous look, Amazons who are more skilled in battle than any man. Women whose black skin is caused by day-long sunbathing sessions (white European writers are endlessly fascinated by what might cause darker skin). And we hear tell of fabulous and fantastic creatures from Africa and the Far East: people with only one large foot, which they use to run as fast as they can or, like an inbuilt umbrella, to protect them from the sun; mysterious, headless men with eyes in their shoulders and mouths in their chests; men and women with the heads of dogs who bark instead of talking.

None of these mythical creatures existed, of course, although it seems at least some medieval readers believed in them. They reveal a fascination with, and the exoticism of, places that for the general population were beyond reach. In the same way that authors today imagine life in outer space or at the bottom of the ocean, medieval writers let their minds run wild when they described far-flung lands. Even those who we know did visit the places they describe share a tendency for hyperbole, exaggeration or even dishonesty, or they give us frustratingly few details. Margery Kempe, one of the only women from the period to give an account of her pilgrimage, got all the way to Jerusalem; maddeningly, however, she tells us very little about what she saw.

Any reader of medieval travel writing must be prepared to take what they encounter with a pinch of salt. They will also often find themselves reading the experience of women who travelled through the filter of a male author. The genre of travel writing was dominated by men, partly because women were not encouraged to write for public consumption and partly because the prevailing attitude of the time was that women were better off staying at home. However, the stories we find in male-authored accounts show that women did not always take this advice. Women did travel, for all kinds of different reasons. While we do not always get to hear about their journeys at first hand, enough material survives for us to put together a picture of what they may have been like, and why women may have embarked on them in the first place.

· · ·

They hadn't even left Venice yet, and already they were arguing. This did not bode well.

The Arsenale was as loud and busy as always, a chaotic mix of sailors and passengers. Felix Fabri and his group had been standing around for over an hour in the blazing sun, waiting to board the galley ship which would take them to the Holy Land, listening with frustration to the usual tired excuses for the delay to their departure. And now, to make matters worse, they were at odds with each other.

It had all started when seven old women approached them on the dock and humbly asked if they could join the group. Fabri found himself 'astonished at the courage of these old women'. They were so frail that they could scarcely support their own weight, and yet still, 'through love for the Holy Land', they wanted to throw themselves in with a group of young knights.

There were others in Fabri's party, 'wiser and more conscientious knights', who shared his admiration and wanted the game old beldams to join them. But the younger knights among them disagreed vehemently. They were travelling to the Holy Land to receive their knighthoods, and they did not want to obtain this honour in the company of old women. 'These haughty spirits', Fabri tells us, 'endeavoured to persuade us not to take our passage in the ship in which the old women meant to sail.' This all led to a huge row which, according to Fabri, 'lasted until it pleased God to remove those proud men from among us'.[21] In other words, the women won.

Many writers and commentators shared the attitude of the younger noblemen in Fabri's party. According to the popular medieval proverb, the definition of a harlot was a woman 'talkative and wandering, not bearing to be quiet, not able to abide still at home'.[22] Being too much out of the house and talking too much were qualities directly associated with loose morals, one of the best examples of this being Alyson, Chaucer's Wife of Bath, whose refusal to stay at home made her the epitome of medieval men's fears about women. Chaucer tells us that Alyson 'knew much about wandering along the road', and she recalls how this habit of hers annoyed her last husband, Jankin. He tried to forbid her from going between houses, visiting friends and gossiping. When she argued back, he would get out his Bible and pompously read the Proverbs aloud to her, telling her that 'man should not suffer his wife to go roaming about', an attitude to which she was extremely resistant.[23] We find a similar stance in the male-authored French satirical poem 'The Fifteen Joys of Marriage', which details fifteen different ways in which women make their husbands miserable.[24] One particular complaint is that women who gad about are far more likely to succumb to the sins of pride, lust and deceit. In the eighth 'joy' a wife forces her husband to let her go on pilgrimage, because she and her friends want to get away with doing all kinds of things that they shouldn't.

Despite being an entrepreneur who would have routinely ventured into the book-manufacturing district to manage the making of her manuscripts, our Parisian widow, Christine de Pizan, was careful to warn other women about the dangers, both moral and physical, of too much time abroad. She is scornful of the 'gossip sessions' that women seek out, condemning them as a waste of money and time of which no good can come. And while pilgrimages may be a worthy endeavour in and of themselves, she counsels that a wife should not use them 'as an excuse to get away from the town in order to go somewhere to play about or kick up her heels in some merry company'.

Women should be ever wary of the dangers of travel, the thoughtlessness of youth and the nefarious men who lurk around every corner, waiting to seduce and prey on them. Considering all these risks, 'the very safest course for women' was to stay at home.[25]

From what we know of Christine, she was not interested in too much travel herself. She made the journey from Venice to Paris with her family when she was just a little girl, to join her father at the court of King Charles V. But she soon fell in love with her adopted country and was reluctant to ever leave it. When she was at the height of her fame as an author, she received two invitations to royal courts abroad, one from King Henry IV of England and one from Gian Galeazzo Visconti, the duke of Milan, which she politely declined. Moreover, the bulk of her political writing is devoted to trying to convince the fractious leaders of her country to make peace with one another and bring instability to an end. She ends a long appeal to the influential duke of Berry, embroiled in the conflict, by referring to herself as a 'poor voice crying in this kingdom, desiring peace and welfare for you all'.[26] Despite many opportunities to go and leave the political infighting and constant warfare behind her, she was clearly devoted to France, preferring to stay and to exert her influence to try and help. Her own lack of interest in travel may well explain how quick she is to follow the misogynistic party line where women and the home are concerned, rather than advocating for women to travel more freely.

Writing a couple of hundred years before Christine, Marie de France filled her stories with the dark realities of women who were forced to stay at home against their will, imprisoned by tyrannical husbands or overprotective fathers. She used birds, a symbol of flight and freedom, to highlight the restraint that such women felt in their everyday lives. In *Laustic*, set in the Breton town of St Malo, an unhappy wife stands by her window every night to commune with her lover in the adjoining house.[27] They could never physically meet, because she was 'closely guarded' by her husband, but 'when she stood at her bedroom window' the two could talk to one another, swap endearments and throw each other gifts. One summer, 'when the copses and meadows were green and the gardens in full bloom', her husband starts to grow suspicious. He becomes angry, asking her repeatedly 'why she got up and where she went'. Thinking on her feet, the lady replies: 'Lord, anyone who does not hear the song of the nightingale knows none of the joys of this world. This is why I come and stand here. So sweet is the song I hear by night that it gives me great pleasure.' Either because he doesn't believe her tale or because he's jealous even of the bird, her husband catches the poor creature in a trap and kills it, 'breaking its neck wickedly with his two hands' and silencing its song for ever. He then throws its body at his wife, spattering her dress with blood—a visceral representation of her own clipped wings.

Lais like this one are fictional (and often fantastical), but the recurring image of the bird serves as a particularly poignant metaphor for women who are trapped not only by circumstance, but also physically and geographically. The men in the *lais* of Marie de France travel the world on knightly adventures, but the women tend to be tied to a particular spot, usually by men. Her tragic tales may well have had an especial resonance for brides at the Angevin court who, for the benefit of their families, had been married off to strangers far from home.

Marie herself may well have been an unhappy wife or, as some historians have imagined, an enclosed nun. But her writing suggests that, whether married to a man, God or no one, she certainly had exposure to different languages and cultures. She was part of what became known as the Plantagenet Empire, a huge collection of states ruled over by Henry II, including Normandy, England, Wales, Anjou, Maine and Aquitaine. It brought the Celtic world together with that of northern France and with Occitania (southern Europe), in a way that is reflected in Marie's own stories, translated from Welsh and Breton into French, which, at that time, would have been the language of high status in England. Nor are her stories limited to the Plantagenet empire in scope. While most of the protagonists hail from Brittany and England, her interweaving of the exotic materials and people—Phrygian silks and Spanish mules, patterned silks from Constantinople and mysterious, witchy aunts practicing herbal medicine in Salerno—makes them a globetrotting set of narratives. Such references suggest an author who was familiar with the trade and literature flowing in and out of England and France from all over the world, an author who had read about and had perhaps even met people from foreign climes at the king's multicultural and multilingual court, even if she had never visited them herself.

By adding 'de France' to her name, Marie advertised that she was originally from France. This suggests that she was probably living and writing elsewhere, probably in England, entertaining the court of King Henry II. Henry, whose mother was English and of royal blood, had spent much of his young life in France, but in 1153, fortified by the wealth, talent, beauty and status of his new wife, Eleanor of Aquitaine, he invaded England and successfully claimed the throne. He was famously restless, constantly travelling on a whim in a manner that astonished the French king, Louis VII—'now in England, now in Normandy, he must fly rather than travel by horse or ship'— and anyone who wanted to thrive from proximity to the glittering royal court was forced to follow, including Marie.[28]

The journey from France to England is one that many of the noblewomen made, both before and after the Norman Conquest of 1066, testament to the close relationship between the two countries during the Middle Ages. While no record of Marie's own journey remains, it would undoubtedly have been lengthy, costly and potentially dangerous, even for a noblewoman travelling in style.

A few hundred years later Margaret of Anjou herself made the journey in the winter of 1444. After she had been married to King Henry VI by proxy, a temporary household was set up to organize her passage to England. We know from a book of receipts and accounts collated for this trip by the royal clerks that it exceeded the significant funds it had been assigned (£5,563 17s. and 5d.—the rough equivalent of £3.5 million today) and that it involved over 300 people. Led by the duke of Suffolk, William de la Pole (a military commander, statesman and favourite of the king), the envoy sent to collect Margaret from France also included the duke's wife (none other than Alice Chaucer, granddaughter of Geoffrey) and her ladies, 5 barons and baronesses, 17 knights, 65 esquires and 204 valets. These numbers only increased on the return leg of the journey, as the new queen of England was accompanied by her own retinue, and the entire expedition took four months. Despite the pomp and circumstance of the journey, Margaret's arrival ended up being something of a damp squib. She was violently ill on the crossing and had to be carried off the ship to a dock which, because of a thunderstorm, was empty of crowds to welcome her. It didn't matter how much money you had to throw at it, the voyage from France to England could still be a challenging one.

It was not unusual, then, for women of the court to travel around Europe, whether they were journeying to meet their future husbands, accompanying them on diplomatic missions or simply following the court. But, for ordinary women, the most likely reason for travel was pilgrimage.

According to the Christian Church, pilgrimage was supposed to be a devotional exercise, not an excuse to get out of the house and have fun. The longer the journey and the greater the time spent away from work and family, the more potential there was for spiritual reward. But despite its ascetic origins and intentions, pilgrimage had become a huge, commercially successful industry across the globe by the fourteenth century, with holy sites in

Jerusalem, Rome and Santiago de Compostela attracting the biggest crowds. Fabri movingly describes what happened on his galley ship when Jerusalem finally came into sight: 'On hearing this shout all rushed forth from every corner of the galley, men and women, old and young, sick and well, and climbed aloft so they might behold the land for whose sake they had left their native country, and exposed themselves to many hardships and to the danger of death.'[29] As they watched the Holy Land approach, all the passengers on the ship joined in a hymn of celebration, accompanied by flutes, bagpipes and trumpets.

The suspicions surrounding unsupervised wandering women meant that they were more likely to go on pilgrimage closer to home; however, their presence at shrines all over the world is well documented. 'I have seen women', Fabri tells us, 'who at first were full of fears, and scarcely dared to look at the seas but who nevertheless became so bold by practice that they would venture to jump from a galley into a boat.'[30] There were enough female pilgrims in Jerusalem to warrant a separate dormitory for them. And chroniclers record the dangers of overcrowding at the more popular sites. The French statesman Abbot Suger recalls the hideous sight of watching women being crushed and almost trampled to death at St Denis and, in an even more tragic crush, 11 women were found dead at the entrance to the shrine of St Florian.[31]

More evidence of women's presence on pilgrimage comes in the form of pilgrim badges. Shrine managers across the Christian world made a fortune selling off holy relics—drops of blood from a particular saint, a piece of Jesus's foreskin or a holy finger—as well as little badges, cheap and easy to mass-produce, made of pewter, tin or lead and imprinted with an icon relevant to the shrine. No one knows why, but many of these badges found their way to the bottom of rivers; hundreds have been washed up on the shores of the Thames over the years, indicating that pilgrims may well have thrown them into the water for luck.

These pilgrim badges could be surprisingly irreverent. Quite often they boasted either male or female genitalia—or both. A particularly bizarre and bawdy badge found in the Netherlands sports a jaunty vulva, dressed up as a pilgrim complete with hat, rosary and trademark wide-brimmed hat. Another proudly displays a vulva on horseback, drawing a bow and arrow. And the vulva depicted on a third wears a crown and is carried aloft by three weary looking men with penises for heads. Some historians have interpreted these badges as a satirical commentary on female pilgrims, suggesting that women who went wandering were sexually voracious and morally loose.

However, if we bear in mind the fact that penis badges were even more common than vulvas, and that no one took issue with male travellers, then this interpretation isn't entirely persuasive. We know from surviving manuscript marginalia that medieval people scribbled genitalia on the pages of their books just as some do today on the back of toilet doors. These pilgrim badges are likely to have been more of the same—a vulgar joke to be shared with friends and family when one got home.

However, it is easy to understand why they have sometimes been interpreted as a warning against wandering women. Mariners believed that women were a liability on board ships; it was thought that their presence would anger the water gods, who might unleash their wrath by whipping up a storm. There were also concerns that they'd distract the men trying to work on board. To this end, women were expected to stay in the hot, foetid and cramped lower berths of the boat rather than eating at the common table to eat or going on deck for fresh air.

Not only did the fairer sex board ships to go on pilgrimage, to aid their male relatives with trade or even to relocate; they could also be found as pirates, striking fear into the hearts of other travellers. While it's certainly true that medieval piracy was, for the most part, a male occupation, there were a handful of women who made their name committing crimes at sea. One particularly notorious example is that of Jeanne de Clisson, a French noblewoman and wronged widow.

On 2 August 1343 Jeanne's handsome and charismatic husband, Olivier, was executed in a marketplace in Paris. Suspected of plotting with the English against the French in the ongoing Hundred Years War (an accusation that both he and Jeanne vehemently denied), his trial was a sham. Despite his pleas of innocence, and although he had risked his life for years defending Brittany from English invaders, the French king decided to make an example of Olivier. His head was sent to Nantes and attached to the city gates by a lance, a warning to other traitors.

When Jeanne received news of Olivier's death, she was both distraught at his loss and incandescent with rage at his cruel treatment. They had been married for 13 years, and it seems their marriage had been happy. Legend has it that Jeanne, who was also wanted by the authorities for purportedly traitorous activities, braved capture to take her two young sons to Nantes and show them their father's decapitated head, hoping to stoke within them the vengeance already burning within her own chest. Together, she and her sons swore to avenge Olivier by wreaking bloody ruin on France and all her allies.

Jeanne managed to raise enough money to purchase a small fleet of ships by selling off her land; it is also believed that King Edward III of England provided her with a fleet of ships, black with red sails, the flagship of which which she dubbed 'My Revenge'. Populating her ships with ruthless seamen and fighters, Jeanne and her sons brought terror to French vessels for 13 years. Not only would she rob them, but she ruthlessly murdered almost everyone on board, leaving only a handful alive to spread the word that all should beware the 'Lioness of Brittany'.

Jeanne's career as a brutal and merciless pirate ended when the French navy eventually managed to sink her ship. She escaped with her two sons but, adrift on the high seas without any food or water, one of them died in her arms before they were rescued by allies of the English, five long days later.

Jeanne was unusual. More common are the accounts by men like Felix Fabri of ordinary women who decided to go on pilgrimage. From them we can learn how women were received on these journeys by the male passengers who accompanied them, and who were often expected to protect them. Fabri was repeatedly 'astonished' by the courage of the old women who joined his party in Venice, and at how quickly they 'forgot their own frailty', despite their age and their gender.[32] He describes the famously arduous passage back to Jerusalem along the River Jordan, which, because it wound its way through the desert, was viciously hot in the daytime and bitterly cold at night. Pilgrims needed armed local guards to accompany them, and there were rumours that terrifying beasts like scorpions, dragons and crocodiles could be found in the area. 'During all these labours', Fabri informs us, 'the ancient ladies outdid all of us, wrested the first place from the knights, neither groaned nor bewailed their toils, but went on first in the whole line of march, stronger than men and braver than knights.'[33] One knight exclaims: 'my brother, I don't believe these old creatures to be women at all, but devils, for women, especially old women, are frail, tender and delicate, whereas these women are made of iron and are stronger than all us knights.'[34]

Fabri's companions are not the only tough female pilgrims that we encounter in medieval literature. Another particularly impressive example is the adventurous and stoical Yorkshire-woman Margaret of Beverley. Margaret's story comes down to us in a Latin text, which is purportedly authored by her brother, but because it's written in the first person it's tempting to imagine that Margaret herself was the author and only gave the book her brother's name in the hopes that it would be taken more seriously.[35] Margaret was born in Palestine while her parents were on pilgrimage to

Jerusalem, and she later returned to the Holy Land in 1187, a few hundred years before Margery Kempe. On this trip Margaret got caught up in the famous siege of the city. Rather than cowering in a corner somewhere, she sprang into action and helped to fight off the invading army, with a cooking pot on her head for protection. 'Though a woman, I seemed a warrior', her book tells us. 'I threw the weapon; though filled with fear, I learned to conceal my weakness.' The siege lasted for 15 days before the city finally fell to Saladin, the sultan of Egypt and Syria; all the while, Margaret 'carried out [...] the functions of a soldier'. She 'wore a breastplate like a man', 'came and went on the ramparts' and carried water to the other soldiers. It was unbearably hot, there was no rest for anyone and she was almost killed when a stone the size of a mill wheel was lobbed at the city walls.

Margaret survived the siege but was seized soon afterwards while trying to escape. She spent over a year in captivity, as a prisoner and slave, suffering torture throughout that time. She remembers being 'forced to carry out humiliating tasks' such as gathering stone and chopping wood. If she refused, she was beaten with rods: 'I endured the blows, the threats, the heat, the cold, in silence. My chains rusted from my tears. The work and slender diet tired my limbs. The long days were boiling hot and rest was rare and brief.' When she was finally released, thanks to a charitable Christian man from Tyre who paid her ransom, she lived in fear of being captured again as she tried to make her way home. 'I walked always in hiding,' she recalls, 'garbed only in a sack that I had worn when captive.' Margaret's only possession was a psalter (a prayer book), which she called her 'one companion in the wilderness'. She subsisted for five days on just one loaf of bread and then had to eat the roots of plants for nourishment. She nearly gave up when she was forced to cross a fast-flowing river: 'What to do? Would the fear of dying make me risk the danger of dying? [...] I could not turn back. I feared staying there and becoming a meal to the wild beasts.' But fear made her bold. She girded her loins and crossed, making her weary way home to England.

While the account of Margaret's pilgrimage and imprisonment is riddled with exaggeration and historical inaccuracies, there is no reason to doubt that she existed and that she travelled to Jerusalem, even that she was captured. European pilgrims did get caught up in the siege of the city and, in the years following, had trouble visiting the Holy Land. Years later, in 1366, another female pilgrim, Isolda Parewastell from Somerset, sent a petition to the pope asking for permission to establish a new chapel in her name. She describes how she was also captured when visiting the Holy Land and held prisoner for three years, tortured on the rack, beaten and humiliated. Still, she survived, and returned home even more willing to do God's work.

Felix Fabri may have been full of praise for the old matrons who forged their way through Jerusalem in his company, but his astonishment at their behaviour is revealing. He seems to see them as the exception rather than rule because, elsewhere, his attitude to travelling women is much more misogynistic. In an account of his second pilgrimage, he describes how everyone on the journey became quickly irritated with the wife of one of the male passengers. The problem wasn't just her gender (although that seems to have been troubling enough); it was also her 'restless and inquisitive' nature. She ran 'hither and thither' around the ship, wanting to see and hear everything, asking lots of questions and generally annoying everyone.[36] Her relationship with the rest of the troop became so strained that they abandoned her on the island of Rhodes. According to Fabri, 'because she had rendered herself odious beyond measure by her silly talk and her inquisitive prying into unprofitable matters' no one except her husband (who, inadvertently, deserted her too) was remotely sorry to see her go.[37] A cruel thing to do, but especially so at a time when travel was so dangerous and difficult.

. . .

Margery Kempe was also deserted by her travelling companions.[38] Robbed of both money and a maidservant, she was terrified of carrying on her journey alone. She had been abandoned because her companions felt she took the pilgrimage too seriously. She felt the journey should be sombre, full of holy talk and contemplation. And she wasn't the only one; Fabri heard and recorded a sermon in Jerusalem that advised pilgrims to be 'grave and devout', as such a sacred journey warranted, and to 'beware of laughing together'.[39] But Margery's group felt differently. Pilgrimage was a holy endeavour, but that didn't mean they couldn't have a good time on the way. They grew tired of Margery trying to curb all their fun, talking about God and weeping at the dinner table, and so they got rid of her.

Margery was panicked. She prayed to God in desperation and, as usual, he was quick to deliver. He promised her a new guide and companion, and not long afterwards an old man from Devon with a white beard crossed Margery's path. His name was William Wever and, after some persuasion, he agreed to accompany Margery on her onward journey. She set off with him 'with a very long face [...] because she was in a strange country and did not know the language or the man who was going to escort her'. William was equally sombre, worried that he wouldn't be able to protect Margery from any miscreants on the road, because of his age: 'I'm afraid you'll be taken from me,' he moaned to Margery, 'and I'll be beaten up because of you and lose my coat.' However, their journey went remarkably smoothly; they 'met many excellent people' who didn't have a bad word to say about Margery, who provided them with food and drink and who gave up their own beds so that she could rest her head for the night. Things went so well, in fact, that Margery beat her old travelling companions to Bologna. When they arrived and heard about the hospitality she had received on the road, and how comfortable her journey had been, they were astonished and decided to extend an invitation for her to rejoin them, hoping to share in her good fortune. However, rather than going to Margery with their tail between their legs (as one might expect), they had a caveat. 'If you want to travel in our party,' they told her, 'you must give a new undertaking, which is this: you will not talk of the Gospel where you are, but you will sit and make merry, like us, at all meals.' If she broke her promise, they would have no qualms about abandoning her again.

Women were not the only travellers to face discrimination on the road. Descriptions from various travel guides make the prejudice of Europeans at the time abundantly clear. The *Codex Calixintus* describes the Navarrese people as a 'barbarous race' who were 'repulsively dressed' and 'full of malice', not to mention 'swarthy in colour, evil of face, depraved, perverse, perfidious, empty of faith, corrupt, libidinous, drunken'.[40] And in his account of his travels to the Holy Land, Fabri makes frequent reference to the hot temper and jealousy of the locals, whom he calls Saracens, a catch-all term used by Europeans to delineate any Muslims: 'Let the pilgrims beware of gazing upon any women whom they may meet, because all Saracens are exceeding jealous, and a pilgrim may in ignorance run himself into danger through the fury of some jealous husband.'[41]

As today, the concepts of race and ethnicity in the Middle Ages were complex and often confused. Traits such as 'treacherous' or 'noble' were thought to be inherited, but skin colour was imagined to be more related to environmental factors than due to an idea of 'race' as we would recognize it. According to the Hippocratic *Airs, Waters, Places*, a foundational text for physicians in the West, 'in general you will find assimilated to the nature of the land both the physique and the characteristics of the inhabitants'.[42] Cold was associated with whiteness and paleness, heat with blackness, and these elemental properties determined character. Indians are proficient in mathematics because a little heat leads to intelligence—too much heat, however, was believed to lead to stupidity. Their understanding of race might be along different lines to our own, but the foundations of racism as we know it are nevertheless discernible within it.

For the most part, European travel writers rarely mentioned skin colour; however, the references we do get range from ignorant to prejudicial. Albertus Magnus claimed that 'since black women are hotter and more swarthy [...] they are the sweetest for mounting, as the pimps say'.[43] Not only were black women considered to be more pleasurable to have sex with, but they were thought to be more highly sexed themselves. John Mandeville describes the women of Chaldia in Arabia as 'foul and evil arrayed', and Marco Polo, a famous explorer of the time, qualifies his description of Kashmiri women as very beautiful with *'as dark women go'*.[44] Accounts from Europe are even more vicious when it comes to religion. For medieval people, differences in religion were often far more charged than what we would now term 'race' or ethnicity. Across Christian Europe, Jews and Muslims were forced to mark themselves out through their dress and were increasingly ghettoized and ostracized.

It is easy to see why Jewish travellers had to secure their own cabins on board ships, rather than risk harassment on the lower decks. John Mandeville gives credence to vicious rumours circulating at the time by telling a fictional story about how some Jewish people put poison in the drinking fountains of Christians. In his fifteenth-century travel guide for priests, canon Pietro Casolo recalls visiting Modon, a Venetian town halfway between Venice and Jaffa with a diverse religious population made up of Christians, Muslims and Jews. Casola describes the Jewish community there as 'filthy', 'very dirty' and 'full of bad smells'.[45] This kind of anti-Semitic feeling was widespread, and its consequences could be deadly.

Nor did medieval writers reserve their suspicion and vitriol exclusively for Jewish communities. There were concerns that increased travel might lead to undesirable marriages between Christians and non-Christians, with especial anxiety about black Muslims. There were penalties across Europe for religiously mixed couples (who were banned from joining in holy matrimony), and in Spain they were especially severe—if caught having sex, they could be executed, either by being burned alive or thrown off a cliff.

The idea that medieval Europe was a whitewashed, purely Christian zone is an illusion, increasingly peddled by extreme right-wing groups across the West. In the late fifteenth century there were about 2,700 resident aliens living in London. That made up about 6 per cent of the population, which means that London was more multicultural in the Middle Ages than it was for much of the twentieth century. However, it cannot be denied that the Church was a powerful and ruthlessly self-preserving institution, and while not everyone living in Europe was white and Christian, they certainly made up the majority. Travelling the world, encountering different peoples and religions, was something that many medieval people wanted to do. But there was an underlying distrust of difference. It was something to marvel at from a safe distance—or so many people imagined. Travel writing from the period is endlessly fascinated with those who didn't fit the parameters, swaying between well-meaning ignorance and exoticism on the one hand and vindictive condemnation on the other. At both ends of the rhetoric, women are high-profile, functioning as a temptation as well as a danger.

. . .

When Margery Kempe returned from her first pilgrimage, she was so grateful to have made it back to English soil unscathed that she fell to the ground and kissed it, 'highly thanking God who had brought [her] home in safety'.[46] Her ship docked in Norwich, and she spent a few weeks there visiting friends while she waited for her husband to come and escort her back to Bishop's Lynn. Over dinner Richard Caister, one of her favourite priests and confessors, expressed surprise that she was in such high spirits after all the hardships she had endured. 'Margery,' he said, 'I am amazed how you can be so merry, when you have had such great troubles and travelled so far.'

'Sir it is because I have great cause to be merry and rejoice in our Lord, who has helped me and succoured me and brought me home again in safety,' Margery replied.

The travel sickness, money troubles, bullying and anxiety had all been worth it. She had seen, with her own eyes, the place where God laid down his life for the sins of mankind. She had every reason to celebrate. It was not long afterwards that she set out on pilgrimage yet again. It seems that Margery Kempe had been bitten by the travel bug.

FIVE

Hustling

'Rimez en ai e fait ditié,/Soventes fiez en ai vieilié'*

MARIE DE FRANCE, *Lais*

'Death deprived me of [Étienne] when he was thirty-four years old', Christine tells us in her *Vision* (1405), an allegorical dream sequence about the civil strife tearing through France, which she begins with the story of her own life. Her husband's passing left her 'burdened with three small children and a large household' and unsure of how she was going to cope without him. Before his death, he had been 'in the flower of his youth, fit, ready, and on the point of rising to a high rank as much through scholarship as wise and prudent government'. The young couple's star had only just begun to rise. But without him Christine found herself sinking fast. 'I was justifiably filled with bitterness,' she recalls, 'regretting his sweet company and the departed joy that had lasted but ten years.'

She was also hampered by unanticipated financial difficulties. She had lost Étienne's large salary and now found herself besieged on every side by men claiming that he owed them money. 'I could not precisely know the conditions of his finances,' Christine explains, 'for husbands in general do not customarily tell or declare all their business affairs to their wives.' She struggled to mount a defence. 'Lawsuits and legal actions surrounded me', she remembers, and she became an easy target for exploitation. When she entrusted a merchant with her children's inheritance, he pretended that he had been robbed and stole it from her.

Overwhelmed, Christine admits that she 'longed for death more than life'. The money was running out, the debts were piling up and her old friends at court were beginning to close ranks, leaving the de Pizans out in the cold. Our widow was no fool. She knew that a new, wealthy husband would alleviate the pressure. But she had made a vow that she would never marry again.

* 'I have made rhymes from them and written poems/Many a time I worked late into the night'

And so, to get her family back on their feet, she was going to have to roll up her sleeves. 'Now', she tells us, 'I had to work.'[1] Christine was ready to hustle.

. . .

One of the most popular medieval images, riddling manuscripts in iterations large and small, is the *Rota Fortunae* (Wheel of Fortune). The wheel itself may vary in size and colour, adorned with different decorations against different backgrounds, but it is usually overseen by a woman, clothed in a beautiful dress of blue or red (the most expensive dyes of the medieval world). She is Lady Fortune, and she is a cruel mistress.

The Wheel of Fortune dates from Ancient Greece and Rome but was made popular in the Middle Ages thanks to the writing of Boethius, a Roman philosopher who was wrongly imprisoned for treason. He spent his sentence composing a book called the *Consolation of Philosophy*, which was widely read throughout medieval Europe and translated into English by Chaucer. Before his arrest, Boethius had been a powerful and influential man. When he found himself wasting away in jail, he reached for the image of a wheel to explain his sudden change in fortune, lamenting 'fortune's universal instability'.[2] This image shows up in medieval manuscripts of all different genres—Arthurian legends, guidebooks for royalty, historical chronicles and allegorical poems. Despite its pagan origins, it folded neatly into Christian thinking as a warning against earthly ambition and served as a reminder that, in heaven, wealth and status would be meaningless.

Perched atop the wheel there is usually a man or woman in sumptuous clothing, perhaps a king or a queen, enjoying the providence and favour they found in life. But underneath the wheel, crushed by its weight, are ordinary people dressed in the rags of poverty or nothing at all, trying to make their slow and steady ascent. These images are not some kind of socialist allegory. This was a time in which social structures and hierarchies were strictly observed and social mobility was possible but difficult, and certainly never stretched to a commoner ascending to royalty; a peasant could never have usurped a king or queen. Rather, these images served to remind medieval people, from peasants to kings, that the wheel of fortune was always turning and that everyone, regardless of their wealth or social status, could experience a downturn in fortune. What goes up must come down, and Lady Fortune never smiles on anyone for ever.

Christine de Pizan experienced the fickleness of the Wheel first hand; she even used the analogy to describe the trajectory of her own life in various writings. Her first 16 years had been blessed with money, royal favour and a loving husband. But her luck began to change in 1380, when Charles V, a king who greatly favoured the de Pizan family, passed away to be succeeded by his son. The new king, Charles VI, did not hold them so dearly, and Christine's father lost his pension and many other benefits. As Christine tells us: 'my father's large pensions disappeared [...] And as for the hope that the good king had given of settling 500 livres of land on him and his heirs, his untimely death prevented the realization of this and other benefits.'[3] Her father died not long after the king, and the family flailed financially for the next ten years, struggling to hold on to their comfortable position at court, until the sorrowful day when Christine's husband also passed away. While they were far from the breadline, the surviving family had become accustomed to a life of nobility and luxury, and this was not something that any of them were prepared to give up. And so Christine picked up a pen—or, rather, a quill. Through her talent, hard work and a dogged perseverance, she put her shoulder to the Wheel of Fortune and, inch by agonizing inch, managed to grind it back around.

She became one of the most popular and prolific writers of her time and, while many women did write for pleasure or edification, she was the first (that we know of) to make money from her writing. Christine was canny. She networked hard, using her family's royal connections to full effect by dedicating her works to the most influential noblemen and women in the literary world, including the king and queen of France and the king of England. Rather than trying to disguise the fact that she was a woman, she used it as a selling point. She remarks that princes presented her work to other royal figures not because of the quality of their content but 'more so because of the unusual and rare event that a woman should write', and she tells us that her works were disseminated throughout Europe because they represented 'new things deriving from a woman's perspective'.[4]

Not only was Christine the first woman to earn a living from her words but she can also be considered the first female publisher. To ensure her products were of the highest quality she had a hand in almost every stage of the composition process, from book production to marketing. This was no mean feat. Book production in the medieval period was laborious, time-consuming and eye-wateringly expensive, an entirely different prospect from the mass production of printed books today. For a start, it all had to be carried out by hand. Paper was rarely used in Europe until the advent of the printing press, around 1450. Instead, animal skins needed to be turned into parchment or vellum and prepared for use. The pelts would be soaked in a lime solution so that the fur could be removed. They would then be stretched out and carefully scraped, using a special knife with a curved blade, then re-tightened, a process that would be carried on over several days until the skins were flat and thin enough for use. Once they had been properly treated, they needed to be ruled, usually in red ink, to help scribes keep their lines as they copied out their text by hand with a quill pen made from the feather of a goose or a swan. Once the words were on the page, it was time for decoration. Coloured dye or pigment would be mixed with egg white to brighten the more luxurious manuscripts—rusted iron was used to make green, brazilwood from Ceylon for red, saffron for yellow and, most costly of all, crushed lapis lazuli imported from Persia and Afghanistan for ultramarine. Painted over a gold leaf base, these decorations were known as 'illuminations' because of the way they shimmer when they caught the light. When the ink had dried, the manuscript could be bound and sent to its new owner.

Book production was an art form, and each stage in the process required a different artisan. This meant it was very expensive, and only the wealthiest could afford to own manuscripts—religious institutions, universities and royalty. The fact that Jean de Berry, brother to the king and renowned literary patron, collected almost all of Christine's works in his famous library is a testament to how much he esteemed her writing. Their high price tag also meant that manuscripts were usually commissioned. A rich individual might order a manuscript of the collected works of a single author, but more usually (and more cost-effectively) they would request a miscellany, a compilation of all their favourites. There were price scales, depending on how much you wanted to spend. While some manuscripts were opulent, filled with gold and ultramarine, others were devoid of any illumination. It was also very common for a customer to run out of money before a manuscript was completed. There are numerous surviving manuscripts that have gaps where illuminations were supposed to be added, or that have luxurious pages early on only to peter out into something far plainer as the book goes on.

Paris was the book production capital of Europe, and Christine took full advantage of having this thriving trade on her doorstep. Between 1399 and 1420 she supervised the creation of at least 54 manuscripts, deciding what should be included, penning passages in her own hand, making corrections and additions, and collaborating with artists to find the right images to decorate them. She also deliberately sought out female artisans:

> On the subject of women who are expert in the art of painting, I know a woman right now of the name of Anastasia, who is so talented and skilled in painting decorative borders on manuscripts and landscape backgrounds that one cannot find an artisan to equal her. [. . .] She so excels at painting flower motifs in the most exquisite detail and is so highly esteemed that she is entrusted with the richest and most valuable manuscripts. I know this from my own experience, because she has done work for me that is considered exceptional among the decorations created by other artisans.[5]

Christine worked hard to create a brand for herself. At a time when most authors neglected to sign their manuscripts and many works remained anonymous, she was careful to insert her name into titles, to cast herself as a protagonist and to commission images of herself in many of her manuscripts. Usually dressed in expensive blue and surrounded by books, either presenting them to patrons or speaking to a captive audience about them, Christine made herself instantly recognizable, fashioning herself as an elegant literary powerhouse. Which is exactly what she became.

Christine was unique in the sense that she was a woman making money from authorship, but plenty of other women earned their living, regardless of how many surviving medieval writings minimized, belittled or completely ignored their work. In Chaucer's *Canterbury Tales*, the pilgrims who journey together to a shrine in Canterbury are defined by their employment. Out of thirty characters, which include a miller, a knight, a physician and a shipman, there are only three female pilgrims: a nun, a prioress and a wife. This casting suggests that only two paths were available to medieval women— marriage or the church. The few trades that women *were* known for were frequently demeaned. Margery Kempe recalls how men would often order her 'to go and spin and card wool, as other women do', telling Margery to stay in her lane while, at the same time, dismissing the lane itself.[6] Similarly, in a tract about famous women in history (one of the libellous books that Christine rails against in her *City of Ladies*), the Italian poet Boccaccio praises notable heroines by denigrating other women and their occupations. When describing Proba, a female prophet and poet, he remarks that 'If we consider the ways of women, the distaff, the needle, and weaving would have been sufficient for her had she wanted to lead a sluggish life', belittling the vital trades of needlework, embroidery and silk which were so essential to daily life.[7] And writing on the Roman poet Cornificia, he permits himself the following tirade:

> She brought honour to womankind, for she scorned womanly concerns and turned her mind to the study of the great poets. Let slothful women be ashamed, and those who wretchedly have no confidence in themselves, who, as if they were born for idleness and the marriage bed, convince themselves that they are good only for the embraces of men, giving birth and raising children, while they have in common with men the ability to do those things which make men famous, if only they are willing to work with perseverance.[8]

The underlying assumption is that women are less likely to be worthy of celebration because they do not push themselves to work hard but are idle, content with the marriage bed and childcare. Women have all the same abilities as men, Boccaccio argues, but they don't have the willpower.

We shouldn't take this famously misogynistic man's words at face value. Not only do his writings devalue the important work of women, the trades and skills honed over hundreds and thousands of years, but the vocation he *does* celebrate in the case of Proba and Cornificia (authorship) was one that was almost impossible for most medieval women to access. If women lacked confidence and felt themselves only fit for marriage and children, or spinning and weaving, it was no doubt because medieval society was designed to make them feel that this was the case.

The prevailing attitude, among lettered men at least, seems to have been that women's work was less valuable than men's. Moreover, there were certain professions—writer, lawyer, physician, shipman, to name but a few—that were kept woefully out of reach for most women, by law. In the *City of Ladies* Christine asks the allegorical figure of Reason why women are not allowed to present a case at trial, act as a witness or pass sentence. 'You might as well ask why God didn't command men to perform women's tasks and women those of men,' Reason replies. God 'gave men strong powerful bodies to stride about and speak boldly, which explains why it is men who learn the law and maintain the rule of justice'. As if sensing this isn't quite sufficient—why would a lawyer need to be physically strong?—Reason adds that women are intelligent enough to work in the legal profession, but there is simply no need for them to. 'It would not be right for them to abandon their customary modesty and to go about bringing cases before a court, as there are already enough men to do it.'[9]

Medieval society had clear ideas about what professions were suitable for men and women. But that's not to say that working women didn't exist, or that there weren't women who managed to smash those gates into smithereens. In fact, there were plenty of other medieval women besides Christine de Pizan, from a broad spectrum of society, who hustled.

One historian has dubbed the fourteenth and fifteenth centuries a 'golden age' for women.[10] While this feels like something of an exaggeration at a time when a woman's property belonged to her husband, and she had to defer to him in any employment she engaged in, it's certainly true that various happenings during the high Middle Ages led to more options for women. The Black Death, a gruesome illness that did not discriminate between men and women, rich and poor, decimated Europe. It was a catastrophe and must have felt, to those living through it, apocalyptic. Once the telltale black spots—an 'infallible token of approaching death', according to Boccaccio—appeared on your body, there was nothing a physician could do to help you.[11] And every time the epidemic seemed to abate, a fresh wave of deaths would follow. Historians estimate that around a third of the population of Europe died in the first wave alone. As devastating as the Black Death was, it did—much like the First World War—free up the labour market. All of a sudden there were a lot of job vacancies in professions previously closed to women, which they were quick to fill.

There were also some legal changes in England that had a direct effect on the women living there. In the fourteenth century *femme sole* (the Norman French for 'single woman') was introduced and it formalized a woman's right, whether single, married or widowed, to trade as an individual rather than under the governance of her husband. Because of this, any woman could technically run her own business, earn her own money (even if these wages still fell under the jurisdiction of her husband), rent a shop for her own use and even train apprentices and servants herself. According to existing records, in London, women were trading in a wide variety of professions as *femmes soles*, from cloth weaving to upholstering, embroidering to brewing ale.

Women had been working for hundreds of years before the Black Death, and *femme sole*, helping their husbands in the fields, assisting their male family members with whatever trade they happened to be peddling, keeping accounts, acting as nurses and midwives, running community hospitals, doing laundry and heading up households. Much of the buying and selling of street food and small items had long been dominated by female 'hucksters', especially when it came to bread, fish, poultry, ale and dairy goods. But these events were nevertheless responsible for facilitating social mobility and creating new opportunities for women—opportunities that became increasingly inscribed in labour laws.

The form of work most associated with women in the Middle Ages, and the one which crops up the most in literary and artistic depictions, was labour involving textiles, and especially spinning, the art of producing thread from wool and flax to be used to weave into cloth. Of all the medieval sexist stereotypes, one of the most common (and the most frightening to men) was that of the 'dominatrix', the woman who upturned the status quo by domineering over, even beating up, her spouse—a right that, legally speaking, only belonged to him. In an image displayed on a fifteenth-century copper plate from the Netherlands, a man kneels on all fours as a woman straddles him—but he doesn't look like he's having a good time. The woman on top of him has pulled down his trousers to expose his rear end, which she cheerfully beats with a foxtail. He, looking aghast, clutches a spindle, which suggests that he's been spinning wool and perhaps also that he is being punished for messing up his task. As spinning was deemed to be 'woman's work', this detail alone would have amused a medieval diner looking down at their empty plate.

In other similar images, which can be found carved into stone and copper as well as illuminated in the corners of manuscripts, the spindle itself becomes an instrument of violence. Bearing in mind that the word 'spindle' (perhaps because of its shape, size and appearance) was a euphemism for 'penis' in much of medieval Europe, we can see how the comedy of these images hinged on the reversal of existing power structures and an upheaval of the status quo. However humorous they are, such depictions also issue a warning. Spinning may appear to be a safe occupation for a woman, they tell us, but be warned: to endow any female endeavour with too much power was to relax the threads binding medieval society together, and to set loose a disruption and chaos that could only lead to male humiliation. An even darker edge to this symbolism is that men as well as women could be punished for crimes of sex and violence by being paraded through the streets, carrying a distaff as a mark of their shame. The humble spindle carried a great deal of metaphorical weight in the Middle Ages, representing not only women's labour but also sex, danger and violence.

While artists, authors and legal authorities may have represented the dangerous potential of the spindle as a tool for women's power, it is safe to say that women's work with textiles was essential, and so was the work of peasant women in the fields, of female traders in the medieval streets, and medical caregivers. Like it or not, medieval society was reliant on their labour. And, thinking back to Chaucer's pilgrims, and the suggestion that there were only two real options for women (marriage and the Church), it is worth remembering that both of those options involved a lot of hard graft. Being a medieval housewife didn't just mean looking after the children, preparing meals and keeping things clean and tidy. Women were expected to pursue other occupations to help keep the family afloat.

. . .

A husband returns from work and is furious to discover that his dinner is not on the table. He's had a long, hard day labouring in the fields, but what, exactly, has his wife been doing?

Their subsequent argument is straight from the playbook of misogyny, versions of which have been repeated for thousands of years across literary depictions as well as real households. But in this medieval iteration the wife doesn't offer the chastened apology her husband clearly expects—she fights back.

The Ballad of the Tyrannical Husband is an English poem we find in a fifteenth-century manuscript belonging to a London merchant.[12] It tells the tale of a peasant husband and his wife. She, the poem tells us, was 'fair and bold'. He, on the other hand, was 'an angry man, and easily vexed'. The two of them get into an argument one night, when he comes home to find that supper isn't already on the table, over who does the most work. He wishes she could spend a day in his shoes, to see what hard labour is really like: 'I would that you should go all day to plough with me,/To walk in the clods that are wet and boggy,/Then you would know what it is to be a ploughman.'

At these unfair allegations the wife loses her temper. She reminds her husband that because of their baby she only gets 'a little sleep', and yet she still has many other tasks: 'I milk the cows and turn them out in the field/While you are quite sound asleep', she tells him, 'I make butter,/Afterwards I make cheese.' When all this has been done, the children are crying, and she must get them up and out of bed. Then there are more jobs to do. While minding them she also bakes, brews ale, spins cloth to make clothes for them all and feeds the livestock. And all this before noon and without any help.

Unimpressed, her husband proposes that they switch places to discover, once and for all, who has more work to do. 'Tomorrow with my lad to the plough you shall go,' he tells her, 'and I will be the housewife.' She readily agrees, knowing full well that her life is the harder.

Like many medieval works, this poem is unfinished, either because the author moved on to another project, or because they died before they could complete it, or because the money ran out before the manuscript could be finalized. We'll never know for sure how the argument ended, but we can make an educated guess. The poem begins with a preamble sympathetic to women: 'God protect all women that are in this town/Including maidens, widows, and wives/For they are much blamed and sometimes wrongly.' And the tone gives the distinct impression that the husband is going to end his day as a housewife exhausted and repentant. Not only does the poem set a medieval precedent for arguments about whose turn it is to do this or that chore, but it also reveals just how varied the life of a medieval housewife was. Farming, brewing, making cloth, cheese and bread, tending to the animals— the wife in the *Ballad* does far more than cook, clean and look after the children. She is a peasant, but for wealthier women too the to-do list could be daunting.

In the *Treasure of the City of Ladies*, Christine de Pizan outlines the daily duties of 'housewives' from peasants to princesses, in exhausting detail.[13] Because barons, knights and squires are frequently called away—to court, or abroad on royal missions, or to fight in wars—their wives 'should be wise and sound administrators and manage their affairs' while they're gone. Such a lady should be knowledgeable about the laws of fiefdom and taxation and, although she shouldn't get involved with peasant labour herself, she should be aware of all the work on the land of her estate, and at what time and during what seasons this work needs to take place. She should rise early and make an appearance at her window, to set the servants and labourers a good example, and she should busy herself around the house, giving orders and checking up on things. 'She will go in the evening with one of her women to see how the sheep are being penned up,' Christine tells us, 'and thus the shepherd will be more careful that there is nothing for which he may be reproached.'

The wives of artisans should not only support their husbands but directly involve themselves in their trade: 'the wife herself should be involved in the work to the extent that she knows all about it, so that she may know how to oversee his workers if her husband is absent, and to reprove them if they do not do well.' And Christine impresses on all women, regardless of their social status, the importance of keeping abreast of their husband's business affairs:

'The wise lady ought to persuade her husband if she can by kind words and sensible admonitions to agree to discuss their finances together and try to keep such a standard of living as their income can provide.' That way, if the husband needs to leave home on business, or if he passes away, the wife will not be left in the dark, as Christine herself had been.

. . .

Margery was a complex woman. She had decided to dedicate her life to God and pursue a religious vocation, but as much as she wanted to be holy, she struggled. It was difficult in those early years to give up the luxuries she had become accustomed to as the daughter of a wealthy merchant. 'She would not leave her pride or her showy manner of dressing, which she had previously been used to', her *Book* tells us.[14] She wore gold piping on her headdress, and the tippets (long, narrow strips of white cloth) on her hood were fashionably slashed and underlaid with various bright and expensive colours. These little details were deliberate. They showed her to be a woman not just of style but also of means. Almost as much as she wanted to be chosen by God, Margery wanted to catch the eye of her peers, to be the object of envy and desire. Never content with what she had, her *Book* tells us, 'she always craved more and more'.[15] In order to get it, she took up brewing.

While brewing today tends to be associated far more with men than with women, the production of ale was one of the most popular trades for house-wives in the Middle Ages. In the fourteenth century, when Margery was born, very few men brewed on their own and most male brewers worked alongside women. If more affluent women hired servants to help them with their brewing, then they almost exclusively looked to other women. When one particularly successful 'brewster', Denise Marlere of Bridgwater, Somerset, died in February 1401, she left behind her prosperous brewing business and bestowed most of it to her servant, Rose, including half of a tenement and almost all her brewing equipment (including a furnace, three sacks of malt, a pan, a silver goblet, a chafing dish and two silver spoons). What remained, she left to her daughter. To Denise, brewing was a woman's work. And her attitude is reflected in surviving medieval legislation and reports, which, until the sixteenth century, tended to treat brewers as an exclusively female group.

Brewing ale proved popular as a trade among women, but especially among wives (Denise was married, to a butcher called Nicholas).[16] For a start, every household needed large quantities of ale. Water was usually too polluted to drink, and only those who could not afford to do otherwise relied on it for hydration. Milk was reserved for making cheese and butter, and wine was too expensive for the majority of people to consume on a daily basis. That's not to say that all medieval people were rolling around drunk every day—their ale was much weaker than the pint you might order in your local pub—but still, they probably had a high tolerance for it because of their regular consumption. Because ale was such a commonplace in the medieval kitchen, it made sense for wives to save money by producing it themselves.

Second, the process of brewing, while time-consuming, was relatively straightforward, widely known and easily taught. No specialist training or equipment was required. Those running a more professional enterprise might have special materials, such as troughs, malt mills and mash tuns, to ease the process, but most domestic brewers found household utensils perfectly adequate and could embark on their trade for minimal expense. It made sense for a wife to produce a large batch regularly (the wife in *The Ballad of the Tyrannical Husband* brews twice a week) and sell the excess to their neighbours for a profit. Finally, ale does not travel well; it spoils very quickly (which is why smaller pubs today still struggle to sell real ale), and it doesn't react well to the changes in temperature and jostling of transportation. Bearing in mind that women, especially wives, were expected to stay close to home, it makes sense that the production of ale became part of their wheelhouse.

Brewing was also flexible: women could stop doing it and start up again very easily, taking breaks to look after small children and then resuming as they got older and more able to look after themselves—or to help. A wife still needed her husband's permission, of course, and her husband had overarching control of the business, as he did any of her financial endeavours. But although he was technically entitled to the final say on when, how and to whom his wife should sell ale, it seems that most men were happy to leave their wives to it, as long as the business didn't prove too disruptive to daily life and brought in some extra coin.

For a while then, at least, brewing was a nice side-hustle for medieval housewives, a way of putting their labour to good use and finding a little bit of autonomy for themselves. But whereas the Black Death changed things for the better for women in other trades, it had a negative effect on female brewsters. Before the plague swept the land, profits from brewing were fairly modest, and so the trade escaped the interest of men. Afterwards, however, brewing became much more lucrative. More people than ever were drinking ale (unlike in most of the rest of Europe, wages in England stayed high even when the population started to recover, which meant more people than ever had disposable income), and as the profit margins of brewing grew, so too did male interest in the profession. Seeing the potential for making a serious amount of money, men started to get in on the action. Unrestrained by the governance of a husband, or the necessity of staying close to home, they were able to brew on a far more ambitious scale, setting up brewhouses, hiring large numbers of servants (rather than just one or two) to help and making ale in far larger batches. Women, who lacked the investment capital or managerial authority to keep up (and who were confronted with an increasingly pernicious rhetoric associating female brewsters with sexual licence), were gradually squeezed out of the trade. It wasn't long before brewing had become a profession from which women found themselves largely excluded.

Operating at the turn of the century, Margery was not yet a victim of this downturn. And yet her brewing enterprise was not successful. Things seemed to go well for the first three or four years (or so she tells us): 'Out of pure covetousness, and in order to maintain her pride, she took up brewing, and was one of the greatest brewers in the town of Lynn.'[17] But then she began to haemorrhage money. Her failure in the *Book* is explained in part by her lack of experience but also, and more importantly in terms of her life's trajectory, by divine providence. However hard-working, knowledgeable and careful Margery's servants were, things never went right for them. Just when her ale had as fine a head of froth on it as anyone could hope for, and the customers started rolling in, it would suddenly and inexplicably turn flat, and an entire batch would be lost. This happened time and time again until her servants decided to seek employment elsewhere.

Undeterred, Margery turned her attention to a different industry. For a brief time she became a miller. Yet again, God had other plans for her. Although the two new horses she purchased were strong and healthy, and her new servant was well versed in his profession, he could not get them to cooperate. 'When he took one of those horses and put him in the mill as he had done before, this horse would not pull in the mill in spite of anything the man might do.' He tried everything, with both horses, but nothing worked. The man quit in frustration, and word soon got out about Margery's failures: 'Then it was noised about the town of Lynn that neither man nor beast would serve the said creature, and some said she was accursed.'

It may well have been that Margery just wasn't a particularly good businesswoman and had no talent for brewing or milling, that she hired the wrong servants and bought the wrong equipment. But she frames these events as the acts of God, who wanted to prevent her from becoming an entrepreneur and keep her as his handmaiden. While some of her neighbours wondered if she had been cursed, or was suffering from 'vengeance from God', others thought differently: 'some wise men, whose minds were grounded in the love of our Lord, said it was the high mercy of our Lord Jesus Christ that called her from pride and vanity of this wretched world.'[18] Her disappointments in these industries become a vehicle, leading her to a vocation in which she truly excels: the life of a religious woman. If at first you don't succeed, don't give up, just try something else.

. . .

Chaucer wasn't entirely wrong, however, in suggesting that medieval women were either married to a man or to God. While lower-class women did join the workforce more than we tend to think—whether they had a husband or not—it's true that unmarried wealthy women did often end up entering a convent. This wasn't a life of leisure, however. Much like being a wife, being a nun was hard work.

Girls could become nuns as young as 14, and were usually offered to convents by parents who didn't have enough money for a dowry, or who aimed to add an air of devotion to their family name. While it may have been less expensive than attracting a good husband, it still came at a price. Parents had to pay an entrance fee, buy their daughter her own habit and bed and throw a grand feast on the day she took her vows, inviting not only their family and friends but all the nuns from the convent too. During her first years, a novice would be taught how to sing and read, and to speak French—skills that, when she was older, she might pass on to novices.

Her days in the convent, both before and after she took her official vows, were long and hard. There were seven 'monastic offices' (services involving lengthy prayers and song) each day, with one in the middle of the night. At 2 a.m. all the girls would tumble out of bed into the cold air of the dormitory to go and say the night office. Then they'd be allowed to crawl back under the sheets to snatch a few hours of sleep before rising at 6 a.m. to say 'prime', another prayer. In and among these seven services, nuns were expected to devote themselves either to study (reading in French, English and sometimes Latin) or to manual labour, from spinning and embroidering to gardening, or even haymaking. Much of the day would pass in strict silence, although we know from records of visiting bishops that the nuns were often caught breaking this rule, gossiping before going to bed or even during the services themselves.

All convents would be overseen by a woman elected by her peers and known as a prioress. There were perks to this position, of course. A prioress would get her own room, or in some convents a whole series of them, equivalent to a flat or small house, with a private kitchen. All the other nuns had to defer to her, calling her 'Mother' and doing her bidding. But that's not to say that being a prioress was easy. Alongside setting a good example at the seven monastic offices, it would be up to the prioress to make sure the nuns under her care behaved themselves and that the finances of the convent were in good health. She had to know whether the farms were making money, whether the bailiffs were following orders and looking after the estate properly and whether the merchants buying the wool that came from the sheep in the fields were giving a fair price. If a prioress wasn't keeping abreast of all her duties, then her nuns would be quick to shop her to the local bishop. Every year he would visit the convents within his jurisdiction to check up on things, inspect the property and interview all the nuns.

Records from these visitations across the country show that, while some convents were full of praise for their prioress, others were quick to complain: she was a bad businesswoman, running the convent into the ground and getting them into debt; their habits were worn and full of holes; she cared more about herself than the convent. According to the report of one nunnery, who found themselves in £20 of debt (equivalent to the annual rent for three London taverns, or the price of two thoroughbred horses), the nuns blamed their prioress for frittering away the finances: 'she frequently rides about and pretends that she does so on the common business of the house although it is not so.' When she leaves the priory, she 'tarries too long abroad and she feasts sumptuously' with 'a train of attendants much too large', wearing garments far too grand for her profession.[19] The fur trimmings of her mantle alone, the nuns tell the bishop, are worth hundreds—enough to wipe out the convent's debts.

Chaucer paints a vivid picture of his prioress, the graceful, sensitive and beautifully dressed Madame Eglentyne, with her 'simple and modest' smile.[20] The most serious oath she ever utters is 'by Saint Loy' (a medieval way of saying that she never really swears at all) and 'her greatest pleasure' is in 'good manners'. Surely, Chaucer tells us, she is 'of excellent deportment, very pleasant and amiable in her demeanour', and she is also very well dressed and attractive, 'her nose well formed, her eyes as grey as glass, her mouth very small, and moreover soft and red'.

Reading between the lines, however, we can see that Chaucer, playful as ever, is not only poking gentle fun at Madame Eglentyne but is also suggesting that she is guilty of many of those misdemeanours that nuns would complain about, from excessive travel to expensive clothes. While Chaucer tells us that she is 'charitable' and 'compassionate', the example he gives is not of her humanitarian work but rather her attitude towards some pet dogs. 'She had some small hounds that she fed/With roasted meat or milk and fine white bread.' Here is our first clue. We know that bishops tried to ban small dogs and other pet animals from nunneries, believing them to be a distraction from devotion and a frivolous expense. In a visitation report sent to Romsey Abbey in 1387, Bishop William of Wykeham writes: 'we have convinced ourselves by clear proofs that some of the nuns of your house bring with them to church birds, rabbits, hounds and such like frivolous things, whereunto they give more heed than to the offices of the church.' The nuns do this, the bishop chides, 'to the grievous peril of their souls'.[21] Madame Eglentyne's hounds might have been tolerated—perhaps even doted on—by the nuns within her care, even if they were frowned upon. However, it's likely that the nuns would have been less pleased with the money their prioress spent on dog food. The roasted meat and fine white bread she treated them to are a far cry from the simple food of poverty on which the nuns themselves were expected to subsist.

Julian of Norwich, enclosed in her cell until her death, would never have been able to count herself among Chaucer's pilgrims. However, the life of an anchoress was just as heavily regulated as that of a nun in her convent—if not more so. As with most professions, there was an application process for becoming an anchoress (or, if you were a man, an anchorite) and, because it was one the most prestigious roles in the Church, it was a rigorous one. Julian would have applied to her local bishop, offering references and a testimony of her own to convince him that she was of good character, well suited to the contemplative life and could support herself financially, either with a private fortune or patronage. Her fare may have been meagre, but she still needed daily meals as well as a servant or two, and it was up to her to cover those expenses for the rest of her life.

Once an anchoress had been accepted into the fold, her existence would have been a gruelling one, marked by strict rules and regulations, as several different guidebooks make clear. Two of the most widely read of these were the twelfth-century *De institutione inclusarum* ('A Rule of Life for a Recluse'), by Aelred of Rievaulx, and the anonymous thirteenth-century *Ancrene Wisse* ('Guide for Anchoresses'), which was heavily influenced by Aelred's earlier work.[22] Both are written by men who took it upon themselves to offer spiritual direction (and regulation) to women who had taken up a religious life. Aelred frames *De institutione* as a letter to his sister, although it is not clear if she is a biological sibling or a 'spiritual' one. *Ancrene Wisse* is addressed to three enclosed women who, according to the author, were well catered to by a patron, with servants and even a cat: 'you do not worry about food or clothing', he writes, 'either for you or for your maidens. Each one of you has all that she needs from one friend.' It seems that the original addressees of *Ancrene Wisse* had also made a name for themselves: 'There is much talk of you, what noble women you are, sought after for your goodness and generosity' because 'in the blossom of your youth you forsook all the world's joys and became anchoresses'.[23]

In the fourteenth century, a hundred years after it was first written, *Ancrene Wisse* was copied and revised by a scribe to cater to a wider audience. It speaks to all the anchoresses in the country, who might be living apart but are joined in one spiritual community: 'You are the anchoresses of England, so many together, twenty now or more. May God multiply you in good, among whom there is the greatest peace, the greatest unity and single-mindedness and concord in your common life according to one rule.' They might be physically separate but thanks to the rules which they all follow, they have 'one way of life', just as if they were all part of 'a convent of London, and of Oxford, of Shrewsbury or of Chester'.[24]

De institutione inclusarum, Ancrene Wisse and other similar guides cater to both the 'outer' (day-to-day practicalities) and the 'inner' (emotional, spiritual) lives of their enclosed readers, often treating the two as interrelated. They warn anchoresses against the sin of idleness, which, according to Aelred, stirs 'unclean affections' (lust). To ward off this 'inner' spiritual disease, they prescribe 'outer' occupations, humble diversions to keep the anchoress busy and out of trouble. Alongside a daily sequence of prayers, she should dedicate time to contemplation, to reading holy books, to mending church vestments, making cloth and, if she was lucky enough to have a small garden, tending to it. She should also talk to the visitors who came to her cell for blessings and advice. All of this toil was to be completed against a backdrop of regular fasting and sleeplessness—anchoresses were told to sometimes sleep standing up, sometimes lying on the floor with their arm as a pillow, and never with anything softer than a rush mat beneath them, to test their endurance and devotion. Aelred tells his sister to 'flee delicate meat and sweet drinks' as if they were 'venom and poison' and another fifteenth-century guide, *Speculum Inclusorum* ('A Mirror for Recluses'), advises that the enclosed should 'immediately read or perform some kind of manual labour' if they find that 'their taste for prayer or delight in meditation decreases'.[25] All the guides are united in their emphasis on chastity and hyper-vigilance. Anchoresses shouldn't rest on their laurels, just because they have shut themselves away from the world. Devils will continue to attack them, just as an army besieges a castle, and it is up them to ward off their blows: 'Do not turn to flee, my dear sisters, but resist the devil's army face to face.'[26]

Despite the extreme nature of the vocation, becoming an anchoress was popular in the Middle Ages. Twice as many women as men enclosed themselves in the fourteenth and fifteenth centuries, and almost three times as many in the thirteenth, perhaps because it was one of the only professions that offered an escape from marriage and children but also, perhaps, because of the position's prestige and esteem. 'The anchoress is called an "anchor",' *Ancrene Wisse* tells us, 'anchored under the church like an anchor under the side of a ship to hold the ship, so that waves and storms do not capsize it.'[27] The good and devoted anchoress was the backbone of the most powerful institution in medieval Europe, holding it steady and keeping it safe from tempest and storm. We'll never know how this kind of reverence affected someone like Julian of Norwich. But in a world where women were so frequently denigrated or dismissed, it must have felt powerful.

.   .   .

In the only image we have of her, Marie de France is writing. Sitting in front of a large manuscript, she has a quill in one hand, a stylus in the other and a look of intense concentration. She wears a long, pale gown over a bright blue tunic, and a lock or two of fair hair has escaped from the front of her short, white veil. All these details are deliberate. Blue was the most expensive dye on the market and here it speaks of wealth but also, as the colour of the Virgin, of modesty and devotion. The veil is an unusual choice, particularly for a court writer, designed, perhaps, to keep people guessing. Was she a widow? Did she have designs on a life of religion? And if so, how did that tally with her stories of love and infidelity? It's easy to read the tantalizing glimpse of her hair, curling out to frame her face, as a reflection of her stories:

good and proper on the outside, but with a whisper of freedom, rule-breaking and disruption of the status quo underneath.

One can imagine Marie dressing herself in just this way to recite her *lais* at court, perhaps even for the king. Minstrels—also known as *jongleurs* or *trouvères*—were professional storytellers and entertainers who would travel around delighting elite households with tales of courtly love and chivalric deeds set to music. A lucky few might be employed by the nobility, which meant they could dedicate more time to literary creation rather than constantly having to earn their keep on the road. The *Roman de la Rose* describes *jongleurs* everywhere, at hunts, tournaments and court events, 'circulating' through the rows of barons, playing one piece or another.[28] There is even mention of a female minstrel, Doete de Troyes, who sings a song at the May Day celebrations. We don't know whether Marie ever performed herself or delegated her creations to a paid minstrel. But without doubt she intended her stories to be heard. Dedicating her *lais* to King Henry himself, she writes: 'In your honour, noble king, you who are so worthy and courtly, I set myself to assemble lays, to compose and to relate them in rhyme.' Boldly, she makes her last line a command: 'Now *hear* the beginning.'[29]

The women in the stories that follow do not work. They are elegant ladies, wives of kings and noblemen. Any tedious details of their daily lives—looking after their households and estates, managing staff, assisting with their husband's accounts or political affairs—are omitted, and while her heroines may be feisty, even powerful, they are not hustlers. From what we know of Marie, who was writing almost three hundred years before Christine de Pizan was born, the same cannot be said for her. In the prologues to her works, Marie offers different reasons for writing.[30] 'Anyone who has received from God the gift of knowledge and true eloquence has a duty not to remain silent,' she writes. Rather, those with talent (and here, of course, she is referring to herself) should be happy to reveal them. Arduous work is the perfect way to keep safe from vice and vanity; old stories should not be forgotten but should be translated and revived, to keep them alive. Alongside these more noble intentions, however, Marie also hopes her compositions will bring her fame and renown. She had originally intended to translate stories from Latin into French. However, knowing that many others had undertaken a similar task before her, she thought she would win more 'glory' by writing down, in her own words, songs that she had heard performed—and 'she worked late into the night' to perfect them.

We do not know if the king ever did 'hear' Marie's *lais* performed, but she definitely made a name for herself, becoming the target of envy and jealousy:

> Whoever has good material for a story is grieved if the story is not well told. Hear, my lords, the words of Marie, who when she has the chance does not squander her talents. Those who gain a good reputation should be commended, but, when there exists in a country a man or woman of great renown, people who are envious of their abilities frequently speak insultingly of them in order to damage this reputation. Thus, they start acting like a vicious, cowardly, treacherous dog that will bite others out of malice.[31]

While much of the malice Marie encountered would have been whispered in the banquet hall or the corridors of court, we do catch some glimpses of it in the writings of her peers. Denis Piramus, a male lyric poet who was attached to the same court as Marie, is dismissive of her *lais*. In his biography of Edmund, an Anglo-Saxon king, he mentions how he spent his youth as a courtier listening to and emulating songs, before moving on to more serious subjects and genres. Among these, he mentions Marie's stories: 'Dame Marie [...] turned into rhyme and made verses of "Lays" which are not in the least true. For these she is much praised and her rhyme is loved everywhere [...] These *lais* are wont to please ladies, who listen to them with delight, for they are after their own hearts.'[32] Piramus's compliment is backhanded. Her stories may be well liked, but they're not remotely true, and they're really tailored to women. Just as men devalued spinning, embroidery, housewifery and other 'female' endeavours, so here Piramus downgrades Marie's work as frivolous fodder for women—entertaining, perhaps, but not serious or accomplished.

We know from social commentary of the time that the court of King Henry II was marked by intense rivalry and competition. Marie wasn't alone in becoming the target for bitterness and slander as her reputation grew, but the tenor of that bitterness was undoubtedly shaped by her gender. It is clear from her writing that she was well educated, multilingual, highly literate, sophisticated and clever, but despite all this she is dismissed as silly and frothy not only by her male contemporaries but also by scholars hundreds of years later. Writing in 1950, William S. Woods makes no mention of Marie's artistry, but instead praises her 'endearing feminine attitude [...] and style', and comments on her 'womanly interest' in cloth, clothing, furniture and children.[33]

· · ·

Women's work, when and where it existed, was often heavily regulated, devalued or—as in the case of brewing—taken out of their hands if it became especially lucrative. There is also evidence that women were exploited in the workplace, particularly when sex was involved. Despite the Church's seeming distaste of sex, even within the sacred bonds of marriage, it tolerated sex work throughout the Middle Ages as a necessary evil. To remove prostitutes from society, as St Augustine dramatically put it, 'was to destroy everything with lust'. He compared sex work to a sewer in a palace: 'Take away the cesspool', he warned, 'and the palace will become an unclean and evil-smelling place.'[34]

Most of what we know about medieval brothels comes from their regulation rather than from first-hand accounts. In 1310 a royal command in London ordered all 'stews' to be closed, and that any 'common woman' caught within the city walls would be sentenced to 40 days in prison. This didn't mean, however, that the brothels ceased to exist; they just moved outside the city walls, to Southwark. In the fifteenth century, a legal document was drawn up to try and keep the brothels under control—and to make the bishop of Winchester, who had them under his jurisdiction, some profit on the side. There were 36 regulations, covering what the prostitutes could wear, where they should sleep and when they could work. Any infractions were punishable by a fine, to be paid directly to the bishop—which is what led to these women being referred to as 'Winchester Geese' ('goose' being slang for 'prostitute'). However, while most of the regulations were restrictive, some were designed to offer the women protection. Stew owners found to be forcibly detaining women or making them sleep in the 'stew' instead of in their home would be fined.[35]

We don't know how women felt about their work in these brothels. Were they forced into it? Did they enjoy it? Was it a choice, or did they feel they had no financial alternative? The legal documents from a small town in southern Germany allow us to glimpse the troubling realities for at least some of the women involved in European sex work.[36] In 1471 the owner (Lienhart Fryermut) of a brothel in Nördlingen and his partner (Barbara Tarschenfeindin) were accused of imprisoning the women, treating them cruelly and forcing one woman (Els von Eystett) to have an abortion. Twelve sex workers, including Els, were interrogated, and their testimony is harrowing. Els describes how she was forced into prostitution after being sold as a slave to the brothel. When she became pregnant, Barbara mixed her a drink to bring about a miscarriage and forced her to take it. Afterwards, Els was sworn to secrecy and made to continue working. The other women questioned by police corroborated Els's story and also made allegations of their own. Anna von Ulm reported that almost all the women had been sold to the brothel. They 'force the women to let men come to them', she informed the authorities, 'and when they do not want to, they are beaten.'

Women's involvement in sex work was as complex an issue in the Middle Ages as it is today. For some, it was likely to be preferable to marriage or religious enclosure. There was always a high demand for prostitutes, which meant there was no shortage of customers, and the profession could prove lucrative. However, when a woman's choice was taken away, or she became exploited by nefarious brothel owners (many of whom would deliberately get the prostitutes embroiled in debt to retain them against their will), then her life could quickly become unbearable.

. . .

In her semi-autobiographical work *The Book of the Mutability of Fortune*, Christine offers one of the earliest accounts of transgender transition. She explains her entry into the working world through the analogy of becoming a man, with a stronger and more agile body, and a deeper voice: 'Who I am, who speaks, who from female became male by Fortune, who willed it so; she changed me both body and face into a perfect natural man; while I was formerly a woman, I am in reality a man.'[37] Her allegory makes clear that, to become a successful writer, she had to emulate the opposite sex.

Hustling was easier for men than it was for women. Women had jobs, but there were a great many professions that were closed to them, and they had to work twice as hard as their male counterparts to make a living or to gain any sort of recognition. It is ironic but unsurprising that of the four women whom this book follows, it was Julian, the one safely tucked away behind the walls of a cell, who faced the least number of challenges in the workplace. But regardless of the barriers in their way, they all hustled. Whether they were in search of money, fame or heavenly recognition, they worked hard to make their words and voices heard. Their names may not be as famous as those of Geoffrey Chaucer or Dante, but the fact we know them at all means that, at least to some extent, their hard work paid off.

SIX

Making Friends . . .

'her kynred and thei that had ben frendys wer now hyr most enmys'*

MARGERY KEMPE, *The Book of Margery Kempe*

In 1413 God came to Margery Kempe in a vision and told her to make the 50-mile journey to the bustling market town of Norwich.[1] There she should seek out an anchoress called Julian, who was living out her days in a small cell adjoining a church. Julian was already a household name to any Christian worth their salt because God had appeared and spoken to her in a series of visions, which, rumour had it, she was now writing down to share with the world.

Since her conversion to the religious life, Margery had met many holy people, with mixed results. Some believed in her, but others condemned her as a fraud or deserted her when she most needed them. Not long before, she had stayed with an anchorite and his servant—a holy man in his own right—while she was travelling around England. Both men were so impressed by her that, when she finally left, the anchorite decided to accompany her. But at the first sign of trouble, he turned on her:

> as soon as people [. . .] spoke against this creature because she wept so grievously, and said she was a false hypocrite and deceived people, and threatened her with burning, then this man, who was held to be so holy, and in whom she trusted so much, rebuked her with the utmost force and scorned her most foully, and would not go any further with her.[2]

The thought that Julian, another woman who, like herself, had conversed with God might not believe in her—might not even like her—was painful.

As she approached the window of Julian's cell, she fell to her knees. Barely pausing for breath, she told her everything. Of 'the grace God had put into her soul', of the 'compunction, contrition, sweetness and devotion,

---

* 'her kin and those that had been her friends were now her greatest enemies'

compassion with holy meditation and high meditation' she had experienced, of 'the very many holy speeches' God had made to her and the 'wonderful revelations' he had bestowed on her. She asked Julian's advice. Could she trust these visions?

Julian listened carefully as Margery unburdened her soul and became convinced in her heart that what this younger woman said was true. 'Set all your trust in God and do not fear the talk of the world,' she told her. 'The more contempt, shame and reproof that you have in this world, the more is your merit in the sight of God.'

Margery faced much criticism throughout her life. Unlike other religious women she insisted on living an active, often disruptive life out in the world. Because of this, she was accused of preaching and heresy more than once. She was nearly burned at the stake twice. People said that her outbursts, which she claimed were a visitation from God, were really a sign of madness, or drunkenness or possession by the devil. Her visit to Julian, whether it was really God's idea or her own, was therefore strategic. By receiving her sanction, Margery was arming herself against criticism, cladding her reputation in iron. If a respected anchoress like Julian believed in her, then others would surely follow suit. But, reading between the lines, I think their meeting meant more than that. While Margery's account is brief, she does tell us that she and Julian 'had much holy conversation in talking about the love of our Lord Jesus Christ for the many days that they were together'. Where so many people she came across ridiculed and abandoned her, Julian listened and encouraged her. In Julian, Margery found not just an ally but a friend.

There is a resounding silence surrounding female friendship in the Middle Ages. While this silence is not dissimilar to the chasm surrounding same-sex romantic relationships between women, it is more puzzling. Homosexuality was considered a sin, even a crime, but female friendship certainly wasn't. So why the glaring gap? While there are pages and pages written on the ideal form of male friendship (usually inspired by the classical theory that true friendship needed to be between two similar men of equal social standing), it is very difficult to find anything comparable written about women's friendships in medieval Europe. Far more letters between men survive than between women; trying to find a medieval image of female friendship— whether in a manuscript illustration, a stained-glass window or a work of art—is like trying to find a needle in a haystack; and even literary depictions favour friendships between men. A woman's role in literature tends to be as wife, lover, meddler, mischief maker or hag rather than friend. But it goes without saying that medieval women did have friends, that they supported, cared for and looked out for one another, just as we know that they had romantic relationships with other women. We just have to dig a little deeper in order to uncover these friendships.

In fact, not only did female friendship exist but it was often a crucial step on the ladder for any woman looking to make a name for herself. In a world where men tended to hold all the cards, the forging of female friendship was essential to advancement, particularly for those who were not following the playbook, such as the radical women that make up the contents of this book. This companionship could certainly be mutually beneficial—you scratch my back and I'll scratch yours—but it also played a far more important role, providing women with support and validation, allowing them to share experiences and have the kinds of discussions from which men often excluded them.

．　．　．

To the minds of most medieval writers, friendship was the preserve of men. Popular classical writings such as Cicero's *De amicitia* ('On Friendship') understood a successful platonic relationship to depend on exact reciprocity and to be based on similarity, virtue and public life. 'Without true virtue', Cicero writes, 'friendship cannot exist at all', and 'he who looks upon a true friend, looks, as it were, upon a sort of image of himself.'[3] They also believed that, in its most perfect form, it only occurred between men. Boncompagno da Signa, a teacher of grammar and rhetoric from the university town of Bologna, penned his own guidebook to friendship in the twelfth century, which was heavily influenced by Cicero. He waxes lyrical about the special bond of friendship as 'a heavenly power which chooses to dwell only among the virtuous'. Friendship is 'the root of innocence', 'the dispenser of all joy', 'the strength of eagerness' and 'the source of all good things'.[4] It is also, in its most perfect form, something that only exists between angels—and men.

Female friendship, on the other hand, was not only frivolous but might even be dangerous. In medieval culture, gossip was, for the most part, a gendered language associated with women and, although it wasn't technically a sin, it was consistently deplored by Christian writers. In a popular anthology of sermons by the prominent churchman John Mirk, women are criticized for whispering to each other and distracting the congregation rather than listening to the sermon. Thanks to them, Mirk says, the church has become a labyrinth full of vain speech and filth. In his guidebook for enclosed women, *De institutione inclusarum*, Aelred of Rievaulx paints a vivid picture of a wayward anchoress gossiping with an old woman through her window, allowing idle tales to pour into her ear like poison. Together they dissect the appearance of priests and monks, the frivolous behaviour of a local young girl, the widow who is sleeping around and the cunning ways of a wife who is cheating on her husband. Aelred tells us that the old woman's tales of the outside world fill the anchoress with 'sensual pleasures'; she will go to bed exciting herself with thoughts of the sexual misbehaviour of others, tormented by the sin of lust.[5] Aelred was not alone in such thinking—according to medieval conduct manuals, women could often incite each other sexually with their gossipy tales of what other women were up to.

Men were also worried about what women might say to each other behind closed doors. Married men were afraid that their wives would tell all their most embarrassing secrets to their girlfriends—and then cackle with laughter at their shortcomings over a glass (or bottle) of wine. Alyson, Chaucer's Wife of Bath, tells us that women can keep nothing to themselves, and two popular medieval proverbs gesture to similar anxieties: 'Where there are women, there are words; where there are geese, there are turds' and 'garrulous women are seldom chaste.' Women can't keep their mouths shut and are as likely to be as indiscreet in the bedroom as they are in their speech. Sex and words therefore enjoy a heady mix in the medieval imagination when they pertain to women.

'Alehouse poems' or 'gossip songs' are the term given to poems, usually written by men, which tend to feature women gathering together over copious amounts of alcohol, making each other laugh with stories about their husbands. These poems usually survive in isolation, and so we don't know if women ever heard them—and, if they did, whether they were insulted or laughed along. One alehouse poem, 'A Talk of Ten Wives on Their Husbands' Ware', survives in a miscellany from the mid-fifteenth century.[6] The manuscript contains a chaotic assortment of different texts, from political prophecy to astrology, from Arthurian legend to medicine. Alongside, we find a poem about ten married women who meet up at their local alehouse to hold a storytelling competition, facilitated by gallons of wine. The women decide to try and determine whose husband's penis is the best—'Since we have no other song/To sing amongst ourselves/Let us tell tales/Of our husband's ware'—but the game very quickly takes the opposite turn. One wife is 'full of woe' to hear her friend lament her husband's poor performance in bed.

Another swears that her little finger is larger than her husband's erect penis. And while another does offer some praise, describing her husband's penis as 'white as milk, soft as silk', she sorrowfully confesses that this is all for naught—however silky soft it might be, he just can't get it up. Safe to say, none of the husbands come off well in this storytelling game.

A poet at the court of the charismatic King James IV of Scotland, William Dunbar, wrote 'Two Married Women', which begins with a male narrator taking a walk on a midsummer evening.[7] He overhears three women talking in a hedged garden. In the conversation he eavesdrops on, all the worst stereotypes about women are realized. None of the wives is happy or satisfied, and they make their displeasure clear in the crudest of terms. 'Though his penis pays me poorly in bed', one reveals, 'his purse pays me richly in recompense afterwards.' One of them is a manipulative and cunning widow who offers the others marital advice. She confesses that she had a secret lover while she was married to her first husband and knowingly convinced him to make the illegitimate child his heir. As an aristocratic lady, she made her second husband, a rich merchant, feel beholden to her by harping on about his social inferiority: 'I put into his mind', she laughs, 'that I married him out of charity', and she jokingly tells the other women that she used to call him her 'wife' and that she could order him around at will.

These poems are alcohol-fuelled and crude—'A Talk of Ten Wives', for example, repeatedly uses the most explicit medieval words for penis ('pentyl' and 'tarse')—and men are nowhere to be seen within them, except as part of derisory gossip. They are undoubtedly humorous but, rather than reflect women's concerns, they feed into male anxieties about what women might do and say out of earshot—and out of their husbands' control. Moreover, *all* that women talk about in poems of this kind is their husbands; as 'A Talk of Ten Wives' puts it, these women 'have no other song'. It seems impossible for men to imagine women talking about anything other than them, which might put modern readers in mind of the Bechdel test. While husbands are the most obvious butt of the joke, women, who are only capable of vicious gossip and can't think of anything to talk about except men, don't come off well either.

However, by depicting the possibility of women getting together, whether their husbands like it or not, these poems offer some glimmers of subversion too. In fact, their very existence suggests that such gatherings were commonplace, whatever the topic of discussion may actually have been. And alongside fulfilling stereotypes of wayward, gossipy women, they also show women listening to one another, offering comfort and reassurance, affection, even instruction—swapping ideas for routes they can take to and from the ale-house, so that their husbands won't guess where they're going. The loyalty of these women lies firmly with their friends, not their spouses.

Literature from other genres also provides insight into the support and guidance women offered one another. Many of Christine de Pizan's poems are framed as dream sequences in which allegorical women visit her to bestow their knowledge and advice. We've already seen how the *City of Ladies* combats medieval misogyny. Centred on an imagined female community, it also offers a vision of women's friendship, a place where the inhabitants celebrate one another's virtue. The three allegorical women who help Christine to build it—Reason, Rectitude and Justice—appear to her in a dream after she falls asleep in her study. Frightened they might be an apparition, or devils, she immediately makes the sign of the cross, but Lady Reason is quick to reassure her. With a smile, she speaks to Christine: 'My dear daughter, don't be afraid, for we have not come to do you any harm, but rather, out of pity on your distress, we are here to comfort you.'[8] As they help to build the city, they remain true to their word. All three show Christine kindness and understanding.

They also remind Christine of the various Roman women who looked after one another during the reign of Diocletian, an emperor who made it his mission to persecute Christians, and, in particular, of a noblewoman named Anastasia.[9] Every day, Anastasia would 'disguise herself as a pauper and go off accompanied by a young girl to visit the martyrs in their cells and try to comfort them with costly wines, food, and whatever else she could find.' She 'washed and dressed their wounds and anointed them with precious ointments' and generally did everything she could to alleviate their suffering. When she was finally caught, she was imprisoned for 30 days without food. But her spirits lifted when the ghost of Theodota, one of the women she had helped before she was executed, came to her aid. This 'saintly companion' set out a table of delicious food for her friend and kept her company.

Another noble Roman woman named Cloelia is likewise worthy of mention—for her bravery but also for her friendship.[10] When she and some other high-born virgins were sent as hostages to an enemy king, she concocted a plan of escape. After tricking the guards and ushering the women out of the palace, their getaway was nearly derailed when they reached the River Tiber and found themselves unable to cross it. Although Cloelia had never ridden a horse before, she found one in a nearby meadow and jumped on its back to wade through the water: 'Unafraid and undaunted by the deep water, she had one of her companions sit behind her as she rode across to the other side.' She then rode back and forth with every single one of her friends, to make sure they all made it home to their families.

Even the Virgin Mary herself is framed as a friend in Christine's city. In a speech to its inhabitants, she announces 'I will gladly come to live among these women, who are my sisters and friends.' Rather than establishing her authority as a queen and leader, she takes her place 'at their side'.

Christine's book finishes when 'the construction of [the] city is finally at an end'. A sanctuary for women past, present and future, it is a place 'where all [women] who love glory, virtue and praise may be lodged in great honour'. New members can and will be admitted—but they must be 'deserving'.[11]

As the creator of the city, it is up to Christine to decide what 'deserving' means. Hers is one of the first Western imaginings of what a place occupied by women could offer, and what women might be able to achieve in a space with friendship and collaboration at its heart. However, it is not a perfect utopia. Most of the women who make their way into its hallowed halls are educated, wealthy and elite, much like the recently defunct American women's club and workspace network The Wing, whose workspace for women was burdened with a hefty price tag and exclusionary behaviour. Christine's city of ladies could easily be accused of reaffirming divides of class and race.

Female friendship in Marie de France's writings also seems to flourish most, if not exclusively, among the upper classes. Most of her *lais* focus on heterosexual love. But in the final *lai* of her collection, *Eliduc*, the real love story is a platonic one between two women.[12] It begins with the eponymous handsome knight, who is so beloved at court that the other knights get jealous and make up lies about him to tell the king. Believing their slanderous words, the king banishes him. Hoping that one day he will be allowed to return, Eliduc leaves behind his beautiful and faithful wife, Guildeluec, to look after his land and property in Brittany. Guildeluec 'bewail[s] her husband's departure' and escorts him to the dock with a heavy heart. He reassures her that he will 'keep good faith with her', despite the distance between them, and takes his leave.

Away on new adventures, Eliduc is presented with a dilemma when he meets and falls in love with another woman. 'Now his heart was firmly trapped', Marie tells us, 'for he wanted to remain faithful but he could not refrain from loving the maiden Guilliadon, who was so beautiful, from looking at her and talking to her, kissing and embracing her.' Meanwhile, the king who had banished Eliduc was having second thoughts. 'He was losing all his castles and all his land was being laid to waste.' He asks Eliduc to come back. Faithful to his lord, if not his wife, he returns to Brittany, bringing Guilliadon with him. On the journey to her new home she discovers, much to her horror, that Eliduc has a wife already and falls 'face down' in a swoon. She is so still and so quiet that Eliduc believes she has died. Heartbroken, he places her in a hermit's chapel deep in the woods, making a pilgrimage to see her every day.

Reunited with his patient wife, Eliduc spends all his time pining after Guilliadon. Guildeluec is no fool, and she soon realizes that something is amiss. She follows him and discovers the hermit's chapel. Entering it, she finds Guilliadon lying on a bed and raises the covers to see 'the body so slender, the long arms, the white hands, the fingers, slim, long, and full'. Confronted with such beauty, she understands, 'why her husband had grieved'. Filled with sorrow that such a beautiful young woman has died, she begins to weep, but is interrupted when an inquisitive weasel comes scurrying out from under the altar. Seeing it run over Guilliadon's body, one of Guildeluec's servants attacks it with a stick and kills it. Another weasel quickly appears from the same place and, visibly distressed, tries and fails to rouse its partner. It then races out the chapel and returns with a bright red flower, which it places in the dead creature's mouth and which brings it back to life. Astonished, Guildeluec snatches the flower from the weasel's mouth and uses it to revive her young love rival. As soon as she awakes, not realizing who she's speaking to, Guilliadon tells Guildeluec everything.

What happens next is surprising, especially given the stereotypical stories of female love rivals. Rather than attacking Guilliadon for stealing her husband, Guildeluec comforts her. She reassures Guilliadon that Eliduc hasn't abandoned her. He believes that she is dead but, deeply distressed by her loss, he has been visiting her every day. 'I am overjoyed that you are alive,' she tells her rival, 'and shall take you with me and return you to your beloved. I shall set him free completely and take the veil.' She sets up a nunnery and inters herself within it, making Eliduc free to marry Guilliadon, and Marie describes the love they have for one another as 'perfect'. Towards the end of their lives, they both turn to God. Eliduc joins a monastery and Guilliadon joins Guildeluec, who 'receiv[es] her as her sister, and show[s] her great honour'—and the two live happily ever after.

'From these two the lay of *Guildeluec and Guilliadon* takes its name', Marie tells us. 'It was first called *Eliduc* but now the name has been changed, because the adventure upon which the lay is based concerns these ladies.' While editors have tended to ignore her directive, and continue to use the original title,

Marie couldn't be clearer about who the real protagonists of this story are. The relationship between these two noblewomen might be platonic, but in terms of its depth of feeling, affection and generosity, it is one of the most memorable, and surprising, in all of her *lais*. In *Bad Feminist* Roxane Gay urges readers to '[a]bandon the cultural myth that all female friendships must be bitchy, toxic, or competitive' because, 'like heels and purses', it is 'pretty but designed to slow women down'.[13] Writing hundreds of years earlier, Marie de France refuses to make Guilliadon and Guildeluec into the bitter, toxic rivals one might expect. Their relationship is strong enough not only to subvert the status quo but to overturn the sacrament of marriage itself. Rather than being branded a whore, Guilliadon is able to marry her lover and find sanctuary in a convent at the end of her life, all thanks to her friend Guideluec.

All these literary depictions show us that female friendship not only existed but was something on which women depended. However, they also expose the entrenched demarcations of class in medieval society. The bawdy, alehouse poems might be a welcome indication that social gatherings between women did exist. But they also poke fun at the lower and middle classes who frequented local taverns, made lewd jokes and generally embarrassed their husbands. In the literature where female friendship is truly celebrated, portrayed as an ennobling and virtuous bond, it is usually to be found in courts and palaces rather than out on the city streets.

. . .

Religious men like John Mirk and Aelred of Rievaulx may have warned women that female friendship could defile the church or incite them to lascivious behaviour, but some of the most compelling instances of female friendship also emerged from the realm of religion.

Anchoresses such as Julian of Norwich were often reliant on networks of supplementary patronage and material support. At least one of Julian's patrons was a woman, although we know nothing of Isabel Ufford, countess of Sussex, except that she left 20 shillings in her will to 'a Julian recluz a Norwich'.[14] Moreover, anchoresses were expected to be available to those who came to visit them and to seek their counsel, either from their home town or from farther afield. They were a status symbol for their town and were expected to show their faces—literally, at their window. Some anchorholds even had double cells in which anchorites could live near one another.

While guidebooks for anchoresses often warned their readers to be careful when interacting with men—even priests, monks and bishops—and discouraged gossip, many of them encouraged their readers to foster relationships with other women. Richard Wich, bishop of Chichester, wrote of anchoresses: 'We permit them to have private conversations with only such persons as whose gravity and honesty admit of no suspicion.'[15] Socializing with other devout people was an integral part of the anchoritic vocation, so long as they were discerning about who they received and talked with. It was not unusual, then, for an anchoress like Julian to meet with a woman like Margery, and to offer advice and support. But for Margery, Julian's warmth and acceptance is a defining part of her life, because of her often fraught relationship with other women.

Countless people Margery meets in her *Book* find her behaviour infuriating, but she seemed to struggle especially with making female friends. Unlike the harmonious world that Christine de Pizan imagines in her *City of Ladies*, women were as likely to attack Margery as to defend or comfort her. Early on in her *Book* she recalls visiting London with her husband to meet the archbishop. When they enter the hall, there are many of his clerks and men around who are swearing and cussing and generally acting in a raucous fashion. Margery boldly rebukes them, telling them they will be damned if they don't stop blaspheming. In answer to her chiding, a woman curses Margery with malicious glee: 'I wish you were in Smithfield [prison], and if you were, I would bring a bundle of sticks to burn you with. It's a shame you're even alive.'[16]

Not all of Margery's altercations with women involve fire and brimstone, of course. Some of her earliest attempts to create an unofficial community of pious women end in much more mundane disaster. When she tries to create friendships with three local, devout widows, all end badly.[17] She finds herself in a 12-year feud with the first widow when she hears 'in her spirit' (through God) that the widow should find a new confessor. The widow, who likes her confessor, not only refuses to believe Margery but is furious with her for meddling, and tells her to stop coming to her house. Margery tells the second and third widows that their husbands will remain in purgatory for many years unless they have 'better friends on earth'—by which she means, unless the widows do a better job at praying for their souls. According to medieval Christian belief, souls could end up in purgatory for an indeterminate amount of time before making it to heaven. Families and friends could accelerate their ascension by praying for them and earning them a swifter exit. Neither widow takes kindly to Margery's critique of her shortcomings.

It's easy to see both sides here. On the one hand, Margery is just trying to offer divinely inspired advice—and she's distraught when her attempts to help her friends are met with such scorn. On the other, one can imagine how Margery might have come across as 'holier than thou', however pure her intentions. By speaking to the three widows so plainly, Margery is unwittingly breaking an unspoken code of acceptable behaviour between female friends. Just as her religious endeavours fell outside the usual mould, so too did her attempts to forge connection with others—much to her detriment.

According to classical models of friendship, it must be equal and reciprocal, but Margery often finds herself giving more affection than she gets. When travelling alone in Germany, she meets a 'worthy woman' from London, a widow with a large retinue who had come to see the holy relics.[18] Margery approaches the woman, who receives her kindly. They eat and drink together, and the woman is 'very friendly', but Margery wakes up one morning to find that the widow has already left Aachen, the town in which they were staying. Margery, who had thought that they would travel back to England together, is very distressed. She quickly hires herself a wagon and gives chase, hoping that she might catch up with the widow, but to no avail. Margery bumps into this woman again later in their journeys and approaches her eagerly, 'thinking to have been very kindly received', but instead the woman is short and sharp with her, saying, 'What! Do you think to go with me? No, I'll have you know that I'll not get involved with you.' One of the most difficult challenges to navigate in any friendship, at any time, are the different levels of expectation or affection that each party brings to the table, and here we may just be seeing Margery grapple with that age-old problem. Her experience of friendship is often marked by feelings of abandonment, competition or mistreatment.

One of the ways Margery makes sense of her loneliness is to frame it as an essential part of her Christian vocation. After being released from prison by the archbishop of York, she is treated to his hospitality. Almost everyone in his household has been won round to the idea that Margery is a holy woman, and they ask her to pray for them. But the archbishop's steward remains unimpressed. Hearing her laugh, he shouts at her, because 'holy folk should not laugh'. She replies, 'Sir, I have great cause to laugh for the more shame and scorn I suffer, the merrier I may be in our Lord Jesus Christ.'[19] Time and again in her *Book*, Jesus tells her that, the more she suffers on earth, the happier she will be in heaven. In fact, almost every time that Margery uses the word 'merry', it is in conjunction with ostracism. She tells us that she was 'as merry when she was reproved, scorned, or ridiculed for love of God' as she had ever been in her previous life as a worldly woman. She thought it was 'right merry to be reproved for God's love', and when she was 'chided and scolded for the love of Jesus' she found solace in the knowledge that it would be 'full merry' in heaven, when she was finally united not only with God but with every holy person who had ever starred in her visions.[20]

Even though Margery tries to welcome her friendship misfires as a route to spiritual reward, they still cause her pain, which makes it all the more poignant when she *does* manage to forge connections with other women. After being released from her trial in York free of charge, Margery is arrested again very soon, this time in Hessle by the duke of Bedford's men.[21] She is escorted to Beverley to await another round of interrogation from the archbishop (who, by now, must have been fed up with questioning her). While some women in the town run out of their houses to shout and jeer at Margery, there are other women who offer her real kindness. She is detained in the homes of one of the guards, where she has a 'nice room and a decent bed in it' but nothing to eat or drink. For a while, Margery stands at the window, 'telling many edifying tales to those who would hear her, so much so that women wept bitterly and said with great heaviness of heart: "Alas, woman, why should you be burned?"' Finding herself very thirsty after all this holy talk, she begs the wife of her jail-keeper to bring her something. Her husband has hidden the key, but she risks his wrath by getting a ladder and setting it up against the window, to pass through a pint of wine.

Some years later, when she is alone and destitute in Rome after giving away all her money to the poor, Margery relies on a network of women, who offer her sustenance and support without expecting anything in return.[22] One wealthy woman, Margaret Florentyne, invites Margery to eat with her every Sunday, allowing her to sit at the head of the table and serving her with her own hand, even though the two women can barely understand each other because of the language barrier. After every meal Margaret gives Margery a hamper of food with which to make stew, enough to last her for at least two days, as well as a bottle of good wine. In the same city a poor woman with an infant invites Margery into her humble home to 'sit by her little fire' and drink wine with her, as they watch the baby play. Despite having so little of her own, this poor woman makes space and time for Margery, and offers her sustenance. And, of course, there's Julian, whose words of validation and comfort come at exactly the right time for Margery, when she is feeling abandoned and disbelieved by so many.

Margery never finds the kind of female spiritual community she yearns for on earth, never manages to uncover anything equating to that convivial 'merriness' she had spied in heaven. But women like Julian offer her a glimpse of what is to come when she does finally reach the afterlife.

Across Europe, religious women were reliant on one another to make their way in a male-dominated sphere. At 17 a young Italian woman called Margaret ran away from home with her lover. Her mother had died when she was very little, and she'd been miserable ever since, thanks to her unkind and neglectful stepmother. When her youth and beauty caught the eye of a nobleman from the nearby town, she was quick to leave her old life behind and become his mistress. Although they never got married, they lived happily together for ten years, and even had a child together. A biography of her life, written by her confessor Fra Giunta, describes how she lived in a castle in Montepulciano and, not remotely ashamed of being a concubine, made a spectacle of herself riding through the streets 'in all the glory of fine clothes', with 'her face painted and her hair decked out with ornaments of gold'.[23] But Margaret's fortunes changed again when her lover was murdered, leaving Margaret alone, without a friend in the world, and with a son to care for. Neither her own family nor her lover's would help her—in their eyes, she was a whore. And so, like many other young Italian women in the thirteenth century, Margaret turned to God for help.

God led Margaret away from Montepulciano to the steep, cobbled streets of Cortona, a small town nestled on an Umbrian hillside. It was home at that time to a powerful community of Franciscan friars. Here, God told Margaret, she could begin a holier life. Not long after she had arrived, she worked up the courage to go to the friars and ask permission to wear their habit and become an official Franciscan penitent. This would have allowed her to join the Franciscan community and entitled her to their care and support. Full of trepidation and hope, she 'knelt before Fra Rainaldo' and 'with clasped hands and with tears' begged for admission to the Third Order.[24] However, knowing nothing of Margaret except that she had an illegitimate son and a scandalous past, the Franciscans refused.

Margaret was alone in a strange town, with no money, no job and nowhere to live—until, in her hour of direst need, she was rescued by two local well-to-do women, Marinaria and her daughter-in-law Raneria. They took Margaret into their home and helped her to establish herself as a midwife, using their connections and circle of friends to secure wealthy clients. Thanks to these women, Margaret had more time to establish herself as a devout and respected woman, and she was eventually permitted by the local Franciscans to enter the penitential life. Unlike Margery, Margaret proved popular with the local women of Cortona—too popular, if anything. God kept instructing her to withdraw entirely from secular society, but her popularity made this nearly impossible. At church 'the women would out of devotion crowd round her, and often she could not pray because of their talk', and she had to entertain an endless stream of female visitors at her door, who came to bring her food and to seek her advice.[25]

Margaret serves as a visual reminder of what could be possible for an ordinary laywoman in the Middle Ages; with a little help from her friends, a woman could climb the social and religious ladder in order to achieve great respect and admiration within a predominantly masculine world. Margaret's religious life was only made possible thanks to her original sponsors, Marinaria and Raneria, women-of-means who took her under their wing, and used their connections to elevate her. And while Margaret's popularity with the women of Cortona made it difficult for her to follow God's order of solitude, the friendship of these women was also essential to establishing her as a respected holy woman.

· · ·

There are no surviving letters between sisters in the wealthy Paston family, and very few between mothers and daughters or female friends (it is likely that such letters did at one time exist but were not saved, or have been lost in the intervening years). Nonetheless, the letters they penned to male relatives, and the few letters between women that do remain, reveal how women relied on and helped one another in the secular as well as the religious world. Agnes, the wealthy matriarch of the Pastons, and her daughter-in-law Margaret (mother of John III and mother-in-law of Margery Brews, author of the Valentine missive) were both formidable women. Agnes was tough and quick to anger, endlessly quarrelling with her neighbours and even her own children. However, she had a soft spot for Margaret, the wife of her eldest son— perhaps because Margaret was pretty tough herself. During the Wars of the Roses, when her husband was away from home, Margaret found her manor house under siege from the Yorkist duke of Suffolk and his men. Anticipating an attack, she wrote to her husband asking for supplies—including crossbows, armour, ammunition and pole-axes—so that she and the rest of the household could defend themselves.[26] It is one of the most famous letters in the Paston collection, and the impression it leaves of Margaret is awe-inspiring.

Margaret and Agnes were close. When Margaret appeared before the bishop of Norwich to try and annul her daughter's scandalous marriage to Richard Calle, Agnes went with her to offer her support. And they were both good friends with a woman named Elizabeth Clere, an independent widow who had inherited her late husband's property. Elizabeth and Agnes both had houses in Norwich, and they would dine or have supper together regularly, sometimes inviting Margaret to join them, when she was in town. Other members of the family bear witness to their closeness, often linking their names together in their correspondence. Such letters reveal a picture of Agnes, Elizabeth and Margaret in and out of each other's houses, business and pockets. Elizabeth was very generous to the Pastons. She loaned Agnes large sums of money when the family found themselves in dire financial need. She only asked for repayment once—and only because she needed the money for another friend in trouble. She also lent Margaret a necklace when the queen, Margaret of Anjou, came to visit the town and her friend was ashamed to wear the second-rate beads from her (apparently quite stingy) husband.

However, Elizabeth wasn't above interfering with Paston family goings-on, even at the risk of her friendship with Agnes. After seeing how cruelly Agnes treated her daughter (also called Elizabeth), she reached out to Agnes's son, John I, for help. Concerned that Stephen Scrope, a 50-year-old ex-soldier-turned-writer, might have lost interest in marrying Elizabeth, she asks John if he can do anything to intervene. 'I think he [Scrope] would be good for my cousin your sister, unless you can get her someone better. And if you can get her someone better, I would advise you to try and achieve it in as short a time as you conveniently can, because she is never so sorrowful as she is nowadays.' Elizabeth reveals to John that since Easter, his sister 'has for the most part been beaten once or twice a week and sometimes twice in one day', so badly that 'her head has been broken in 2 or 3 places'.[27] At the end of this letter Elizabeth asks John to burn it after reading. She is frightened of angering Agnes and losing her friendship, but fond enough of her young namesake to risk her friend's wrath.

For the elite, well-to-do Pastons, female friendships hinged on the discussion of domestic matters and socializing; when business was involved, they tended to turn to fathers or husbands instead. But in the working world, beyond the Paston letters, female friendships also thrived, and relationships were formed across the entrenched class divides that usually propped up medieval society. We know, for example, from the wills of medieval silk workers in Paris that close-knit communities of women were formed via their trade. While many professions were closed to women, and especially single women, widows and immigrants, the silk trade was unusually welcoming to them. Responsible for the manufacture of headdresses, altar cloths, belts, ribbons, gloves and purses designed for the highest echelons of society, the silk trade, unlike other 'female' crafts, was profitable and well respected. It acted as a powerful magnet drawing women from all over the world to its hubs (such as Paris), providing them with the opportunity to give and receive training, to manage their own workshops and to rise among the ranks. While we tend to imagine medieval households as defined by family, in which women contributed as wives, widows, daughters, sisters, mothers or aunts, the silk trade led not just to communities but to actual households of single women, bound together by their training, who worked, prayed and ate together. These women established a life for themselves beyond the usual social norms and supported one another in their endeavours.

Their households could often cut across class and social divides too. In Paris, for example, more affluent silk merchants would hire poorer women as spinners, weavers or servants, sometimes rewarding them with generous gifts and remembering them in their wills. Before becoming an influential silk merchant, Jeanne du Faut had lived at the royal beguinage in Paris, an institution sponsored by the royal family for women who had not taken formal religious vows but who wanted to dedicate their lives to God.[28] Sometime before 1292, perhaps seeking more freedom than the community offered, Jeanne left the beguinage behind, but she carried its spirit of female camaraderie and friendship with her. She bought a house on the rue Troussevache, at the centre of the Parisian silk-making district, and set up her own workshop, hiring several other women as silk-workers and apprentices.

Her will makes clear what a strong network of female silk-workers—and friends—she managed to establish during her time in the silk trade. She bequeathed gifts to several different religious houses and the poor, but she also distributed money and property to her female employees, as well as writing off their debts. Even though she still had living male relatives who would have had a legitimate claim to Jeanne's property, she essentially made her friend and business partner, Beatrice la Grande, her heir. Evidently, Jeanne favoured her female employees and partner over her male kin, and in her will (made in 1330) she describes Beatrice as her 'beloved', to whom she wants to bequeath property. The term 'beloved' and the generosity of the gift suggest that Beatrice was far more than just Jeanne's colleague—perhaps she was her lover as well, but she was certainly her friend.

A medieval English poem called *Emare* explores the transnational and multicultural relationships that silk work could foster among women. The verse is anonymous, and exists in only one manuscript, which dates from the fifteenth century and includes various romances (including English adaptations of two of Marie de France's *lais*, *Lanval* and *Le Freine*).[29] It tells the story of a young Christian princess, Emare, whose mother died before she had even learned to walk and talk. She was brought up by Lady Abro, a kindly local noblewoman who taught her the arts of courtesy and how to embroider silk. She was very happy in the noblewoman's household, and had many friends there, but, as soon as she was grown up, she was sent for by her father, King Artyus. It was time to go home.

Back at court, Emare made quite the entrance—she was, according to the poet, 'the fairest creature ever born'. Upon seeing his daughter's beauty, Artyus was filled with lust. Rather than trying to control these inappropriate feelings, he petitioned the pope for a special dispensation that would allow him to marry her. Shockingly, the pope granted his petition, and the lecherous king began to prepare for a wedding to his daughter. But Emare, horrified, refused to have anything to do with the plans—or with him. Unable to persuade her, and furious that he couldn't fulfil his desire, Artyus sent her off to sea in a rudderless boat.

A material object serves as a backdrop to Emare's unhappy tale. Right from the start, the poet describes how, in a land far away, a young Muslim noblewoman spent seven years making a beautiful piece of silk cloth as a present for her beloved. Glistening, golden and covered with precious jewels—topaz and rubies, azure and agate—she embroidered this cloth with images of legendary lovers, and even weaved her own love story into its folds. She then presented it to her fiancé, the son of a Babylonian sultan, as an engagement gift. However, when the king of Sicily invaded the sultan's home, he stole it. The king gave the cloth to his son, who in turn bestowed it to Artyus, as a wedding gift—who, delighted, ordered that it be transformed into a wedding robe for his daughter. In her rudderless boat Emare was stripped of any money, food or water. The sumptuous robe, wrapped tightly around her shoulders, was the only thing she was allowed to keep.

Rather than becoming her death shroud, this cloth proved to be a lucky talisman. When God heard her prayers and washed her boat up on a distant shore, the beauty and intricacy of her robe marked her out as a woman of nobility and status, someone worthy of protection. Discovered by a foreign king, and in a full-circle moment, Emare pretends that she is the daughter of an earl, sent to teach his daughters courtesy and silk work—just as Lady Abro had taught her when she was a girl.

Of course, there are multiple ways we can interpret this story. On the one hand, it is a testament to the caring relationships between women, symbolized by a product of 'feminine' craftsmanship. Lady Abro takes in the young Emare and looks after her, teaching her skills that will one day help to save her life; and Emare, in turn, does the same for the daughters of a foreign king. And although Emare never meets the Muslim woman who embroidered the beautiful robe, she feels her hand of friendship in its charmed and protective folds. However, it should not escape our notice that the cloth was stolen, and that we never even learn the name of the woman—described only as a 'heathen'—from whom it was taken. Her fate remains unknown, and the love she poured into the cloth is diverted from the intended recipient and bestowed instead on someone else—a white, Christian princess who by the end of the poem is married and living happily ever after.

. . .

Virginia Woolf famously lamented the lack of female friendship she came across in her reading: 'All these relationships between women, I thought, rapidly recalling the splendid gallery of fictitious women, are too simple. So much has been left out, unattempted. And I tried to remember any case in the course of my reading where two women are represented as friends.'[30] For much of history, it has been hard to find examples of women who were friends—and, where they do exist, references to them are usually fleeting or one-dimensional. The Middle Ages went further; their writers didn't just neglect or devalue female friendship, but often even warned against it. The consequences of women getting together and sharing too much could prove dangerous—especially for men.

That didn't mean, however, that women weren't working hard to carve out space for one another. They found ways to reach out, to offer support, comfort and advice—in essence, to be friends with one another. Female friendship in the Middle Ages wasn't always straightforward—far from it. We've seen how feminist utopias such as Christine de Pizan's *City of Ladies* could be exclusionary, how women like Margery Kempe found it hard to form female friendships that weren't fraught or marked by competitiveness and how men tried to discourage too much intimacy between women, afraid of what they might discuss or disclose behind closed doors. But, while the evidence for it is slim, it's clear that female friendship did exist. So often excluded from the networks and communities of men, women didn't give up but found ways to make their own.

SEVEN

. . . And Influencing People

'Oëz, seignur, que dit Marie,/ki en sun tens pas ne s'oblie'*

MARIE DE FRANCE, *Lais*

Lanval couldn't believe his luck.[1] For a long time now the handsome knight had been living at King Arthur's court in abject misery. He'd journeyed from a foreign country to seek out Camelot—renowned throughout the world for its brotherhood, its fraternity and its egalitarian spirit—hoping to become part of its story. But, after an initially warm welcome, things went downhill rapidly. He was a stranger in a strange land. The other knights, whose praises were always being sung, excluded and neglected him. Even the famously noble Arthur kept forgetting to make provision for his new knight, leaving Lanval disappointed and destitute.

But now, it seemed, his fortunes had changed. Away from court, lamenting his lot, he'd been approached by two beautiful women. They told him that their mistress had sent for him and led him to her tent, which was so luxurious 'that neither Queen Semiramis at the height of her wealth, power and knowledge, nor the Emperor Octavian, could have afforded even the right-hand side of it'. Perched on the top was a decorative golden eagle and inside—oh, inside! There the lucky Lanval had found a maiden more beautiful than a new rose who, out of the blue, declared her love for the bemused knight. 'Lanval,' she said, 'for you I came from my country. I came far in search of you and if you are worthy and courtly, no emperor, count or king will have felt as much joy or happiness as you, for I love you above all else.'

Lanval had no idea why she'd chosen him, but he knew better than to question her. This enchanting mistress had already offered him a boon. 'Henceforth,' she told him, he 'could wish for nothing which he would not have, and however generously he gave or spent, she would still find enough for him.' For the rest of his life, Lanval would be able to enjoy

---

* 'Hear, lords, the stories of Marie/who is not forgotten in her own time'

everything this bountiful lady had to offer—on one condition. He had to keep her a secret.

It's at this point in Marie de France's story that the nobility, listening enthralled at court, might well have breathed a collective 'uh oh'. For, as we all know, when a promise is made in a fairy tale, it is bound to be broken.

Thanks to his newfound wealth, and the newfound sparkle in his eye, Lanval attracted the attention of Queen Guinevere. She opened her heart to him: 'Lanval, I have honoured, cherished and loved you much. You may have all my love; just tell me what you desire!' At first, out of respect, Lanval tried to be polite. 'I have long served the king and do not want to betray my faith,' he told her. 'But Guinevere saw his refusal as a personal slight, and angrily accused him of being a '[b]ase coward'. Lanval likewise lost his temper. He told Guinevere he already had a mistress who far excelled the queen in every possible way: 'You can be sure that one of her servants, even the very poorest girl, is worth more than you, my lady the Queen, in body, face, and beauty, wisdom and goodness.'

Well, as can be imagined, Guinevere didn't take this well. Spurned and humiliated, she ran to her husband in tears and told him that Lanval had made advances on her and then insulted her when she had refused him. This, of course, was no small accusation—Guinevere was knowingly accusing Lanval of treason. Arthur was furious with his knight. He swore an oath that, unless Lanval could defend himself at trial, he would be executed.

It was bad enough being in prison but worse still to know that, because of his actions, his mistress had abandoned him. 'He lamented and sighed, fainting from time to time; a hundred times he cried to her to have mercy, to come and speak with her beloved. He cursed his heart and mouth and it was a wonder he did not kill himself.' But still she would not come. At the trial, after much heated debate, the jury decided that Lanval must produce his mysterious lover to absolve himself—the one thing he could not do.

Not all of Marie de France's *lais* end well. But this one, thanks to the nameless fairy princess who takes Lanval as her love, has a happy ending. Just when the jury is about to announce their verdict, a beautiful maiden on horseback enters Camelot. She enters the court, gives testimony to save Lanval's life and then, with barely a backward glance, remounts her horse to leave for ever. But the knight refuses to be abandoned for a second time. 'Outside the hall there was a large block of dark marble on to which heavily armed men climbed when they left the king's court', Marie tells us. Quick as a flash, Lanval mounted it and 'leapt in a single bound on the palfrey behind her'. She carried him away to Avalon—to live, we presume, happily ever after.

Lanval may have lent his name to this story, but the two most powerful characters in it are women. When Lanval finds himself neglected by the king, it is a woman who lifts him up again. Thanks to his mistress, he can perform enough honourable and generous acts to reassert himself at Camelot: 'Lanval gave costly gifts, Lanval freed prisoners, Lanval clothed the *jongleurs*.' And it is a woman too—the spurned Guinevere—who almost gets him killed, so great is her influence on the king. Medieval legends and fairy tales written by men would usually end with damsels rescued by handsome knights. But in this female-authored story, a happy ending is secured by a woman. She is more beautiful than any other, has more riches than anyone on earth and is not remotely daunted by legal procedure. Lanval is at her mercy. He must beg for her help, and throw himself onto the back of *her* horse, so as not to be left behind. The role reversal is striking and feels, however anachronistic the term may be, *feminist*. The woman is sexualized, but she is always in control of her sexuality, inviting Lanval into a relationship rather than being claimed or pursued. She is the one who provides the wealth. She is the one who sets the terms. She is the one with the power to forgive, when Lanval breaks his promise—and she is the one who holds his life in her hands.

Because of their resourceful heroines, the stories of Marie de France are ahead of their time. Aside from *Lanval*, her stories are full of influential women who are not content to sit around waiting for things to get better, who may not have superpowers but still manage to have an impact on the world around them. Take, for example, the young maiden in *Les Deux Amanz* who works with a mysterious aunt from Salerno to secure the husband she wants. Or the wife in *Bisclavret* who traps her husband in lupine form so that she can marry someone else. Or the noblewoman in *Milun* who manages to sequester away an illegitimate child to protect her reputation.[2] All of these women, with varying degrees of success, steer their own narratives.

Such heroines may have been a form of wish-fulfilment, a fantasy that could never be realized outside of fiction. In reality, women were excluded, by virtue of their sex, from universities as well as from various professions and positions of power. But that's not to say that no woman ever managed to influence the patriarchal society in which she lived. We know for a fact that there were various medieval women (including Marie herself, the only known woman to author Arthurian legends) who had an active and traceable impact on the lives of those who admired them, looked up to them and followed their lives and work. Such women made it possible for others of their sex to imagine how they might achieve more than what society had allocated for them.

. . .

As we've seen, medieval literature tended to view women as fickle, changeable, physically, and mentally weak, sexually voracious and deceitful. A medieval leader was wise, strong, brave and skilled in battle, prudent, generous, well educated—and male. That's not to say that women were never in positions of power; throughout the period, women regularly had responsibility for governing kingdoms and countries, whether as regents or in their own right. But, too often, they needed to adopt 'male' qualities in order to secure such positions. Medieval commentators were willing to believe that women could be powerful, but only if they overcame their natural 'feminine' proclivities. And so women who sought power and influence had to construct themselves in one of two ways: as exceptional paragons of feminine virtue, on the one hand, or as an embodiment of masculine ideals, on the other.

Ideally, a paragon of female virtue would look a lot like the Virgin Mary. Meek and mild, quiet and unassuming in her beauty, a devoted wife and mother who was happy to act as a vehicle and vessel for a male God. In its campaign for celibacy, *Hali Meidhad* draws on the Virgin to paint a picture of the perfect woman, prescribing virtues such as 'righteousness and wariness against vices; moderation and temperance and spiritual strength, simplicity of manner and obedience and tranquility, endurance and sympathy for every man's sorrow'.[3] Gentle and kind, her serene smile encouraged medieval women to be help-meets, guides, intermediaries, to take a graceful back seat to husbands, fathers and sons while supporting them from the wings. In a world of cut-throat politics, of warfare and Machiavellian machinations none of these qualities would produce a trailblazer.

At the opposite end of the scale there is the *virago*. Meaning 'man-like, warrior woman', this Latin word could be used positively to describe female leaders who successfully emulated the superior male sex and who therefore assumed more power (albeit while reinscribing patriarchal structures). But it could be wielded as a dangerous stereotype, a stick to beat women with rather than a means for elevating them.

Joan of Arc was a woman who embodied both the positive and the negative aspects of the *virago*. At the age of 16, this young French shepherdess had visions of the archangel Michael and various saints, encouraging her to take up arms and help drive the English from France. She went to the dauphin (the future Charles VII) to offer her allegiance to him and, according to various reports, the future king was seriously impressed by her knowledge of military technique, which she claimed had been revealed to her by angels while she tended her flock. 'There will be no help from France if not from me,' she declared. 'Although I would rather have remained spinning at my mother's side. Yet must I do this thing, for my Lord wills that I do so.'[4]

What is perhaps most astonishing about Joan's story is that, although she was young and inexperienced, her military strategies worked. Dressed in armour, like a man, and carrying a religious banner as her heraldry, she fought her way across France, pushing back the English forces and enabling France to make real progress for the first time in the infamous Hundred Years War. Leading the charge on horseback, she chased the English from the Loire Valley, allowing the dauphin to be crowned king at Reims, as was traditional for all French kings. It looked as though the tide was finally turning for the French, all thanks to an illiterate peasant girl.

However, on 23 May 1430 Joan was captured by the enemy. Charles, whom she had helped become anointed king, refused to pay her ransom. The crimes for which she was prosecuted were not to do with battle or warfare, but rather with religion and gender. Threatened with torture, she briefly agreed to wear women's clothes and denied the validity of the angelic voices that had spurred her into the fray. But four days later she had a change of heart; she put her male clothing back on and took back her recantation: 'what I said, I said for fear of the fire,' she admitted. 'I was damning myself to save my life.'

Joan's story is heartbreaking. A teenager, deserted by a king who owed his crown and possibly his very life to her, she was surrounded by enemies on every side, accused of lies and fantasies proceeding from evil and diabolical spirits. 'Alas!' she declared on the day of her execution. 'Am I so horribly and cruelly used, that my clean body, never yet defiled, must this day be burnt and turned to ashes?' Despite her pleas for mercy, Joan would never return home to spin wool with her mother. She was burned alive. Her tragic life and death expose the double bind of the *virago*—women felt the need to adopt male qualities to exercise successful leadership, but the consequences of doing so could be disastrous. Her execution, when it came, was attributed as much to her adoption of male clothing as it was to her political and religious actions.

She was tortured and killed not just for winning battles (Joan's involvement is often cited to a key contributor to France's eventual victory) but for having the audacity to believe she could lead those battles in the first place.

In general, it was safer to follow the example of the Virgin Mother rather than trying to be a *virago*. Queens and noblewomen were encouraged to be obedient and submissive to their husbands. They should act as mediators, offering male relatives moral guidance while helping to keep their tempers even or persuading them to be merciful. They shouldn't exert too much political authority unless they wanted to set themselves up for vitriol and attack. European commentators, when musing on what made a good queen, focused on marriage and children, rather than considering women as independent agents.

The satirical poem *The Mirror of Marriage*, by French poet Eustache Deschamps, was popular in medieval Europe.[5] Hostile towards women as a collective, Deschamps complains that they are full of vice and make marriage miserable for men. He saves some rare praise, however, for Blanche of Castile, who twice acted as queen regent of France during the reign of her son. He recalls how, when the death of Blanche's husband threatened the position of her five-year-old son Louis, she persuaded the barons to uphold his right to the throne as heir. She took Louis to Parliament and constructed a melodramatic tableau: placing the little boy in a bed, she knelt before him in supplication and framed herself as a desperate and dejected widow, appealing to the great men of government to have mercy on them both. Her careful stagecraft worked its magic. The noblemen, persuaded by such a pathetic scene, banded together behind Louis and, by extension, his mother. Louis was only five and too young to rule—and so Blanche took up the mantle (an outcome she had, of course, been seeking all along). She became queen regent until her son was old enough to assume the crown and, according to Christine de Pizan, she governed France 'with such skill and care [. . .] that no man could have done better'.[6] By all accounts, Blanche was an excellent and beloved ruler. But to become one, she had to lean into her role as a widow and a mother.

Two hundred years later, Margaret of Anjou did not fare so well. At the tender age of 15 this feisty French princess (who would later become known as the Red Queen) was married to King Henry VI of England, to seal a truce between the warring countries. Margaret, being a Frenchwoman in England during the Hundred Years War, was never especially popular; but while she played the traditional role of dutiful intercessor and mediator, keeping her head down and staying out of politics, she was tolerated. This all changed, however, when the king had a mental breakdown, leading to various attempts to usurp him. Margaret worked tirelessly to maintain her position and protect her son Edward's inheritance. In the infamous Wars of the Roses, which came about after her husband's illness, she emerged as a leader of the Lancastrian party, pioneering a campaign of propaganda to attack the rival Yorkists' credibility and leading her side into combat. Because of her involvement in battle, she is explicitly linked in fifteenth-century historical commentaries with Joan of Arc, and she even compared herself to Joan in a speech to her troops: 'I have often broken [the English] battle-line. I have moved down ranks far more stubborn than theirs are now. You once followed a peasant girl, follow now a queen.'[7]

However, unlike Joan, Margaret was on the losing side. After her husband lost the throne, she spent years in exile in both France and Scotland, trying and failing to reclaim the kingdom in various campaigns until her army was eventually defeated for good at the Battle of Tewkesbury in May 1471. Despite (or perhaps because of) her determined efforts, she became a scapegoat for a civil war that decimated England. She was dubbed a she-wolf, a snake, an adulteress who brought ruin to her adopted country and then, ruthlessly sidelined, impoverished and all but forgotten, she died in France at the age of 52. For a long time, the Red Queen was memorialized, thanks to Shakespeare, as a 'foul wrinkled witch' and 'hateful withered hag', rather than as a fearsome fighter and resolute leader.[8]

. . .

When she was joined to King Henry in holy matrimony, Margaret of Anjou was given a copy of Christine de Pizan's *Livre des faits d'armes et de chevalrie* ('The Book of Feats of Arms and Chivalry'), which describes the perfect chivalric knight and encompasses military strategy and warfare.[9] Not only does this book seem like an unusual wedding gift, but it tackles an incredibly rare topic for a female author. In writing her *Faits d'armes* Christine was deliberately distancing herself from earlier, 'feminine' love literature and entering into the more 'masculine' genre of advice literature for kings, which covered, among other things, combat and political strategy. Her confidence shows how popular and well respected Christine was in her own time. It's hard to imagine any other female author being taken seriously on this subject, especially one who had no experience of battle.

Despite throwing herself into a male-dominated field, Christine seemed to accept the general medieval worldview that women were less equipped to be in charge than men. In her *City of Ladies* she acknowledges that 'God created man and woman to serve him in different ways' and that 'he endowed each sex with the qualities and attributes which they needed to perform the tasks for which they [were] cut out'.[10] Following this train of thought, Christine praises the female influencers of her own time for their roles as supporting ladies to leading men. Of Isabeau of Bavaria, queen of France, she writes: 'She has neither a shred of cruelty or greed in her body nor a single evil trait, for she is full of kindness and benevolence towards her subjects'; the duchess of Orleans is 'not only steadfast and constant, but also very loving towards her husband and a fine example to her children'; and the countess of Clermont 'is everything that a noble princess should be in terms of her deep affection for her husband'.[11] Christine stresses the roles of these women as wives and mothers, and commends their tenderness and benevolence, rather than their strength, intelligence or leadership. And in *The Treasure of the City of Ladies,* Christine's guidance for noblewomen and princesses also tends to follow the medieval party line.

'Sometimes it may happen', she cautions, 'that the prince, by bad counsel or from some other cause, will try to oppress his people with some expense.' In such an instance, the kingdom's subjects 'will realize that their lady is full of pity, goodness and charity and will come to her and very humbly beseech her to represent them to the prince'. The princess will receive them kindly, as it is a princess's job to play the card of mercy and to show her husband 'how it is necessary, if he wishes to reign long in peace and glory, to be loved by his subjects and his people'. If a war is brewing, she must 'ponder long and hard whether she can do something (always preserving the honour of her husband) to prevent [it]'. And she should do works of charity, and visit those who are suffering and ill, to 'comfort them sweetly', because, as Christine puts it, 'women are by nature more timid and also of a sweeter disposition'.[12]

Christine argues that, although women may be physically weaker, they can still contribute to the governance of a kingdom because they are more compassionate (more emotionally intelligent, we might now say). Even if a princess or queen doesn't have the political power to create and enact policy herself, she can exert gentle pressure on her husband and encourage him to favour diplomacy over war and promote fair justice. Christine is also quick to assert that, if they were given the same educational opportunities, women could even surpass men in their intellect, because 'their minds are in fact sharper and more receptive [than men's] when they do apply themselves'.[13]

And we do get glimpses of formidable heroines in the folios of Christine's manuscripts, especially when it comes to women from long ago. She describes Nicaula (or, as she's better known, the queen of Sheba) as 'wise', 'powerful' and 'extremely well-versed in both the arts and the sciences' and is careful to mention that she refused to tether herself to any man: she was 'so proud that she never condescended to take a husband nor wanted any man to be at her side'. Christine dares the reader to name any king 'who was more skilled in politics, statesmanship and justice who maintained a more magnificent court' than this great empress.[14] Unlike the contemporary French princesses and countesses, described as loving mothers and wives, Nicaula is an independent and intelligent powerhouse, gifted in politics and the art of war.

Even more dramatic are Christine's descriptions of warrior women. One of the first inhabitants to be admitted into her allegorical city is the 'heroic' Queen Semiramis, who excelled in 'the practice and pursuit of arms'. When her husband was killed, Semiramis refused to lay down her weapons but instead 'took them up with renewed vigour'. She 'seized the reins of power' over the countries and territories that she and her husband had conquered together and took over a whole host of new ones. 'No man could match her in strength and ability', Christine tells us. Courageous and 'undaunted by anything', she 'crushed' her enemies and was quick to quell any rebellions in the lands she had claimed as her own.[15]

Hot on Semiramis's heels entering the city are the mythical Amazons. In a country near the land of Europe called Scythia, Christine tells us, all the greatest male inhabitants were killed during a fearsome war. 'When their womenfolk saw that they had lost all their husbands, brothers, and male relatives', they took matters into their own hands. They 'called together a great council of women' and resolved to 'lead the country themselves, free from male control'. They forbade any men from entering their territory and turfed out any male children that were born, and they raised their daughters as warriors. These fearsome women 'took up arms', Christine recounts, 'and waged war on their enemies, laying waste to their lands with fire and sword and crushing all opposition'.[16]

Two particularly powerful Amazon queens were Lampheto and Marpasia, whose armies conquered large swathes of Europe and Asia, 'subjugating many kingdoms to their rule'. Marpasia's daughter, Synoppe, was equally tough; a beautiful and noble maiden, she was so proud that she chose never to sleep with any men, 'preferring instead to remain a virgin until her death'. Warfare was her 'only love and sole pleasure', and 'she never tired of going into battle and seizing new lands'. When her mother was killed, Synoppe wasted no time in avenging her death, 'by putting to the sword the entire enemy population and laying waste to their whole country'.[17] The colonialist imagery of conquering armies and devastated countries is rightly galling for modern readers, but at the time they would have been cause for real admiration. Contemporary readers would have been amazed that women could show such prowess on the field and astonished by their dismissal of male companionship and their domination of typically 'male' arenas.

Queen Hypsicratea went even further than Semiramis and the Amazons. To accompany her beloved husband into battle, she changed her physical appearance by dressing up as a man. Giving no thought to her complexion, she strapped on a helmet and let her skin get covered in dirt and sweat. She weighed down her small body with chainmail, took off her rings and jewellery, roughened up her hands by carrying axes and spears and swapped her girdle for a sword. 'This lady so thoroughly adapted herself to her new surroundings', Christine tells us, that she becomes the pinnacle of the medieval *virago*, her young and delicate body 'transformed' into that of 'a strong and powerfully built knight-in-arms'.[18]

There is, of course, a middle ground, somewhere between the *virago* and the Madonna. Alongside her stories of demure, contemporary princesses and those historical heroines who waged war as skilfully as any king, Christine also draws attention to women who occupied a greyer area in terms of their gender politics—women like Blanche of Castile. One striking tale from *The City of Ladies* concerns a queen from Roman mythology, a Sabine princess who was abducted by a Roman king to become his bride.[19] At first, she was devastated, torn away from her homeland and family, but she ended up falling in love with her new husband after bearing him children. She was therefore filled with dread when her people decided to declare war on the Romans and rescue her, as well as the many other women who had been captured. Desperate to prevent a bloody massacre, she gathered all the kidnapped women and, urging them to be brave, she led them into the centre of the battlefield:

> The queen therefore undid her hair and took off her shoes, as did all the other ladies. Those who had babies picked them up in their arms and carried them with them. In addition, there was a whole host of children, as well as

pregnant women. The queen walked at the head of this touching procession, and they all headed straight for the battlefield, just as the two armies were lining up.

Having reached their dangerous destination, the women all fell to their knees and cried out for peace, declaring that they would remain unmoved, trampled underfoot by the horses on both sides, if a truce couldn't be reached. Moved to tears by this pitiful scene, the two armies threw down their weapons and rushed to embrace one another. To paint this striking tableau, Christine draws on elements of both the Madonna and the *virago*. These women used their performative role as mothers and wives to elicit pity from the men waging war; but risking their lives to bring about peace also required strength and bravery. In many ways, Christine herself occupies this ambiguous space regarding gender, presenting something of a contradiction in terms of her attitude towards women and influence.

On the one hand, Christine's writing is relatively conservative. While she does champion women, she does so with the caveat that they are, by nature, meeker and milder than men and should therefore emulate the Madonna, who presides over her imagined City of Ladies. It is tempting, when comparing Christine's account of contemporary French queens with conquerors of the past, to draw the conclusion that she only felt able to celebrate *viragos* when they were consigned to the annals of history. Perhaps it was easier for Christine to imagine women being bolder in the past, freed from the constraints of her present.

Despite being a respectable noblewoman, Christine's own life had hints of the *virago* about it. In her early days of authorship she tended to focus on love poetry. However, when her work started to attract the attention not just of nobility but also of royalty, she saw an opportunity to build on her more lucrative readership by delving into the typically male-dominated genres of political and conduct literature. Christine coyly attributes the interest of princes in these new works to her gender, claiming that they read her books 'more I think for the novelty of a woman who could write (since that had not occurred for quite some time) than for any worth there might be in them'. But these words feel like false modesty when coupled, in the same breath, with the acknowledgement that her books 'were soon discussed and carried into many different lands and regions'.[20] However 'novel' the idea of a female political writer may have been, the fact that her books sparked such discussion and dissemination suggests that there was far more to her success than her sex.

One particularly impressive commission that Christine received was from Duke Philip the Bold of Burgundy, a keen patron of the arts, who asked her to write a biography of his late brother, King Charles V—the same king who had shown such favour to Christine's father. It was rare for an official biography of a king to be authored by a woman, and Philip's request is evidence of just how influential Christine had become. She did anticipate hostility from some quarters; in the biography itself she imagines an audience aggravated by her gender. 'They thought it beyond my capabilities', she laments, 'being as I am a woman, to record the names of such important people' and imagines them asking 'Why does this woman write to us about the orders of chivalry of which we are already familiar?'[21] But there is no evidence to suggest that it was anything but well received.

Moreover (and despite her claim that women's influence in politics was 'negligible'), Christine used the biography to exert her own influence on the political troubles that France was facing at the time. It distressed Christine greatly to see her adopted country so war-torn, eaten up by what she considered to be petty rivalries. She described the civil war as a 'sickness' tearing through the land, and in her biography of the late King Charles, known as 'Charles the Wise', she waxed lyrical about his kingship, urging French leaders to follow his example and to heal their country. Elsewhere, in a poem directed at the French nobility, she claimed she was unable to write further, blinded by the tears that streamed down her face when she contemplated how badly their behaviour was affecting her beloved country.[22] Historians have argued over whether Christine was neutral in the conflict or had an allegiance to a particular side. The fact that her position is so difficult to discern is testament to how savvy she was, courting each side to ensure continued patronage from both and to keep her take-home message clear: it didn't matter who was right or wrong, what mattered was peace.

Given the tenor of her advice in these works—and, in particular, her repeated pleas for peace—it's likely that, despite actively trying to influence the political situation of her country, Christine saw her actions as those of a mediator, and therefore in keeping with the role she believed women should play in political life. But since she also described herself metaphorically becoming a man to pursue a writing career, it's also possible that she imagined herself occupying a more fluid space in terms of gender than the average medieval woman. We know that she ventured boldly into male spheres, that she was disappointed not to be able to learn the sciences or to study at a university. And we also know that she admired another, contemporaneous, *virago*—Joan of Arc. Christine's last book, written in 1429, celebrated Joan as evidence of God's favour of women: 'Oh! What honour for the female sex! It is perfectly obvious that God has special regard for it when all these wretched people who destroyed the whole kingdom—now recovered and made safe by a woman—something 5000 men could not have done—and the traitors [have been] excommunicated!' She dubs Joan 'the supreme captain of our brave and able men' and says that 'the prowess of all the great men of the past' cannot be compared to hers.[23] Neither Achilles nor Hector had such strength as Joan.

· · ·

Margery Kempe was afraid. Night was falling, she had no idea how to get back to her lodging and she was surrounded by an angry mob.[24]

While visiting Canterbury with her husband she had found herself, yet again, 'greatly despised and reproved because she wept so much'. Not only monks and priests but secular men too had abused her and hurled insults at her all day, 'so much so that her husband went away from her as if he had not known her, and left her alone among them'. Seeing that she was unprotected, these men chased Margery out of the church, shouting, 'You shall be burnt, you false heretic! Here is a cartful of thorns ready for you, and a barrel to burn you with.' She tried to escape them, but now, hounded to the outer edges of Canterbury, she was lost and frightened. She stood quite still, 'her body trembling and quaking dreadfully'. Turning to God for help, she uttered a silent prayer.

As if by magic, two handsome young men appeared. 'Are you neither a heretic nor a Lollard?' they asked her, and Margery assured them that she was not. Satisfied with her answer, they 'escorted her home to her lodgings and were very nice to her'. Safe at last, Margery gave thanks to God.

Margery Kempe was not an inconspicuous figure. Clad all in white, a uniform usually reserved for virgins, and frequently overcome by bouts of crying so loud that they were described as 'roarings', she rarely went unnoticed. Loved and hated, both in her own time and ever since, reactions to Margery have often been extreme. Many of the people she came across in her travels found her tedious, irritating and loud. Others labelled her a heretic and wanted to see her executed for her crimes. They thought that she must be possessed, or mad, or simply deceitful. 'Her weeping was so plentiful and continual', her *Book* tells us 'that many people thought that she could weep and leave off when she wanted, and therefore many people said that she was a false hypocrite, and wept in company for advantage and profit.'[25] There were, of course, others who supported her: men who, in Margery's words, were 'spiritually inclined' and who therefore 'loved and esteemed her all the more'.[26] But for every believer in her *Book* there seem to be ten more detractors.

Although Margery certainly liked to do things in her own way, her *Book* makes clear she was significantly influenced by other holy women of her time. Not only did she aim to follow in their footsteps; she imitated their behaviour to legitimize her claims in the eyes of religious men. In one particularly revealing anecdote she tells us about the time a famous friar, known across the country for his stirring sermons, came to preach at her home town of Bishop's Lynn.[27] She was very excited to hear him talk, as she'd heard so many good things about him, and she wasn't disappointed; in fact, she was so moved by his words that 'she burst out with a great cry'. The first time this happened, the friar bore her behaviour patiently; he'd already been warned about Margery Kempe and her tears. But when it happened again, and he could see his audience becoming distracted, he lost patience. 'I wish this woman were out of the church,' he snapped, infuriated. 'She is annoying people.' While some of Margery's friends defended her, saying that she couldn't help herself, there were many who turned against her, suggesting that she must have a devil inside her to cause such a racket.

Emboldened by their support, the friar banned Margery from his sermons unless she agreed to stop her crying—which, she claimed, was impossible. Nor did he stop there. In his next sermon (from which Margery was excluded) he only thinly veiled his many criticisms of her: 'he preached a great deal against the said creature, not mentioning her name, but so conveying his thoughts that people well understood that he meant her.' While there was much protest from those who 'trusted and loved her very much', there were others in the crowd who, like the friar, had lost patience with her. As it happened, a priest who was a great friend to Margery and who had, in fact, agreed to write her autobiography at her dictation, was also in the audience. Sensing the growing hostility, he 'was resolved never again to believe her feelings' and temporarily stopped writing for her altogether. He didn't want to be seen offering support to a fraud, who could well be an agent of the devil.

The way in which this priest was won back round to Margery is revealing. We are told that, shortly after abandoning her, he was led by God to a book about another holy woman, someone called Mary, from a little-known town in the north of France. We happen to know a great deal about Mary of Oignies, who died almost two hundred years before Margery was born, thanks to an account of her life written by her confessor. Born of wealthy parents in the Netherlands, Mary was desperate to pursue a religious life, but her parents ignored her wishes and married her off at 14 years of age. Happily (and unusually, under these circumstances) Mary's husband was an understanding man, and he agreed to live chastely with her and to spend their married life tending to lepers.

Alongside her works of charity, Mary had visions from God, mortified her flesh with a hair shirt worn underneath her clothes, donned the white clothing of virginity (despite being a married woman) and was visited by constant bouts of uncontrollable crying. When reading about Mary, 'of the abundant tears that she wept, which made her so weak and feeble that she could not endure to look upon the cross, nor hear our Lord's Passion repeated, without dissolving into tears of pity and compassion', the priest was shocked at the similarities he found between Margery's life and Mary's. In renewed faith, he 'drew towards' his former friend once more.[28]

St Bridget of Sweden, the only woman to be canonized in the fourteenth century, also features prominently in Margery's *Book*. Of noble birth, with connections to the Swedish royal family, she was higher up the social scale. However, like Margery, she was a married woman who would have preferred a religious vocation. Her parents married her off when she was just 13, and while she did manage to persuade her husband into chastity for two years, she ended up bearing him eight children. It was only after he died that Bridget was finally free to pursue the life she had always wanted. She became a visionary and pilgrim and, in 1347, she established a new order of nuns dedicated to study and learning. Her influence and legacy across Europe were undeniable; in England, the Bridgettine monastery of Syon Abbey, one of the wealthiest and most influential religious establishments in the country, was founded by King Henry V himself in 1415.

Margery Kempe did not receive royal favour, nor was she the founder of her own religious order. But the similarities between her own life and Bridget's feel more than coincidental. We know from Margery's *Book* that she was familiar with and interested by Bridget. When she travelled to Rome, as Bridget had done not long before her, Margery sought out Bridget's former maidservant so that she could hear more about the saintly lady. She learned that Bridget was 'kind and meek with everybody', that she had a 'laughing face' and that you'd never know how famous she was because she was so 'homely' and happy to talk to anyone, regardless of their social standing.[29] Margery made a pilgrimage to the chamber where Bridget died and took time out of her travels to listen to a sermon by a German priest about her life. On her return from Europe in 1434, she went straight to Syon Abbey, where we are told that she was stirred to 'great devotion and very high contemplation' as well as 'abundant tears of compunction and compassion'.[30]

Whether or not Margery's tears and visions were genuine, they were not unique. In fact, her manner of living followed a clear pattern which had already been established by famous mystical women on the continent. She is often taken to be an eccentric or a maverick; but her frequent reference to Bridget of Sweden and Mary of Oignies, both of whom were admired and respected by the Church, show that she wanted to align herself with the great and the good. She even goes so far as to suggest that she might be even more special than them. In a vision at her local church, when the priest lifts the holy sacrament, Margery recalls how she saw it shake and flutter before her very eyes, trembling like the wings of a dove. Afterwards, when she thanks God for the vision, he says, 'My daughter Bridget never saw me in this way.'[31] Margery also tells us that her devotion to God feels stronger and more miraculous than any she's ever heard of: 'neither Hilton's book, nor Bride's book, nor *Stimulus Amoris*, nor *Incendium Amoris*, nor any other book that she ever heard read [...] spoke so exaltedly of the love of God as she felt highly working in her soul.'[32] Here she alludes to some of the best-known mystics of contemporary Christian mysticism—St Bridget (Bride) herself, as well as Walter Hilton and Richard Rolle, two male hermits who had visions of God and wrote them down for posterity. Margery suggests that the love she feels, the visions she experiences, are even greater than their own.

The fact that there is a *Book of Margery Kempe* at all indicates that she was positioning herself among the leading figures of medieval Christendom. A person who was exceptionally holy, and therefore a possible candidate for sainthood, required a hagiography, an account of their life, often written by a priest or a confessor. Margery never explicitly makes a case for herself as a saint in her *Book* (doing so would, in fact, have proved her a victim of pride and therefore unworthy). But the way she speaks of her visions, and the fact she made a record of them in a biography, suggests that sainthood may well have crossed her mind.

Saints were ordinary human beings who, thanks to grace and favour from God, became extra-ordinary, bestowed with the power to protect the vulnerable and defend their faith. The most powerful saints were usually those who had been martyred, but they all continued to work miracles for faithful Christians after their deaths—a prerequisite of their sainthood, according to the Church. There were saints who had defeated the devil, saints who had been boiled alive and then emerged from the water without any scars, saints who could smell the difference between a good Christian and a sinner, saints who could levitate and saints who were impervious to fiery flames and other forms of torture. Over 300 are memorialized in Middle English hagiographies alone, and their popularity was immeasurable across medieval Europe. They appeared in urban legend and miracle stories, in religious art, in shrines that became popular pilgrim destinations, as well as on pilgrim badges. Whether young or old, rich or poor, everyone prayed to saints and visited the places where they had lived and performed wonders. They asked the saints to intercede on their behalf in major life events, but they also appealed to them with a myriad of more mundane problems, from locating lost property to easing headaches or cooking a good meal. While some saints were nobility or even aristocracy, there were just as many poor men and women who had set themselves apart through selfless deeds, commitment to the Christian faith and their ability to make magical things happen through the grace of God.

Margery sees and talks to various saints in heavenly visions. Perhaps unsurprisingly, she is particularly interested in female saints; two who bear special witness to her spiritual journey are Margaret of Antioch and Katherine of Alexandria. Margaret of Antioch, the patron saint of childbirth and fertility, was a beautiful and humble shepherdess approached by a nefarious prefect named Olibrius, who offered to either marry her or make her his concubine. Margaret, who had sworn herself to chastity in God's honour, refused him. Olibrius was furious. He had her arrested, tried as a criminal, tortured and finally thrown into a dungeon to rot. While she was imprisoned, Margaret prayed to God for her enemy (the devil) to be made visible to her, so that she could fight him. God obliged and a terrifying dragon appeared. Against the odds, and in spite of the dragon's physical stature and flamethrowing breath, the young, beautiful Margaret triumphed. There are several different versions of what happened next. In one account, Margaret made the sign of the cross and the dragon burst into flames; in another, she ruthlessly cut herself free from the dragon's stomach; in a third, her genuflection transformed the dragon into a dog, which she promptly killed with a hammer. The miracles don't stop there. The next day, the Romans tried to execute her by drowning her and then setting her on fire, but nothing worked.

Margaret emerged from all their tortures unscathed. By the time they decapi-tated her, Margaret's status as saint was firmly established.

Unlike Margaret, Katherine of Alexandria wasn't a humble peasant. Her parents were royalty, King Costus and Queen Meliades of Alexandria, and they both supported Katherine's love of learning, even though she was a woman. When she was a teenager, her father had a walled castle built for her, partly so she could more easily pursue private study but also so that she would be well protected from nefarious men. According to legend, Katherine became so well educated that she managed to best 310 male philosophers and scholars who were gathered by her father to challenge her and to prove her skill in debate and her academic prowess.

When her beloved father died, Katherine laid claim to the throne, but she was not a popular queen. Her subjects were dissatisfied with her devotion to study and her refusal to take a husband. 'We have a queen', they lamented, 'she keeps to herself. She loves nothing but books and school. She lets all our enemies ride and run throughout the land. She is always studying and alone. This will bring us all to wreck and to sorrow! If she had a lord, all might be well.' When Alexandria was invaded by a Persian emperor named Maxentius, who had dedicated his life to persecuting Christians, the people of the country blamed Katherine—she could have protected them better by marrying a man instead of devoting all of her attention to her books. Maxentius, once he'd arrived in Alexandria, made the life of Katherine and her subjects a misery. After she petitioned him to have mercy on her people, he brought together 50 philosophers to debate with her, and to persuade her out of her faith. But his plan backfired when Katherine persuaded all these learned men of Christ's divinity, successfully converting them as well as Maxentius's own wife. The emperor was livid. He had the philosophers burned alive and his wife tortured and beheaded, before throwing her dead body to the dogs.

Katherine was beaten and imprisoned. She was terrified at what fate awaited her but nevertheless fortified by her faith, and by the angels who tended to her wounds. Meanwhile, Maxentius—obsessed with breaking Katherine's body and spirit—turned his attention to creating a torture wheel for her, complete with vicious spikes. He planned to tie her to it, and to make her death as agonizing as possible, but God had other ideas. Much to Maxentius's fury, he made the wheel explode into hundreds of pieces. Like Margaret, Katherine was eventually killed by beheading. But instead of blood, milk and oil flowed from her neck, and her body was carried by angels to Mount Sinai, where an oil-filled font with curative powers appeared as her shrine.

Katherine was immensely popular in medieval Europe, and especially in England. Sixty-two churches were dedicated to her, and 56 of those had wall paintings boasting scenes from her extraordinary life. This was largely due to her wide appeal—she was a princess, and therefore beloved by aristocratic women; a consecrated virgin and bride of Christ, and therefore especially appealing to nuns; she spoke out against her enemies and so was favoured among preachers; and she was a role model for students because of her love of learning. More tangentially, she was thought to hold particular favour for women with evil husbands, for nursing mothers (because of the milk which emerged from her dead body) and to millers and other craftsmen who worked with wheels.

It's not hard to see why Margery Kempe alluded to Margaret of Antioch and Katherine of Alexandria. Margaret was the patron saint of childbirth, and Margery's first vision had been post-partum; both women had sworn themselves to celibacy; and both women had visions and both spoke out for what they believed in, despite violent oppression. Much of Margery's own trouble can be traced back to her speech. Her travelling companions hated her insistence on speaking about holy things over dinner, when they were trying to gossip and make merry. She angered the archbishop of York's men by rebuking them for swearing oaths. And when she was put on trial for treason, her holy speech was repeatedly held up for questioning. Clerics were anxious that Margery might 'lead' the people 'astray', because they had 'great faith in her talk'.[33] In the Middle Ages women were not allowed to preach, and the clerks use this against her, reading out the popular injunction from St Paul's Letter to the Corinthians that 'women [should] keep silence in the churches'.[34] But Margery was always quick to defend herself: for a woman to preach from a pulpit was considered heresy, but she knew that in talking about God in other places, however much it might annoy people, she was breaking no rules. However, the frequency with which other people tried to silence her is testament to how dangerous and subversive women's speech was considered to be.

Equally telling is Margery's account of how her *Book* came to be, especially the challenges involved and how she managed to overcome them. In her prologue she describes the convoluted and often frustrating process of writing her autobiography.[35] Various well-respected men of the Church urged her to make an account of her life for posterity, and 'so that God's goodness might be known to all the world'—the suggestion being that Margery was a vehicle for God's grace, love and power. However, she was illiterate. This didn't necessarily mean that she couldn't read—'illiterate' in the Middle Ages might mean that one could read but not write, or that one could do neither. But either way, she needed someone worthy to dictate her book to. On her travels, she found a suitable candidate, an Englishman living in Germany with his wife and children who was so enamoured by Margery, and by her literary project, that he relocated with his family and moved in with her, writing down as many of her memories as he could.

When he died before her *Book* was finished, Margery was forced to find a substitute. She turned to the priest we met earlier. When he was re-convinced of Margery's authenticity, and returned to the project, he found he could not decipher the previous scribe's notes. Unwilling to give up, Margery prayed to God and, miraculously, the priest was suddenly able to read them. When his eyesight started to fail, she made another prayer, and the man was cured. Together, they finished what would become *The Book of Margery Kempe*, with Margery herself 'sometimes helping where there were any difficulties'.

While neither Margery nor the priest refers to the book as a hagiography, this account of how it came to be aligns the housewife of Bishop's Lynn with various miracles. First, the priest is made able to read notes previously illegible to him, and second, his eyesight is cured. It is not unusual for a hagiography to draw attention to miracles; it is part and parcel of building a case for sanctification. But a surprising number of those in her Book are not altogether altruistic. Rather than protecting the vulnerable or defending the faith, the miracles described in Margery's prologue are concerned with creating the right conditions for her story to be told, making sure that she was heard, read and understood.

If her own account is to be believed, then Margery certainly made an impact in her own time. She was threatened, multiple times, with execution and hounded in various towns by those who thought her a heretic. But there is also a long list of those she has helped through her prayers. A wicked woman on the point of death is 'granted mercy' in the afterlife because of Margery. A mother who has been driven mad by childbirth, who 'saw many devils' and had to be 'bound hand and foot with chains of iron, so that she should not strike anyone', recovers after Margery visits her. And when in 1420 a great fire in Lynn threatens to consume the church of St Margaret, Margery's prayers help to abate its flames, bringing about 'a snowstorm to quench [it]'.[36] The famous friar who came preaching to Lynn certainly took notice of her and various people she met claimed that they had already heard of her. She came face to face with some of the most powerful Christians of her time, from Archbishop Arundel to the bishop of Lincoln; some loved her, some hated her, but they all seemed to know who she was.

While her *Book* gives the distinct impression that her life had a profound impact on those around her, there is no real record of Margery beyond her autobiography. In fact, she was almost entirely absent from the history books until the twentieth century. Before her manuscript turned up at a home in Chesterfield, there were only two existing references to her story. Wynkyn de Worde, a German immigrant in London responsible for the first popular print works in England, distributed some excerpts from her *Book*—but they were so heavily abridged as to be almost unrecognizable. And some years later another printer, Henry Pepwell, gave her a brief mention but mislabelled her as an anchoress. It wasn't until 1934, when Colonel W. Butler-Bowdon was fishing about for a ping-pong ball in a dusty old cupboard that her full manuscript was rediscovered. However, 1930s academe didn't look kindly on the boisterous Margery. Her first editor, Hope Emily Allen, described her as 'petty, neurotic, vain, illiterate' and 'physically and nervously overstrained'.[37] For many years the mystic was destined to be either neglected or condemned, even by those, like Allen, who worked tirelessly to rescue her book from obscurity.

The impression we are left with, then, is of a woman who desperately wanted to be influential: a woman who fashioned herself after other famous holy women across Europe in order to try and make a name for herself, who sought out not just one but two different priests to ensure her legacy was preserved on the pages of a manuscript and who refused to lock herself away in a nunnery or anchorhold but who made her presence known on the streets. But, alas, she was—at least in her own time and the years immediately afterwards— largely unsuccessful in her attempts to exert influence. It seems that Margery, like many women throughout history, was just a bit much for everyone.

Unlike Margery, Julian of Norwich shut herself away and made no pretence to sainthood. The fact that Margery sought her out for authorization and validation indicates that she must have leveraged some influence in her own time as a holy woman. But, aside from this reference, the bequests made to her in the wills of four noblemen and -women, and her own writings, there is almost no trace of Julian in the history books. As far as we know, no one even read the *Revelations* in her lifetime. The original manuscript has been lost, and there is no contemporary mention of the account of her visions anywhere to be found. By the fifteenth century, amid growing anxieties about heresy in England, a woman like Julian may well have been nervous about circulating her religious writing. She certainly seems to have been aware of these risks.

Before entering the anchorhold, Julian had already written an account of her visions. In this 'Short Text', she downplays her role as author and frames herself as a mere messenger. She describes her visions as 'universal' and says that she experienced them 'for the benefit of many others', and not because God loves her any better than anyone else: 'for I am sure there are very many who never had a revelation or vision but only the general teaching of Holy Church, who love God better than I do'.[38] She begs her readers not to think of her ('a woman uneducated, feeble and frail') as a teacher, but says that she is simply repeating the knowledge that she 'received' from God. 'In truth,' she confesses, 'love moves me to tell you about it, for I want God to be known, and my fellow Christians to be helped.' Here she is carefully distancing herself from the kind of holy speaking that could be misinterpreted, as it was for Margery, as heretical preaching. 'But just because I am a woman, must I therefore believe that I should not tell you about the goodness of God, when I saw at the same time that it is his will that this be known?' Where Margery, Christine and Marie all try to make a name for themselves in different ways, Julian's aim is the opposite. She asks that, once the reader has finished her account, they reflect on Jesus and 'quickly forget' her.

While enclosed, Julian wrote a second, longer version of her visions, which contains no reference to her gender at all. While some believe this omission is due to anxieties about female authorship, I think it's the opposite. By this time, if Margery's account is to be believed, Julian had won the respect and admiration of the Church. With the confidence of her new vocation bolstering her, she no longer felt such caveats to be necessary. Her sense of readership, however, remained unchanged. Regardless of her sex, she felt it was her duty to communicate the visions—and what she believed they meant—not just to a privileged few but to all faithful Christians. At the end of her *Revelations* she addresses her imagined readership directly. 'And you to whom this book may come, thank our Saviour and with all your heart that he vouchsafed these showings and revelations of his endless love, mercy and goodness for you and to you, so as to be your and our safe guide and safe-conduct to everlasting bliss.'[39] We don't know why the *Revelations* were not known during Julian's lifetime, although it seems plausible that she was afraid they might be misconstrued as heretical. However, she clearly hoped they would reach a wide audience eventually, so that others could be comforted and inspired by God's love, just as she had been.

Julian did not care whether her name was remembered; in fact, she preferred it to be forgotten. The influence she sought was of a different kind. It might have taken her a few hundred years but, bearing in mind how many Christians today have read and found solace in her *Revelations*, she did eventually find it.

Marie de France, Christine de Pizan, Julian of Norwich and Margery Kempe were all trying to craft a legacy that would endure. They wanted their words to live on, and to influence those who read them, long after they were gone. Marie penned stories about powerful women and signed her name to them, at a time when it was very unusual to do so. 'The one who forgets herself is foolish', she tells us. 'Here I write my name "Marie" so that I will be remembered.'[40] Her popularity at court made her the target of envy but she was undeterred, and bold enough to make a present of her *lais* to the king. Christine de Pizan aimed equally high with her readership. In the *Treasure of the City of Ladies* she expresses her intention to 'distribute many copies [of the book] throughout the world' to 'queens, princesses, and great ladies'. She wrote in French (a language 'more common throughout the world than any other') so that her book wouldn't become 'useless and forgotten', and she hoped that 'many valiant ladies and women of authority' would read her words, 'now and in time to come'.[41] And for a while Christine got her wish. Her writings were translated into multiple languages and read by royalty. She received invitations to foreign courts and managed to excel in the male-dominated arena of political writing.

Despite their successes, however, Marie and Christine both fell victim to misattribution and erasure after their death. While many of Marie's tales were translated or copied abroad in the later Middle Ages, they usually travelled anonymously—and, until very recently, her name had been all but forgotten. Christine's writings, too, became increasingly anonymized in the years following her death—or, worse, were misattributed to men. 'This said book, at the request and prayer of a very wise gentlewoman of France called Dame Cristine, was compiled and created by the famous doctors [. . .] at the noble University of Paris', writes a (male) translator in his preface to one of her political works.[42] It wasn't until Simone de Beauvoir credited her with being the first woman 'to take up her pen in defence of her sex' that she started to enjoy a feminist revival.[43]

Margery had an impact on nearly everyone she met, and clearly aspired to greatness; but she is almost entirely absent from the historical record. Now her fame is growing. There have been academic conferences in her name, plays and novels written about her, the manuscript of her *Book* has been digitized and can be read online, and she even has a Twitter (now X) account. But although many readers have come to love her, others are still quick to dismiss her as fraudulent, mentally unstable or just plain irritating.

The lives and writing of our poet, mystic, widow and wife show that women could—and did—have an influence in the Middle Ages. But they also show how fraught, challenging and disappointingly fleeting such influence could be. Thankfully, artists, writers, editors, translators, academics and performers around the world are now reclaiming and reviving the work of Marie, Christine, Julian and Margery. The award-winning author Lauren Groff has reimagined Marie de France's life in her novel *Matrix*; Christine de Pizan famously took her seat at Judy Chicago's *Dinner Party* (1979) and inspired Tai Shani's Turner-Prize-winning installation *DC: Semiramis* in 2019; feminist artists responded to the writings of Julian of Norwich in an exhibition called *Ecstasies in Norwich*; and the performance artist and musician Cosey Fanni Tutti meditated on Kempe's *Book* in her autobiography *Re-Sisters*. As the writings of these four extraordinary authors continue to enthuse modern-day creatives, their names, at least for now, have not been forgotten.

EIGHT

Having It All?

'Adonc cloy mes portes, c'est assavoir mes sens, que plus ne fussent tant vagues aux choses foraines'*

CHRISTINE DE PIZAN, *Christine's Vision*

There were three windows in Julian of Norwich's cell. The narrowest looked directly into the church after which she was named, and which her rooms directly adjoined. Kneeling at this narrow opening, she could observe Mass and receive the Holy Eucharist from the priest. The second was more pragmatic. Through it, her dutiful maid Alice passed her meals. Hers was the food of poverty: she ate vegetables, never meat, and her diet was designed to keep her alive but never full. Sometimes she and Alice would converse through it, and at the end of the day she would discreetly pass through her waste. The third window was the busiest and the noisiest, host to a parade of visitors who had come from far and wide to seek her advice and guidance. The guidebooks for anchoresses warned of the dangers of entertaining too many visitors, who could serve as a distraction from daily prayer and contemplation. 'How seldom nowadays will you find a recluse alone', Aelred of Rievaulx lamented in his *Rule of Life for a Recluse*. 'At her window will be seated some garrulous old gossip pouring idle tales into her ears.'[1] But Julian often took pity on those who had travelled a great distance, or were in particular distress, finding time to listen to their problems and offer them as much reassurance as she could.

Julian was grateful for this third window, her only real connection to the outside world. But she still looked forward to the end of the day, when she could finally draw the curtain closed, signalling that she was no longer to be disturbed. Because, when she was finally alone, she could cross the cell to her simple bed, take out the manuscript nestled underneath and return to the visions that had taken hold of her so long ago—the visions that had led her here, to this cell, to this new way of life. Left to her own devices, with only a

---

* 'I closed my doors, or my senses, which no longer strayed to external matters'

dripping candle to light her page, Julian could reflect on what she had seen—
and write down what it meant.

This is pure speculation. We have no idea how Julian felt about being an
anchoress, what she missed most about her former life, whether she dreaded
her visitors or looked forward to them. But knowing her vocation allows us
to imagine something of what her daily life may have been like. It was the
duty of an anchorite or anchoress to receive visitors, and to give them counsel
and advice if they came to this third window. However, it was also their right,
when they felt the pull of solitude, to draw a curtain across it and retreat into
the privacy of their cell.

Virginia Woolf famously wrote in 1929 that a woman 'must have money
and a room of her own if she is to write fiction'.[2] Julian might have been
recording heavenly visions rather than writing a novel, but the truism still
applies. She had a 'room of her own', however small it may have been (the
average anchoritic cell is thought to have been around 12 square feet), and she
had her meals and daily needs attended to by her maid. It is difficult for us to
understand why a woman might have chosen to pursue such a strict way of
life, but it afforded Julian the space and time to write the book that has made
her famous today.

According to a guidebook for male anchorites, the *Speculum Inclusorum*
('A Mirror for Recluses'), there were three main duties of the anchoritic life:
fervent prayer, devout meditation and edificatory reading. Revealingly, when
this guidebook was translated for women, edificatory reading was replaced
by edificatory *speaking*, the implication being that a woman was more likely
to have holy books read aloud to her or communicated to her via a holy man
than to read them herself. Neither version mentions writing as a part of the
anchoritic life, but Julian certainly incorporated it into her daily devotions.
Her 'Short Text', written before entering her anchorhold, is terse and often
difficult to follow—as if Julian is just trying to get the words out onto the
page rather than attempting any narrative artistry or significant interpretation of meaning. More famous and far more accomplished is the 'Long Text',
the version she wrote while enclosed.

The product of years of contemplation, rumination and editing, the 'Long
Text' is one of the most accomplished pieces of theology to come out of the
medieval period. Julian explains that she wrote it because she felt 'stirred to
say more'—to add to her initial telling of the visions, and to weave in the
greater understanding that she had reached thanks to the space and privacy
of her anchorhold. It took 'fifteen years' of reflection, she admits, to truly

understand the meaning of the revelations and she still sees the text as a work-in-progress: 'it is not yet completed, as I see it.'[3] Based on how many exact phrases and sentences make their way from the 'Short Text' into the 'Long Text', it seems likely that Julian was working with her original version in front of her, adding in more interpretation and explanation as she went along, to make the visions as meaningful and accessible as possible (remember that she hoped her *Revelations* would help and comfort all Christians, as they had helped and comforted her). She also adds in a far greater sense of time and place, giving each revelation a number and adding subdivisions to each one. This makes the later account much easier to follow and enables her to make the relationship between the different visions far more explicit. When discussing her first vision, in which Christ appears to her bleeding on the cross, she is careful in the 'Long Text' to describe how his suffering body acts as a kind of trailer for the sequence of visions as a whole: 'For the strength and the ground of all was shown in the first sight', she tells us, 'and therefore was this lesson of love shown, with all that followed, as you shall see.'[4] The overarching meaning of the visions, as she understands them, is that 'God is love', and her addition here makes this message clear from the start.[5] Such changes communicate a sense of the visions as a holistic whole, rather than a series of disjointed fragments, with each one informing the rest.

As well as more interpretation, Julian adds more description and imagery. When describing the dehydration of Christ's suffering body in the 'Short Text', she simply writes: 'and it seemed to me that the drying of Christ's flesh was the greatest pain, and the last, of his Passion.'[6] In the 'Long Text', however, she expands the idea of dehydration into a moving and poetical meditation on death:

> The dear body was brown and black, completely transformed from his fair living colour as it dried out in death. For at that same time that our Lord and blessed Saviour was dying on the cross, it seemed to me that there was a dry, keen wind and terribly cold; and it was revealed that when all the precious blood that could bleed from the dear body had bled from it, there still remained some moisture in Christ's dear flesh. Loss of blood and pain drying him inside, and the blowing of the wind and cold coming from outside, met together in the dear body of Christ.[7]

At every turn, she gives the impression that she has only come to real understanding through reflection and contemplation, the kind that a married medieval woman would have struggled to find the time and space for. It's doubtful that she could have achieved such depth of understanding, and such complexity of prose and ideas—which often read as pure poetry—if she had not enclosed herself. She still had duties to attend to, regular prayer and devotion as well as a responsibility to offer counsel and advice to society. But the anchorhold offered privacy, contemplation and the absence of menial chores or family ties. Rather than struggling to 'have it all', Julian turned all her attention to one role. In doing so, she became not just an anchoress but a poet.

. . .

A very old man, descending the stairs from his bedroom bare-footed, slipped and tumbled to the ground.[8] Hearing his anguished cry for help, his neighbours came running. They found him 'lying with his head twisted under himself, half alive, all streaked with blood'. He was so broken and bruised that for many days afterwards he had to keep five rolls of soft material pressed to the wound, to staunch the bleeding. Discovering the man all alone, his neighbours all had the same question—where was his wife?

Margery Kempe had already set tongues wagging years earlier when she refused to have sex with her husband. She and John had been living in different houses for many years before John's fall, because their neighbours refused to believe that they weren't having sex if they still lived together. Finding her husband half-dead in his house, the same neighbours whose scepticism had forced her to move out now blamed her for causing his accident by leaving him. They said that, if John died, Margery 'deserved to be hanged for his death, for as much as she could have looked after him and did not'.

Margery asked Jesus what she should do. He appeared to her in a vision and told her that, to save her reputation, he would grant John another year of life and allow her to take a break from her religious duties so that she could care for him. At first, Margery refused: 'No, good Lord, for then I shall not attend you as I do now.' She didn't want to lose a year of devotion to look after an ailing, estranged husband. But eventually, seeing that it was the only way to put a stop to the endless slander and criticism, she acquiesced. 'Oh Lord,' she begged, 'grant me grace to obey your will.'

Margery took her husband home with her and looked after him until the day he died. She found it difficult, particularly towards the end when he became 'childish' and needed help going to the bathroom, often soiling himself whether sitting at the table or by the fire. While she resented this labour, which took her away from the religious life, she framed it as a punishment from God for lusting after her husband so (to her mind) disproportionately when they were young: 'she thought to herself how she in her young days had very many delectable thoughts, physical lust, and inordinate desire for his body. And therefore she was glad to be punished by means of the same body.'

Margery's situation reveals, albeit in an extreme way, the kind of compromises women were forced to make if they wanted to have a life beyond the domestic. Julian of Norwich was largely shielded from the pressures of the outside world. But working mothers like Christine de Pizan, who wrote prolifically to provide for her family, and Margery, whose religious vocation was so often at odds with being a wife and mother, struggled to navigate the demands of home and work while fending off criticism for not focusing all their attention on their domestic duties. Most women felt pressured to choose, learning to be satisfied with staying at home, minding the children and taking care of the household or giving up the pleasures and security of marriage entirely, as Julian had done. Far more problematic were those women who refused to limit themselves but instead tried to 'have it all'.

A 20-year-old mystic living in Germany approached a learned theologian, who asked her many questions about her religious practices.[9] After listening carefully to her description of visions which brought her enviably close to God, the man began to weep. 'Lady, do you have a husband? Do you live together as man and wife? Do you have children? Do you have property? Do you have honour in the world?' he asked her. Her reply—'Yes, sir, I have all those things'—astonished him. He could not imagine how she could be a mystic while also being a mother, wife and property owner. 'Tell me good lady, how is it possible to reconcile all this?' he asked. She answered readily:

> Good sir, how do these things harm me? Permit me to explain that I give my children what they need and raise them so they are not proud; I do everything for them that is fitting, in praise of God [. . .] When I have done it all and go to church and can manage to find a little place to stand just wide enough for both my feet, then I sink so deeply into God that I find no one exists in that moment but Christ and me alone.

Humbled by the young woman's words and her accomplishments, the theologian replied: 'Lady, you are on a righteous path. Pray to God for me, poor friar, who has worn the cloth for fifty years and is called doctor of divine arts and has not yet been able to attain such perfection of devotion.'

Despite surviving in 30 different manuscripts, very little is known about the context of this brief story. Who was the young woman? Where did she come from? Was she able to continue to fulfil all the competing demands upon her life, or did they start to take their toll on her? Notwithstanding her hazy presence in history, this brief anecdote offers a complex glimpse into the attitude of (and towards) women who attempted to 'have it all'. The learned theologian's questions suggest incredulity that she can reconcile all her different roles, and he only expresses admiration for her once she has put his mind at rest that her husband and children are not being neglected. Her response is a defence and a reality check; only after she has taken care of things at home is she able to find 'a little place' for her mystical pursuits, when the rest of the world (albeit briefly) melts away.

The literature of the time, from sermons to guidebooks, suggests that women were expected to choose a single pathway, and, like Margery, were often judged for splitting themselves into too many different pieces. This anecdote holds up 'having it all' as something that is remarkable and praiseworthy only if the demands of marriage and motherhood do not suffer. For most women, then as now, trying to navigate multiple roles was too challenging to be possible. But that doesn't mean none of them ever tried.

·   ·   ·

The fourteenth-century conduct poem *How the Good Wife Taught Her Daughter* is evidence of how seriously marriage was taken in the Middle Ages, as well as of the various expectations and demands that were placed on wives, in particular.[10] The poetic voice adopted is that of a wife and mother addressing her daughter. In the aftermath of the Black Death, young women were migrating into the towns and cities in droves for jobs, and it is entirely possible that *Good Wife* was designed to help keep them in check. Three of the surviving manuscripts containing this poem are vernacular compilations, the type of book that would belong to the wife of a wealthy merchant or trader. Two, however, are clerical manuscripts, with texts in Latin as well as English; one seems to have been a friar's handbook. The education of young women, away from home and the watchful eyes of their own mothers, may well have fallen to their new mistresses, or indeed to local friars who took it upon themselves to try and keep them on the straight and narrow. Such an audience would also explain why this is one of the only conduct poems written in English addressed to a woman.

The 'teaching' *Good Wife* offers mainly relates to finding a husband. Once a husband has been secured, the poem instructs its imagined reader how to become a good wife and a good mother; according to the poem, being a 'good woman' means being both. The daughter is advised to love and honour her husband in all matters, to answer him 'meekly', to 'quiet his wrath and be his dear darling', diverting his angry outbursts with 'a fair word'. She should not laugh too loud, yawn too widely or be too wild of cheer. She should not spend too much time gallivanting around and, when she does need to leave the house, she should not walk too fast or look around too often. She should not spend all her husband's money drinking at taverns (in fact, she should barely drink at all), and she should certainly never go to lower-class sporting events like cock-shooting or wrestling. Alongside these unpalatable directives, the poem outlines an endless litany of tasks and responsibilities, the kind we have already seen in *The Ballad of the Tyrannical Husband* and Christine de Pizan's written advice to wives.

In one of the manuscripts in which this poem circulates, it sits alongside a companion poem, *How the Wise Man Taught His Son*.[11] Comparing the advice that the two texts offer is revealing. *Wise Man* is as quick to curb late nights spent drinking in taverns as *Good Wife* is, and it also advises its reader not to talk too much. However, the reasons given are tailored to a professional rather than a domestic life. In a public office, a man's tongue can easily become his foe, and staying up partying can negatively affect the quality of his work. When the poem does briefly mention marriage, it makes the anticipated gender dynamic of medieval relationships clear. A husband should 'rule' his wife 'pleasantly and gently', because only 'softly and gently' can a man 'tame' a woman.

According to *Good Wife*, a woman's aim should be to marry, have children and bring them up in accordance with its advice. Being a mother was, of course, a role that brought its own attendant duties and responsibilities along with it. In *The Treasure of the City of Ladies*, Christine tells us that a wise princess should watch over her children and their upbringing diligently. She should make sure that her children are disciplined and that their nurses and tutors are carrying out their duties effectively. Moreover, she should not leave the upbringing of her children to others but should be a hands-on parent: 'She will not wait for a report from someone else, but she herself will often visit her children in their rooms. She will see them go to bed and get up and see how they are disciplined.' In particular, she will be 'diligent about their education', ensuring that they learn to love God, to read and write and to remember their prayers by heart. Communication between a mother and her children is essential, according to Christine: 'She will converse with them in order to sense their understanding and their knowledge', and she will regularly give them books to make sure they improve themselves from day-to-day, while censoring any reading that might contain 'vain things' or 'follies'. It is part of a mother's duty, Christine tells us, to 'try to get their children's father to agree that they be introduced to Latin and that they understand something of the sciences'.[12]

Here Christine tacitly acknowledges that certain aspects of education tended to be reserved for boys and encourages mothers to use their powers of persuasion to alter this status quo. Without the father's go-ahead, a daughter would be unable to learn those subjects, such as science and Latin, that were considered more intellectual and more appropriate for men. These words relate specifically to princesses. But Christine's book also encompasses women from other social and economic circles. A bourgeois mother, just like a princess, 'should see that her children are well taught and disciplined, even if they are small, and that they are not heard whining or making a lot of noise'.[13] Moreover, they should be kept tidy, and in an established routine. If a mother was the wife of an artisan, then she should send her children to school to get an education when they are young, and then later, when they are teenagers, it was her job to find them a trade by which they might earn a living.

From birth, women were expected to be the primary nurturer of their child, or to find a wet nurse to be their surrogate. Wet nurses were common for elite women across Europe, sometimes because the mother could not feed the child herself and other times because of the belief that suppressing lactation would enable the mother to become pregnant again more quickly. However, they weren't always condoned. The English theologian Thomas of Chobham (1160–1233) warned his readers against farming out breastfeeding to someone other than the child's mother, equating it with murder: 'The fact that separating a baby from the [mother's] own breasts is a matter which pertains to killing is clear from the writings of the saints who say that no milk is so suitable for nursing a child as maternal milk.' He further contended that any woman who fed a child in her womb but who refused to breastfeed was neglecting the child, and eschewing 'God-given work'.[14] The Spanish poet and mystic Luis de León was evidently in agreement: in his book *La Perfecta Casada* ('The Perfect Wife'), he dubs children who are sent to wet nurses *bastardos* ('bastards').[15] Paintings of a serene Madonna breastfeeding Jesus graced churches all over Europe, and religious writers used the metaphor of Christ breastfeeding his followers as an expression of his divine love. Such imagery was working overtime to convince mothers that feeding their child themselves was a holy endeavour, and was not for delegation.

Nor was it just breastfeeding that male authors had an opinion about. Before the advent of print, church sermons (delivered by men) were one of the best ways to get information and advice out to the public about all sorts of things, including motherhood. We learn from a medieval English statute from Worcester that priests were encouraged to discuss childrearing in their sermons and, specifically, to warn mothers against placing children beside them in bed, in case they might suffocate them, and instead to make sure they were put down in cradles with strong supports. The punishment for mothers who followed the example of their female relatives instead of observing this advice from the Church was harsh. It was not uncommon for mothers of suffocated children to be prosecuted for their perceived negligence: in 1490 one Joan Foster was prosecuted for tragically crushing two infants in bed with her, one her own child and the other belonging to another mother, Joan Paris.

According to *Good Wife*, it is the mother's duty to make sure her children are behaving, and to discipline them when they are not: 'And if thy children be rebel and will not bow them low', *Good Wife* advises, 'neither curse them nor blow;/But take a smart rod and beat them in a row,/Till they cry mercy and their guilt well know.' The medieval mother is encouraged to resort, immediately, to violence. 'Dear child, by this love,' the poem continues, rather chillingly, 'they [your children] will love thee ever more.'[16] Corporeal punishment is labelled an act of 'love', one that will ensure the devotion of the mother's children for eternity. And this wasn't just a literary trope. We have already seen how Agnes Paston beat her daughter Elizabeth and, according to her biographer, the eleventh-century Queen Margaret of Scotland 'lavished' her children with care 'in order that they be nurtured with all diligence and brought up as much as possible in honourable ways' but was also quick to punish them: 'she had ordered her household steward to punish the children with threats and slapping whenever they were naughty.'[17] While there were debates about how serious violence towards children should be, it was generally considered an important part of their discipline.

Wealthier mothers needed to find their children a good position in a noble household, to help set them on the path to advantageous marriages and to ensure that they were schooled in crucial life skills such as manners, languages and the ability to hold their own in social situations. Rather than learning these skills at home, parents sent their children away, to foster their independence and to grow their social network. From what we know of such placements, and regardless of their status, these children effectively acted as servants while trying to soak up the atmosphere of the house and its family, learning what they could for their future lives as heads of households. Mothers of more modest means needed to seek out apprenticeships or roles of servitude for their children, to set them up for a decent living or good marriage in the future. Male and female child servants working in good households would often end up betrothed to one another.

In its campaign to persuade its readers into a life of celibacy, *Hali Meidhad* describes how mothers are 'always [...] anxious', that their child 'will grow astray'. Even those who are rich and have a nurse should still 'concern [themselves] with everything that [their daughter] has to do'. How unfortunate, he laments, is the wife who comes home to hear her child screaming, to see the loaf burning on the hearth and the pot boiling over into the fire—*and* to find her husband sitting with his feet up, complaining about the noise and his spoiled dinner?[18] Of course, the picture that *Hali Meidhad* paints is deliberately bleak. But it's still hard to imagine, taking account of all the tasks they were burdened with, how wives and mothers could have made room for anything else at all.

. . .

In her autobiographical poem *Christine's Vision* (1405), Christine de Pizan reflects that it was only after she managed to get both of her children out of the house that she had time to dedicate herself to her new profession. In 1397 she secured a place for her daughter Marie at the royal convent of Poissy—a coup for both of them, because membership of this particular convent was largely drawn from the aristocracy and Marie's acceptance there was a testament to Christine's reputation. Not long afterwards, Christine's compositions brought her to the attention of one John Montagu, the wealthy and influential earl of Salisbury, who was also a poet. While visiting Paris in 1398, he asked to meet her, and offered to take her 13-year-old son Jean back to England with him, as a companion for his own son. Christine happily acquiesced, thinking not only of the good such a prestigious placement would do her son but also of the years of respite it would give her from caregiving.

Jean was sent home just three years later, far earlier than intended because King Henry IV seized the throne from his cousin Richard II and had many of Richard's supporters—including Montagu—executed. Christine was worried about him, 'a child in a foreign land at the time of the great pestilence' who had been found in a treasonous household. Her immediate fears were allayed when the new king 'happened to see' some of her books and was so impressed by them (and by her) that he brought Jean to court, where 'he held him dear and in high rank'. He even invited her to visit but, '[s]eeing how things were' politically in England, and certain that a traitorous king would not 'come to a good end', she instead concocted a plan to get her son home safely. 'I did so many things—not without great forfeit, for it cost me several of my manuscripts—that I obtained leave for my son to come and fetch me to lead me there, a place I still have not seen.'

By keeping the king sweet with presents of her manuscripts, and pretending that she was going to visit herself, she managed to get Jean back to France. Naturally she was relieved that her son was no longer in danger. But she was not entirely thrilled at their cohabitation. 'Now I was delighted to see this boy whom I loved, for death had left him my only son and I had been without him for three years,' she writes, 'but the burden of my expenses increased.'[19] It became difficult for her to provide for him while also keeping up with her career, and she therefore made it her mission to find him another placement as soon as possible, eventually securing him a position with the duke of Burgundy.

When she was alone, with no one to look after but herself and her household, Christine's internal to-do list shrank significantly. Her empty nest eased the financial pressure but also created the time and headspace she needed to devote herself to writing more seriously. 'Although I was naturally inclined to scholarship from birth,' she confessed, 'my occupation with the tasks common to married women and the burden of frequent child-bearing had deprived me of it.' But now she could return to 'the solitary and tranquil life' that 'naturally pleased [her] the most'. Able to turn her mind to more scholarly materials, she found 'passages of Latin and the noble sciences' that she had memorized in her earlier days coming back to her, and inspiring her anew.[20] The allegorical figure of Philosophy in her poem reminds her that, however much she had loved her husband, being a wife did hold her back from her vocation. 'By your own words, if your husband had survived until the present, you would undoubtedly have spent less time on your studies; for the household chores would not have allowed you the benefit of scholarship.'[21]

From the outside looking in, Christine seems to be a woman who 'had it all'—as far as was possible. But the autobiographical sections of *Christine's Vision* reveal that, beneath her polished exterior, Christine was struggling to make ends meet, to keep her family afloat and to carve out space and time to juggle all the different roles she was attempting to play.

. . .

The year 1417 was a bad one for heresy. Across the country, those linked with the religious movement of 'Lollardy' were being hunted, imprisoned and burned. Following the teachings of Oxford scholar John Wycliffe, Lollards criticized corruption in the Church, denied the doctrine of transubstantiation (the belief that the wine and bread given at holy communion became the actual body and blood of Christ), argued against pilgrimage and petitioned vigorously for the Bible to be translated into English so that its words could reach beyond the elite. As a movement it was especially attractive to the lower classes, who felt excluded from the Latinate language of the Church and frustrated by the wealth it amassed at the expense of ordinary people. And it was also popular among women because, radically, Lollardy allowed women to preach.

It didn't matter who you were, what status or money you had. If the authorities got wind of a connection to the Lollards, then you were in serious trouble. Take, for example, John Oldcastle, a country gentleman who many believe was the basis for Shakespeare's yellow-stockinged Falstaff—drunk, disruptive, corrupt but charismatic, and eminently entertaining. Oldcastle himself had helped King Henry IV defeat the Welsh during his reign and been promoted to knight for his services to the crown. He had remained a great friend to the royal family, and something of a father figure to King Henry's son, who took the throne in 1413 after his father's death. When the rumblings began that Oldcastle was mixed up with Lollardy, Henry V tried to protect his old friend. But the power of the Church won out. Oldcastle was captured and led into London in chains, where he was 'consumed with fire, gallows and all' for his crimes in December 1417.[22] Neither his wealth nor his status nor his gender could save him.

It was a bad year for Margery too, although, unlike Oldcastle, she survived it. On her return from pilgrimage to Santiago de Compostela she became embroiled in various ecclesiastical trials in York, Hull, Hessle and Beverley, facing serious charges related to heresy, and only managing to escape unscathed owing to her supporters and her powers of persuasion. She found herself going toe-to-toe with the famously zealous anti-Lollard archbishop of York, Henry Bowet, arguing—quite literally—for her own life. It is evident from her *Book* that Margery was not a Lollard. She frequently mentions how Christian images, considered idolatry by Lollards, act as a catalyst for her visions; she goes on pilgrimage; and she tells us that she has only ever 'heard' biblical stories being read aloud to her in sermons (the subtext being that she never read them herself in translation). In trials for heresy a suspect would be questioned in the 'Articles of Faith' to find out whether their beliefs were orthodox. Every time Margery undergoes such interrogation, she answers 'reasonably'. 'She knows her faith,' the archbishop admits.[23]

The term 'Lollard' was a useful label for anyone the Church felt was being a disruptive influence. At her trial in York a preaching friar accused Margery of trying to persuade other women to leave their husbands. According to him, Margery had been entertained at the house of the well-respected Lady Westmorland at Easter and, while Lady Westmorland herself was 'well pleased' with Margery, and 'liked [her] talk', her daughter Lady Greystoke had later revealed that, during the festivities, Margery had advised her to abandon her role as wife and desert her husband.[24] The friar believed that this reported conversation was sufficient evidence to have Margery burned at the stake. To this friar, and to many of her other detractors, Margery was a contagion, liable to infect other good women with her dangerous ideas and her persuasive tongue. She vehemently denied the friar's accusation and was imprisoned.

At first, the authorities considered asking Lady Westmorland to send a letter either in support or in condemnation of Margery; some went so far as to suggest she should be imprisoned for 40 days. Uncertain how to proceed, the archbishop asked Margery to repeat to him the story she told Lady Westmorland: 'I told her a good tale of a lady who was damned because she would not love her enemies, and of a bailiff who was saved because he loved his enemies and forgave them their trespasses against him, and yet he was held to be an evil man.' The (not so) hidden meaning here is that things are not always what they seem. The clerics and the townspeople might call Margery an evil woman and a heretic, but that didn't make it true. The archbishop agreed that this was 'a good tale', dropped the charges and let her go.

In medieval Europe, if you were a man who wanted to follow a Christian vocation, there were numerous options available to you with varying degrees of strictness and interaction with the outside world. For women, however, especially in Britain, there were only really two: a nun or an anchoress. Both involved removing yourself from the outside world, taking a vow of chastity and committing yourself to a fixed abode for the rest of your life. In her *Book*, Margery describes a holy man who, infuriated with her, declares that he wishes she were 'enclosed within a house of stone'. This doesn't just mean that he wanted her out of the way. He is also saying that he wishes Margery would follow a prescribed holy way of life by becoming an anchoress. Even after Margery's lifetime she was wrongly described as an anchoress by Henry Pepwell, who printed a sanitized extract from her *Book* in 1521. It may be that Pepwell genuinely believed her to be a recluse, but it's also possible that he felt Margery's writing would be better received if he marketed her as an anchoress. Either way, Margery's life was one that male authorities found difficult to categorize and therefore threatening.

There was a third, semi-professional route available to women—a vowess. Usually, becoming a vowess was chosen by single women or widows, but wives did too occasionally assume 'the mantle and ring' in a ceremony before a bishop. Vowesses made an oath of chastity but remained domestically and economically independent from the Church. They were able to travel, rather than staying in a convent or anchorhold, and they could even remain married, if they gave up sex with their husbands. Margery's decision not to enclose herself was therefore not as uncommon as the hostility she received might suggest. She posed such a unique problem for Church authorities because, although her life mirrored that of a vowess in many ways, she never officially became one.

Probably in an effort to subdue her critics, she did try. Four years before her altercations with the archbishop of York, she asked the bishop of Lincoln, Philip Repingdon, to perform the vowess ceremony for her. However, at the same time she made an unorthodox request. Alongside the required mantle and ring, she wanted to wear white at the ceremony. Margery often wore white. She was mocked by her fellow pilgrims for doing so, and, more seriously, this habit was held against her when she was on trial, because the colour was reserved for virgins. 'Why go you in white?' the archbishop of York asked her. 'Are you a maiden?'[25]

Margery never got her vowess ceremony. The reasons Repingdon gives for delaying were muddled and many. He needed more time to think; he wanted to consult with other advisers first; Margery was out of his jurisdiction; he should wait until she had proved herself further. But his final words on the matter focus on her attire: 'my counsel will not let me profess you as a vowess in so singular a clothing without better advisement.'[26]

Repingdon hedged his bets with Margery—he stalled rather than refused, in case she turned out to be the real deal. And, in fact, he acknowledged her special relationship with God in his reply, asking her to speak with Him and request permission for a delay. She may have raised suspicions, but she still commanded a great deal of respect for an ordinary woman who wasn't connected to the Church in any official way and who had no fixed vowed relationship with a supervisory male authority. Repingdon's refusal, ironically, gave her more freedom than she would otherwise have had.

Like Christine, Margery was a woman who tried to 'have it all'. While she no longer wanted to sleep with her husband, she didn't want to leave him or to dissolve their marriage. She still wanted to be a wife and a mother, even as she pursued a religious vocation. It was this insistence on doing things her own way that attracted so much attention and anger from both her peers and the authorities; if she was allowed to get away with improvising her own way of life, might not other women follow? Margery, of course, had the ultimate justification for all her deviations from prescribed behaviour. In various conversations with Jesus he validates her unorthodox choices, telling her that her way of life pleases him more than any other: 'I have often told you daughter, that thinking, weeping, and high contemplation is the best life on earth.'[27] However, even with God on her side, Margery's *Book* still shows how hard it was for her to juggle her different roles. For Christine, the struggles are financial and vocational. For Margery, the potential consequences of her decisions are, quite literally, a matter of life and death.

·   ·   ·

Hundreds of years before *Cosmopolitan* writer Helen Gurley Brown made 'having it all' into a household phrase and a feminist movement in 1982, women were expected to choose one pathway—or so the literature suggests.[28] The autobiography of Margery Kempe, and the sheer volume of criticism and hostility she documents within it, reveals how challenging life could be for a woman who refused to stick to just one role. Christine de Pizan managed to juggle motherhood and authorship but admits that it was far easier to think and write with her children out of the house. Julian of Norwich's theology is the product of years of deep and philosophical thinking—the kind of thinking it is hard to imagine anyone managing to achieve while taking care of a medieval husband and household. The lives of all three women show that trying to 'have it all' was not easy. What they managed to achieve while striving for more was nothing short of remarkable.

———————

NINE

Death

'I felt a great louthsomnes to die'*

JULIAN OF NORWICH, *Revelations of Divine Love*

When Julian of Norwich entered her cell, she was halfway dead already. She had bidden her old life goodbye and dedicated all that she had, all that she was, to God. There may even have been a funeral held before her body was symbolically sealed into her new home. Here she would live out the rest of her days until her body was buried in the earth beneath her feet.

To most people, even then, the life Julian had chosen would have sounded like a waking nightmare. Who would want to be trapped within the same four walls of a cell for ever, occupying the same space as a grave waiting to receive their lifeless body? But some women did seek this living death as the most perfect expression of their love for God.

Julian gives us very few details about herself in her writings, but she does share the events that led her to the anchorhold. 'And when I was thirty and a half years old,' she tells us, 'God sent me a bodily sickness in which I lay for three days and three nights.'[1] On the fourth night she became so gravely ill that she 'did not expect to live until morning', and she received the last rites from her priest. She was not ready. 'Being still young, I thought it was a great pity to die,' she admits. But by the time her curate arrived, her eyes were 'fixed' and she 'could not speak'. He placed a crucifix in her eyeline, instructing her to '[l]ook at it and take comfort from it' as her soul left her body.

Julian remembered how everything around her grew dark except for the crucifix and how she 'truly believed that [she] was at the point of death'. But then, suddenly, her pain vanished, and she was well again. The crucifix began to change before her very eyes, and then things got really spooky: 'I suddenly saw the red blood trickling down from under the crown of thorns,' she tells us, 'hot and fresh, plentiful and lifelike, just as though it were the moment in

———

* 'I felt very sorry and reluctant to die'

his Passion when the crown of thorns was pressed on his blessed head.' Bleeding, arms spread wide, Christ was suddenly in the room with her, suffering, but alive—just as she was. And he began to speak.

Thus began a series of visions, directly from the mouth of God. She watched as he held out a hazelnut, nestled in his palm, and helped her to understand how it represented the world, kept safe by his love. She saw him fight and defeat the devil and then stretch open the wound in his side to offer a sheltering space for all humankind. She didn't know why she had been chosen, but she knew she had to communicate all that she'd seen.

. . .

The life of anchorites and anchoresses was imagined as a kind of 'living death', the idea being that they had closed the chapter on their earthly life and were now looking towards the next. We don't know the details of Julian's own enclosure, but she would certainly have participated in a church ceremony, rich in funeral rhetoric, before being interred in her cell, and she may even have had the death rites read over her body by an officiating priest as she entered it. Once inside, she would have been considered permanently separated from the world and, as a symbol of this departure, a grave might have been dug in her new abode before she entered it. Or she may have been required to dig it herself, with her own hands, while meditating on her own mortality: 'Every day they should be scraping the earth up from the grave in which they shall rot', the *Ancrene Wisse* author dictates.[2]

So punishing was this way of life that we know of at least some women who escaped their cells. In a letter from the medieval monks of Whalley Abbey to King Henry VI, we learn that a Yorkshire anchoress named Isold de Heton, interred at her own request in 1346, had 'broken owte' and was living her life 'like as she had never been professed'.[3] The monks, who were seeking the king's permission to close down the expensive anchorhold, claimed that maidservants responsible for taking care of it had 'gotten with child within the said hallowed place'. Although local rumour had it that Isold had run away with a lover, other letters from the time suggest that she had actually abandoned her religious vocation to intervene in her son's marriage. She was a widow who had left her little boy in the care of his grandfather when she became enclosed, and she was horrified to learn that the old man had broken off his grandson's prearranged engagement in order to marry him off to the daughter of one of his friends. Still, it's easy to imagine that

Isold was not in a hurry to return to the severity of the anchorhold once the issues with her son were resolved.

We do not know how Julian of Norwich died. However, given the time and place in which she lived, she probably witnessed more than her fair share of death. The average life span in medieval Europe was much shorter than it is today, and the mortality rate for children, particularly under the age of seven, was frighteningly high. Childbirth, as we've seen, was incredibly dangerous. Countries were often tangled up in bloody wars for long stretches of time; diseases such as dysentery, tuberculosis and malaria ravaged coastal regions after being carried over on ships; and an ever-growing population coupled with poor weather conditions led to significant famines. Between 1310 and 1314 in England, for example, several bad harvests meant that food production fell by 50 per cent while prices rose by a staggering 400 per cent or more. Men carried weapons as a matter of course, and they were routinely getting into fights that ended in tragedy—especially the hot-headed young.

Oxford was the murder capital of medieval Europe, with students constantly getting into deadly brawls with each other as well as with the local townspeople. In 1298 a man named John Burel died in prison from his injuries after he and his friends got into a heated argument in a local tavern with some other students, Nicholas Uilere and John de Suthfolk. On leaving the bar, Burel drew his sword, looking for a fight, and chased them through the streets. When he eventually caught up with Nicholas, he beat him so badly that onlookers were afraid he would kill him. To protect his friend, John de Suthfolk drew his own weapon—a battleaxe, no less—and dealt Burel a mortal blow to the head. All the men were arrested and taken off to prison, where Burel breathed his last. And the following year, further tragedy struck when the prostitute Margery de Hereford was murdered. An unnamed student at the university had sex with her and, when she demanded due payment, he attacked her. These kinds of events, especially in big cities, were not unusual—they are just two examples from one university town.

The ubiquity and visibility of death in the period is made hauntingly clear by its art and infrastructure. Medieval churches were the hub of most European communities, and their central point would usually be the crypt; sermons, hymns and ceremonies were laden with references to death, ensuring that the fragility of life was kept at the forefront of Christian minds. Tableaux in churches and other official buildings, as well as illuminated manuscripts, boasted vicious hellscapes and popular allegories like the *Danse Macabre*, in which the spectre of Death led unsuspecting characters from all walks of life into their graves. It must have often felt as if death was everywhere—especially so once the Black Death arrived. This infamous disease, which is now synonymous with the medieval period, made its deadly way to Europe by sea, on a boat travelling from Caffa (now Feodosija, Ukraine) to Sicily. When it came to England, via the bustling port of Melcombe Regis in Dorset, it marked the beginning of an astounding 300 years (on and off) of endemic plague in London. By the time it finally dwindled, it had taken a third of Europe's population with it.

One thing that stands out about accounts of plague victims in the period was just how revolting the disease was for its victims. According to Boccaccio, both men and women 'acquired certain swellings either in the groin or under the armpits', tumours as big as apples which gave way to 'black or livid blotches', presaging a stinking and painful death.[4] To make matters worse, because of the contagious nature of the disease, its victims often left this world as proverbial lepers, isolated and abandoned. Boccaccio comments on how those who were usually compassionate would shun the sick to try and save themselves: 'for the enormous number of men and women who became ill, there was no aid except the charity of friends, who were few indeed.'[5]

Agnolo di Tura, a shoemaker and tax collector from Siena who lost his wife and all five of his children to the plague, also noticed this tendency towards desertion: 'Father abandoned child, wife husband, one brother another; for this illness seemed to strike through the breath and sight.' Both he and Boccaccio recall how a climate of fear impacted burial practices, making death even more visible. 'None could be found to bury the dead for money or friendship', Agnolo tells us. 'Members of a household brought their dead to a ditch as best they could, without priest, without divine offices', and 'great pits were dug and piled deep with the multitude of dead' on the outskirts of town. Agnolo himself had to act as gravedigger for his own family, burying five of his children with his own hands—and he speaks of how people hurried away after depositing their relatives in shallow graves: 'And there were also those who were so sparsely covered with earth that the dogs dragged them forth and devoured many bodies throughout the city.' So many died, he tells us, 'that all believed it was the end of the world'.[6] His words, and his story, make the scale and terror of the plague painfully clear.

Women's behaviour also came under scrutiny in relation to the Black Death, partly because of run-of-the-mill medieval misogyny but also because the disease seemed to kill more men and children than it did women, especially in its second wave. According to one English chronicle in 1361, women widowed by the disease were, in the eyes of their society, too quick to move on. In a similar vein, the chronicler John of Reading thought the 'greatest cause of all grief' was (rather than the countless gruesome deaths) the behaviour of widows, who, 'forgetting the love they had borne towards their first husbands, rushed into the arms of foreigners or, in many cases of kinsmen, and shamelessly gave birth to bastards conceived in adultery'.[7] If these commentaries are to be believed, the plague made women promiscuous and disloyal to English men. Moreover, it made them immodest. Boccaccio expresses surprise at an 'unheard-of custom' that developed among women. Driven by the 'abandonment of the sick' and 'the scarcity of servants' a woman who became ill—'however attractive, lovely, or well-born' she may have been—would 'exhibit any part of her body as sickness required' to a male servant, 'as if to another woman' and 'without any shame'.[8]

We now know that the humble rat was responsible for the transmission of this deadly disease, slinking under doorways, burrowing into chests of clothes and food and scampering under floorboards. But at the time, the cause was unknown, and this led to desperate speculation. One common belief was that the plague was spread by the power of the imagination. Physicians agreed that anyone who ruminated on, or worried about the plague, made themselves more vulnerable to the infection—by this logic, even thinking about the plague was enough to sign your own death warrant. Others were certain that the plague was an instrument of divine retribution, a way for God to punish people for their sinful ways. One anonymous fourteenth-century poem writes: 'plague is killing men and beasts. Why? Because vices rule unchallenged here.'[9]

It blames, in part, the leaders of Europe, lamenting the 'sloth of shepherds' which left 'the flocks straying' and accuses rulers of being 'moved by favour and not wisdom'. However, it also blames ordinary people. Whereas soldiers of Christ used to dress in rough garments, they now wear soft fabrics; where the youth of the past 'were distinguished by moral excellence', the youth of the poem's author's day 'are learned only in squalid rites'. Women are, yet again, singled out for reprimand, for they are 'no longer bound by the restraints of their sex' but incur God's wrath by acting like whores. Those who were persuaded by this explanation for the plague took to the streets in self-flagellation, whipping themselves in the hope that God would forgive them and relieve them of the pestilence.

The deadliest theory of all was that the plague was caused by Jewish people poisoning the wells and rivers. Some even went so far as to claim that Jewish people were poisoning the air itself with their diabolical powers. This wasn't the first time that, with harrowing results, Jews in Europe became the target of such conspiracy theories. As a marginalized group, they were frequently made scapegoats for anything that went wrong, and this 'theory' that they were responsible for the plague led to nothing short of genocide. As the pestilence raged on, at least 60 Jewish communities were wiped out in Germany; and in 1349 more than a thousand Jews were burned in the town square of Strasbourg, blamed for a plague that had nothing at all to do with them and was killing them too. Across Europe, Jewish people were attacked, killed, wiped out in a persecution that was as relentless as the disease itself.

Between the Black Death, the famines, the wars, the violence and the persecution of marginalized communities in Julian's lifetime, death must have felt part of the very texture and fabric of her daily existence. It is oddly fitting, then, that she chose a vocation so marked by mortality. We know that the city she lived in was the most decimated by the Black Death in all of England. While Norwich's population tried to take shelter behind the city walls, its defences were designed for conquering armies and proved useless against rats. The plague arrived at the city's door on the first day of 1349, and recent estimates suggest that close to 60 per cent of the city's inhabitants were wiped out. It is therefore almost certain that Julian would have witnessed a disturbing amount of sickness and death during her lifetime.

In fact, several historians and authors have speculated that she may well have lost family members to the disease, perhaps even a husband and children. To support their supposition, such theorists often cite her visions, in which she makes frequent reference to Christ as a mother with a tenderness that suggests this is something she may well have experienced herself. She compares him feeding his followers with his body and blood to a mother nursing her child at the breast, 'most courteously and most tenderly'.[10] The mother can lay her child gently to her breast, to feed and soothe her, Julian tells us, but 'Mother Jesus' can go even further, leading Christians 'easily into his blessed breast through his sweet open side'. The word 'mother', she continues, is 'so sweet and so kind in itself that it cannot truly be said of anyone or to anyone except of him and to him who is the true Mother of Life and of all things. To the property of motherhood belong nature, love, wisdom, and knowledge, and this is God.'

Julian was not the first writer to describe Jesus as a mother; in fact, doing so was a very popular convention of mystical and devotional writing of the later Middle Ages, a metaphor turned to by men as well as women.

Speculation on whether Julian had experienced motherhood herself, then, is likely to be gendered—we don't tend to wonder about the parental status of male mystics who wielded the same analogy when describing their revelations or mystical experiences. However, based on the context of disease-ridden Norwich, and coupled with the fact that most women at this time did marry, it is not beyond the realms of possibility that she was a mother, and that she tragically lost her child or children to the plague, or some other fatal illness. Regardless, Julian would surely have been well acquainted with suffering but, through her vocation, she found a way to turn it into something more positive—an expression of the love of a higher power, and the promise of its end in the next life.

. . .

By the time Margery Kempe finally reached the Mount of Calvary, she was exhausted.[11] When she had caught sight of Jerusalem for the first time, she had been so overwhelmed by 'sweetness and grace' that she almost fell off her donkey. Two friendly German pilgrims had rushed over to keep her upright. Thinking she was ill, they put spices in her mouth to revive her, and then helped her onwards into the town. But now, standing in the very place where God had been killed, she was overtaken by a vision so powerful that she did fall. She 'writhed and wrestled with her body' on the ground, 'spreading her arms out wide' and—so loudly it sounded as if her heart was breaking—she wept.

Her vision, which is of the crucifixion, is visceral and painted red. The 'precious, tender body' of Christ on the cross is 'rent and torn with scourges' and 'more full of wounds than a dove-cote ever was of holes'. A twisted garland of thorns is jammed down onto his forehead, from which blood trickles down into his eyes. His 'blessed hands' and 'tender feet' have been nailed into the wood, and there are 'rivers of blood' flowing out from 'the grisly and grievous wound in his side'. This was not the first time that Margery had seen God die. But there was something about being in the very place where he'd breathed his last, that made her vision more potent than ever. She knew that Christ had endured all this pain, all this suffering, out of love—for her, and for all mankind.

Margery's visions of the crucifixion, which punctuate her *Book*, are excruciating in their attention to detail. She recalls watching in torment as Jesus's attackers pull off his clothes, strip him naked and bind him to a pillar 'as tightly as they could', beating his 'fair white body' with rods, whips and scourges, before driving the 'rough and coarse' nails into his hands with 'great violence and cruelty'. Christ's body, she tells us, 'shrank and drew together with all the sinews and veins [. . .] for the pain that it suffered and felt', and then, once he has been fixed to it, his torturers 'let the cross fall down' into the prepared mortise with such a great force that his whole body 'shook and shuddered' and all of his joints 'burst and broke apart'.[12] All Margery could do was watch the blood pour from his wounds and weep.

Even beyond these graphic revelations, you don't have to look far to find sickness and death in Margery's *Book*. Her account of her husband's illness, which temporarily forced her to pause her pilgrimages and her devotional exercises, is pitiful: 'in his last days he turned childish and lacked reason, so that he could not go to a stool to relieve himself, or else he would not, but like a child discharged his excrement into his linen clothes as he sat there by the fire or at the table—wherever it was, he would spare no place.'[13] In typical fashion, rather than focus on her husband's discomfort, she instead complains about how his sickness affected her. And Margery herself is 'punished' by God with a variety of different illnesses throughout her life, including a particularly bad bout of dysentery and an undiagnosed pain in her side that lasted many years and was so acute that 'she must discharge everything that was in her stomach, as bitter as if it had been gall, neither eating nor drinking while the sickness lasted, but always groaning until it was gone'.[14]

Sickness was a catalyst for Margery's mystical experiences, just as it was for Julian's. Her first vision, after the birth of her first child, almost killed her, and she then suffered mental illness and temptation from the devil afterwards, so severe that 'people thought she should never have escaped from them alive'.[15] However, one day, when she was by herself, Christ appeared to her sitting on the side of her bed; 'in the likeness of a man' he was 'the most seemly, most beauteous, and most amiable [thing] that ever might be seen with man's eye'.[16] The fact that both Julian and Margery first see Christ at their sickbeds tells us a great deal about the medieval attitude to suffering. It was ubiquitous, and often mortal, but it could also be perceived in a more positive light, as an opportunity for growth and change. For Christians, it was an expression of Christ's self-sacrificing love for his followers.

This attitude is something that is borne out in women's devotion more generally in the Middle Ages. In Margery's first vision Christ is very much alive, speaking to her companionably as if they were together in the same room. But in many others he is dying. Just as he had appeared to Julian, suspended in time on the cross, so he frequently transported Margery to the moment of his death, evoking for her the smell of sweat, the sound of nails splintering bone, the sight of his blood. Margery and Julian believed their visions to be real. However, their mystical revelations were an extreme version of a wider trend sweeping the later Middle Ages, popular among women from all walks of life, which was known as 'Passion Meditation' (in which 'Passion' refers to the crucifixion of Jesus). Many people, both men and women, were unable to read or write in the Middle Ages, especially among the lower classes. Attending church at least once a week, the average parishioner would sit through the service unable to understand any of the Latin being spoken. However, as the ancient language washed over them, they could gaze upon the artworks adorning the church walls or painted onto their prayer books, telling the story of Christ's death.

It is impossible to stress how saturated medieval Europe was with Passion iconography—it was, quite literally, everywhere. In the early Middle Ages most Christian art depicted God as a stern, even angry figure, drawn directly from the Old Testament. Even in depictions of the crucifixion he tends to look more like a warrior than a victim. But as time went on, Christian theologians and artists were increasingly seduced by the idea of Jesus as a human in pain, just like us. There are countless images of Jesus as a 'Man of Sorrows', naked from the waist up, covered in blood, eyes cast down in pain, treading his own blood in an allegorical wine press or being brutally flogged after his arrest. The *arma Christi* tradition trains viewers to pay attention to detail by depicting each individual instrument of the Passion: the lance that pierced Jesus' side, the crown of thorns placed on top of his head, the nails driven into his feet and hands. And in the pages of devotional manuscripts, one can find the wound in Christ's side as an isolated object (and looking remarkably like a vulva).

Christians were encouraged to tap into their sensory worlds and imagine themselves present at these iconic scenes of Christ's torture and death as a way of deepening their connection with him. And, tellingly, many of the guidebooks for this meditational practice were directed at women. In his guidebook for anchoresses, Aelred of Rievaulx includes a Passion Meditation, instructing his female readers on how best to place themselves at the scene and chastising them for being too passive when they imagine Christ's suffering: 'Why are you standing there?' he asks them. He urges them to '[r]un up, consume [his] sweet drops of blood', and to imagine kissing his wounds one by one, until their lips become stained with blood.[17] These descriptions are not only vivid and gruesome but quasi-erotic.

As a devotional practice, Passion Meditation originally had misogynistic overtones, the idea being that women were generally unable to engage with Christian doctrine on an intellectual level and therefore needed a sensory, imaginative substitute. However, it arguably ended up empowering women rather than condescending to them, allowing them to develop a heightened and additional, special relationship with God. As we've seen, women were frequently defined in the Middle Ages by their superfluity. With their excess speech, excess blood from menstruation, excess tears and excess emotion, women's leaky and incomplete bodies were terrifying to men. However, the misogynistic rhetoric that called their bodies deficient allowed them, ironically, to identify with Christ in more specific and intimate ways. Call to mind any artistic representation of Christ's Passion and Crucifixion, be it from the visions of Margery and Julian or from Mel Gibson's *Passion of Christ*, and it's likely that you'll see a body that is suffering and leaking— blood gushing out from the wound in the side, or down from the crown of thorns, face contorted into a grimace. Women could see, in such evocative images, mirrors of their own bodies, not deficient at all but sacred and holy. Margery's tears, which annoyed so many of her neighbours and travelling companions, flow forth in an excess matched by Christ's prodigious blood on the cross, which he shed to save her soul. In this way, the gruesome and gro- tesque imagery of a dying body becomes something comforting, and even empowering, to the women who meditate upon it, a distraction from their own pain and suffering as well as a reminder that all suffering eventually ends and that what comes after its endurance can be wonderful.

. . .

According to medieval medical belief, lovesickness was a real medical condi- tion that, in its most extreme form, could lead to death. It was a disease of the heart caused by romance (or, rather, lack thereof), but it could be exacerbated by a person's physiological makeup. The four complementary humours of the body existed in a delicate balance; because the body and the soul were thought to be intimately intertwined there could be consequences for both if the humours fell out of kilter. An imbalance could cause a myriad of physi- cal ailments, depending on which direction it fell in—those with an excess of the humour black bile, for example, were of a 'melancholic disposition' and more prone to emotional malaises such as depression, hysteria or lovesickness. Constantine the African, an influential eleventh-century physician and writer, explains the imbalance in relation to lovesickness as follows: 'The love that is also called "eros" is a disease touching the brain [...] Sometimes the cause of this love is an intense natural need to expel a great excess of humours [...] this illness causes thoughts and worries as the afflicted person seeks to find and possess what they desire.'[18] According to Constantine, then, lovesickness was sometimes triggered by a disappointment in love, but it could also be caused by a bodily imbalance.

Some people were not only more susceptible to lovesickness but also more predisposed to its emotional and physical symptoms. Nausea, fever, excessive weeping, fainting, listlessness, inability to get out of bed, loss of appetite—all of these ailments could be signs that someone had fallen prey to lovesickness. Moreover, lovesickness wasn't reserved for earthly attachments. Margery Kempe, Julian of Norwich and other religious women could be described as experiencing a chronic kind of lovesickness. Their beloved wasn't a human man but God, and they were separated from him until the day they died. Those who were lucky enough to have seen him in visions felt this separation even more acutely because they had experienced a taste of what they were missing.

In a series of thirteenth-century prayers known as 'The Wooing Group', a female voice addresses God with yearning, as if he were a long-distance lover.[19] 'Why do I not embrace you with arms of love so fast that nothing can wrench my heart away from you?' she cries. 'Why do I not kiss you sweetly in spirit? [...] Why do I not feel you in my heart, as sweet as you are? Why are you so estranged from me? Why can I not woo you?' The answer is that the author and her lover are separated by sin, of which she will not be fully cleansed (according to Christian doctrine) until after her death. 'My sins are a wall between me and you,' she laments. 'My sins deny me all this sweetness.' These anonymous prayers were originally intended for an audience of female religious professionals (anchoresses and nuns). However, by the later Middle Ages, thanks to their broad appeal, they had made their way into lay hands, and spread quickly among the upper classes, helping to firmly establish the trope of God as estranged lover.

Margery was clearly familiar with this idea. A couple of hundred years after the prayers were written, her desire to be united with God in heaven causes her to weep 'abundantly and violently'; forced to remain on earth without him, she is 'languishing' in love.[20]

For religious women such love-longing was encouraged, as long as it didn't spill too far over into the erotic. But doctors prescribed treatment for earthly lovers, as with any ailment. A sufferer of lovesickness should ensure they were getting plenty of time outdoors, surround themselves with calming influences and get a lot of rest. On the more medical side, many physicians suggested (as always) blood-letting or laxatives, to help the patient purge their excess bile and rebalance their humours. It is not clear from existing evidence how helpful any of these recommendations were for the loveless (although one can easily imagine that calm, rest and time spent in peaceful gardens would have curative properties); but the prescriptions do suggest that this was very much an upper-class illness. In the literature where lovesickness makes an appearance, its victims tend to either be noble or royal, and the only real cure is to secure the object of their desire.

The *lais* of Marie de France are full of knights and ladies suffering from lovesickness. While her stories are set in different places and spaces, with characters of different temperaments, encountering different dilemmas, the pain of love is the thread that ties them all together. One maiden whose lover has been killed swoons not once, not twice, but four times on realizing that he has died; unable to recover from the blow, she herself falls unconscious and later dies. Another young maiden lies down next to the corpse of her beloved and, after embracing him and kissing his eyes and lips, dies of a broken heart. Love is described as 'an invisible wound within the body', causing unutterable suffering and leaving a trail of bodies in its wake.[21]

In *Guigemar* the eponymous protagonist's heart is 'disturbed' when it is pierced by love, and Marie tells us that the feeling 'wounded him so deeply that he had completely forgotten his homeland'. He spends a 'sleepless night sighing in anguish' before confessing his love, terrified that the woman he loves may not reciprocate. When he does eventually reveal his feelings, his language is loaded: 'My lady, I am dying because of you; my heart is giving me great pain.'[22] In *Equitan* the king who falls in love with the wife of his loyal seneschal is caught unawares by the feeling and becomes 'distraught and overcome with sadness'. Just like Guigemar, when he confesses his feelings, he tells his love that he is 'dying because of her'.[23] The only thing that will make his agony disappear is her reciprocation. Women, as the objects of desire, hold the life of these men in their hands and are therefore under heavy pressure to return the sentiment.

However, despite all this pain and heartache, love is still the sweetest and best feeling that a person can experience in the world of Marie's *lais*. The famous quotation 'better to have loved and lost than never to have loved at all' could well have been the subtitle to her narratives. Suffering is framed not only as a necessary evil—something that must be endured in return for all the joy that love can bring—but also as artistically productive. In the prologue to her *lais*, Marie associates the composition of the collection with the avoidance of suffering: 'Anyone wishing to guard against vice should study intently and undertake a demanding task, whereby one can ward off and rid oneself of great suffering. For this reason I began to think of working on some good story.'[24] Here Marie gives us a tantalizing hint that she may have thrown herself into her work to avoid suffering. But she also sets the scene for suffering as the route to composition.

Chaitivel ('The Unhappy One') tells the story of a noblewoman who is courted by four knights, each so valiant and chivalrous that 'she was unable to choose the best'.[25] Wanting to keep the love of all of them, she displayed a 'friendly mien' to each, showering them with love tokens and secret messages. When a tournament is announced, they all enter it, hoping to win her favour with their performance. But when a fight breaks out among the competitors, three of them are unhorsed and killed. There is a huge outpouring of grief from all those involved in the tournament—'a full two thousand men unfastened their visors and tore at their hair and beards, united in sorrow'—and the indecisive noblewoman is likewise devastated, falling to the ground in a swoon as soon as she hears the news.

The fourth knight escapes with his life, but he is wounded in the thigh and rendered impotent. His lover, wracked with guilt about how she treated him, takes him into her care, providing him with the best doctors and visiting him often. 'Because of my great love for you all,' she tells him, 'I want my grief to be remembered. I will compose a lay about the four of you and entitle it "The Four Sorrows".' But the knight has another suggestion. 'My lady', he says,

> compose the new lay, but call it 'The Unhappy One'. […] The others have long since ended their days and used up their span of life. What great anguish they suffered on account of the love they bore for you! But I who have escaped alive, bewildered and forlorn, constantly see the woman I love more than anything on earth […] yet I cannot experience the joy of a kiss or an embrace or of any pleasure other than conversation. You cause me to suffer a hundred such ills and death would be preferable for me. Therefore the lay will be named after me and called 'The Unhappy One'.

In this *lai*, Marie processes her lovesickness through writing, but also to secure a legacy for those who have suffered. The noblewoman in *Chaitivel* works through her own sorrow and regret by telling the story of her four lovers, while also ensuring their great deeds are remembered.

Christine de Pizan's writings about love and loss feel acutely different to the quasi-ecstatic lovesickness we find in much medieval literature of her time, largely because they are marked by a real loss. The opening 20 poems of her first collection, known as 'Cent Ballades' ('One Hundred Ballads'), are all devoted to the unexpected death of Étienne, and the hopelessness she felt in its aftermath.[26] 'Of the sorrow that in me doth breed,' Christine warns us in her first poem, 'I shall speak more than enough'—and speak she does, pouring out her heartache onto page after page of manuscript.

The cause of her grief, she tells us, is Death—who, without warning 'did alight on him whence came my good' and led her to despair. 'What sorrow, pain, and sad mischief, what vile discomfort, and what sad adventure' her untimely parting from her husband has been; she suffers 'more than any creature known did suffer' since harsh death snatched her husband, and therefore all her fair days, away from her. She complains of 'immeasurable pain', laments that she has been condemned to an 'ill life', unable to heal, unable to die, suffering 'dread wakefulness, and restless sleep'. She lives 'without relief, lacking all hope of any end or measure', and cannot even gather the energy to carry out any of her household duties. She feels alone 'everywhere, in every way'; she is one from whom, brought low and defeated, her friends have retreated. It seems that everyone is becoming tired of her sadness, asking her why she, who used to be so cheerful, is now always sad, why she dresses as plain as a nun and no longer laughs or sings. Anyone who thinks her grief is overblown or overstated in these verses is likely not to have encountered a loss as significant as hers. It is true that medieval verse relies on hyperbole but, even so, and despite the hundreds of intervening years, Christine's pain on the page feels blisteringly honest.

According to the 'Cent Ballades' (as well as her other writings with autobiographical elements), Christine suffered from suicidal thoughts in the years after she lost her husband. 'I desire naught in my misery', she reveals 'but my death, caring to love no longer, since that is dead which maintained life in me.' In the end, from what we know of her, the greatest healer for Christine was time. Keeping herself busy with her writing, her family and a new career, she never forgot Étienne, but she found new reasons to live.

. . .

It was 1093 when Queen Margaret, the Pearl of Scotland, realized she was dying. She was 47 years of age. This may not seem very old to us, but in the Middle Ages it wasn't a bad run, and Margaret's life had been a full one.

Her first years had been spent in exile. Before she was even born, her family, as direct descendants of English royalty, had been forced by the invading King Canute and his Danish army to flee England, travelling overseas to Hungary. And, while Margaret grew up knowing she had been destined for greater things than the life of a political refugee, she benefited from the first-class education and social etiquette that Hungary granted its young noble-women. Eventually, her family returned to England, but any hopes they might have harboured of resuming a noble or even royal position were dashed by the advancement of the Normans, who, in their bid to lay claim to England, wanted to wipe out any rivals to the throne. Forced to escape once more, Margaret and her family found themselves not in Northumbria, as they had originally intended, but blown off course—in Fife.

As it happened, this misdirection was the best thing to ever happen to Margaret. Intelligent, pious and beautiful, with the sheen of a continental upbringing, it wasn't long before she caught the attention of King Malcolm III. At first, she resisted his advances, wanting to pursue a life of devotion rather than that of a wife and a queen. But Malcolm didn't give up, and Margaret eventually gave in. Despite her initial reluctance, her marriage to the Scottish king was a happy one, and she spent her adult years in an enviable and admirable fashion, bringing up their eight children, caring for the poor and the sick, reforming the Scottish Church and becoming generally beloved throughout her adopted land. It is safe to say that Margaret's life had been a contented one. And this may well explain why she remained so calm in the face of her imminent death. Her close friend and spiritual adviser, Turgot of Durham, describes her final days in his biography of her:

> There, knowing that death was imminent, she took great care to prepare for her death [. . .] Her face had already become deathly pale when she requested me, and the other ministers of the holy altar with me, to stand by her and to commend her soul to Christ by singing psalms. She also ordered us to bring her cross, which she used to call the Black Cross [. . .] she took it with reverence, embraced and kissed it [. . .] Her death occurred in so much calm, with such complete tranquillity, that there is no doubt that her soul departed to the region of eternal rest and peace. Moreover, amazingly, her face, which had become so pale in death, as is common in the dying, became so flushed and red and white after her death that she might be believed to be asleep instead of dead.[27]

This was, in medieval terms, the definition of a 'good' death. Margaret is lucky in that she has some warning and therefore also time to 'prepare' herself for what is coming. She takes the holy sacrament, as a good Christian woman should; she summons men of God to her bedside to give her the last rites and to join her in holy singing. She asks for a crucifix to be brought to her death-bed, just as Julian did, so that she can contemplate it in her final moments. And, thanks to all this preparation, her death is both calm and tranquil—she departs from this world so peacefully that it seems as if she's only sleeping.

What we can see in this account of an eleventh-century queen's death are the beginnings of something that, by the end of the period, would be known as *Ars Moriendi* – the art of dying well. With shorter life expectancies as well as relentless wars, famines and diseases, medieval people were well acquainted with death, and they sought tools and techniques to help them cope with its reality. Queen Margaret's request for a crucifix, and the unburdening of her soul in confession, are intended to hasten her journey into heaven, and would both become an essential part of 'dying well' by the end of the period. While priests had been encouraging these sorts of practices for hundreds of years, it was a fifteenth-century Christian committee, known as the 'Council of Constance', which decreed that the advice should be consolidated and more widely distributed. To that end, they commissioned the authorship of a prac-tical manual (*Ars Moriendi*) which was designed to support not only priests who routinely assisted the dying but also the laity, who might well find them-selves at the end of their life without a man of the cloth.[28]

The *Ars Moriendi* outlined five main 'temptations' that might cause a Christian soul to stray away from a 'good' death: attachment to worldly goods, infidelity, despair, impatience and spiritual pride. More importantly, it offered techniques for countering these temptations, including church rites like confession and reminders of biblical figures who had successfully resisted them. There are practical tips, such as questions the priest should ask a dying person, prayers for the dying and behavioural advice for their friends and family. It stresses the importance of a priest or a friend at one's deathbed: 'everyone must assiduously take care that he arrange with a devoted, trust-worthy and suitable companion or friend to faithfully assist him in the end to constancy of faith, patience, devotion, confidence, and perseverance by inciting and reviving him and in agony by saying faithfully devotional prayers on his behalf.' There are also contingency plans in place for those who might not be able to speak, or who might be delirious. The list of questions to ask the moribund, for example, are carefully crafted so that all they require is an assent: 'Are you glad that you shall die in Christian belief?', 'Do you know that you haven't lived as well as you should?', 'Do you have the will to change your ways, if you do not die?' Readers are coached on how to deal with common symptoms that beset the dying, such as irritability, agitation, disorientation and the loss of ability to think or reason. And there is an overall ethos that death is an inevitable part of life and that, despite its negative connotations, it can be positive, progressive and affirming, as it helps dutiful souls transition to the next life. Readers should 'be not aggrieved with [their] sickness' but rather 'take it all with gladness'. More than anything, the book aims to help the dying reach heaven as swiftly as possible, rather than enduring years in purgatory for unrepented sins. In this sense, then, the *Ars Moriendi* is a self-help book for the living, not just the dying. It helps people to ensure they are living a good life so that, when their death inevitably comes, they are sufficiently prepared to reach the next.

.   .   .

We do not know how Julian of Norwich, Marie de France, Christine de Pizan or Margery Kempe died. Their writings allow us a glimpse of their lives, but their endings remain a mystery. We know that Julian died some time after 1416, when she was in her seventies, and probably in her anchoritic cell. But the exact year and manner of her passing are lost to us. Christine is believed to have died in 1430, possibly in her daughter's nunnery in Poissy, but we do not know for sure. Margery died sometime after 1438, but we don't know where, or what of. And of the enigmatic Marie's death we know nothing at all. Once again, she slips from view.

However, we do know that all four of these women believed in a Christian afterlife. Heaven and hell loomed large in the medieval imagination. When the *Ars Moriendi* attempts to arm Christian souls against devils visiting their deathbed, and when Margery recalls being besieged by demons after the birth of her first child, neither of them is speaking metaphorically. They describe what they believe to be real devils, clambering up from hell to try and trick humans into sinning and damning their souls for ever. Almost as prevalent as images of Christ's Passion in medieval churches and manuscripts were depictions of hell and the ghastly creatures who populated it. A particularly popular trope was the hellmouth; in these paintings, the entrance to hell was imagined as the large, gaping maw of a monster, filled with fire and the souls of the damned. Demons stretch naked bodies out on torture wheels, throw them screaming over their shoulders, beat and jab them with pitchforks as they lay on the ground, truss them up by their ankles, roast them on spits, chew them up but never spit them out.

Bearing in mind the horror of these images, it's not surprising that there was such an emphasis in medieval literature on avoiding sin. Even those who were confident they would manage to escape the everlasting fire of hell were not safe, because purgatory still lay in wait for most of them. As an idea, purgatory was rooted in Judaism, but was adopted into official doctrine of the Christian Church in 1274. It was an in-between space, reserved for those souls who had not sinned grievously enough for an eternity in hell, but who still needed to atone before heaven could welcome them. The fires of purgatory were designed to purify the soul rather than consume it, but they still burned. And there was no guarantee that a soul would ascend from purgatory to heaven on the Day of Judgement. If a soul still had sins to cleanse when that day came, then they would be sent straight to hell.

Marie was clearly aware of purgatory. *Espurgatoire de Seint Patriz* ('The Purgatory of St Patrick') was her translation into Old French of one of the most popular legends of the Middle Ages. It tells the story of a knight called Owain who sought out purgatory to cleanse his sins, and the fact that the Latin original was a medieval best-seller suggests that there was a real appetite among readers for tales of the afterlife. In the preface to her translation Marie outlines the importance of purgatory: 'it must happen, nonetheless,/ we shall suffer, more or less,/doing our works, in Purgatory;/even those who await true glory/must come to torment, suffer it.'[29] Just as the characters in her *lais* must suffer to experience true love, so human souls must suffer purgatory if they want to experience heaven.

The protagonist of Marie's story is a virtuous knight called Owain. Believing that he 'owe[s]' much more to God for his sins than the penance prescribed by his bishop, he decides to seek out a more severe punishment on his own.[30] Upon reaching purgatory, he sees 'every possible form of pain'. Desperate people crying out for mercy are hung up by their feet, their bodies swinging in 'burning chains' and their heads dangling down into 'infernal flame'. They are 'cruelly struck/upon a burning, flaming hook' by their eyes, ears, nose, breasts or genitals. Their bodies are 'charred and blackened', 'roasted on a grill' and 'impaled on spits'.[31]

It is therefore easy to see why women like Margery were afraid of purgatory. Unlike Owain, she sought to avoid a sojourn there entirely. In one of her visions, she tells God that she's worried she won't make it into heaven because she's not a virgin, and because she has sinned so often in her life. But God is quick to reassure her that her sins have already been forgiven. 'You shall not fear the devil of hell,' he promises her, 'for he has no power over you.'[32] Margery will be spared any time in purgatory because she has already suffered enough from 'the slanderous talk of the world' and from all the times she has been tormented in her visions, night and day, by vicious fiends.[33]

If fear of damnation was the rod steering people to live better lives, then hope for salvation was the carrot. When Owain makes his way through the various torments and is ushered into heaven, he witnesses a celestial realm filled with celebration and love: 'Each of them in that place rejoiced/at their great happiness vouchsafed;/from suffering and Purgatory/they had been freed.'[34] Margery's *Book* offers a similarly joyous vision. After reassuring her that she is safe from the torment of hell and purgatory, God waxes lyrical about how jubilant her passage to heaven will be. She will be escorted by a great host of holy figures—the Virgin Mother, the 12 apostles, St Margaret and St Katherine and Jesus himself; and when she gets there, she will be 'fulfilled with every kind of love' that she desires. There will be 'great joy and melody', 'sweet smells and fragrances' and all the holy saints will rejoice that she is finally coming home.[35] For a woman who is so often lonely and misunderstood, heaven is a place of companionship, belonging and love.

For Christine, unsurprisingly, heaven is a place of learning and understanding, one that she uses to encourage her readers to live their lives more wisely and compassionately. When her lengthy allegorical poem 'The Path of Long Study' begins, she has shut herself away in her study again, grieving the warfare that is tearing her beloved country apart.[36] Seeking solace in her books, she eventually tires herself out and falls into a deep sleep. An ancient sibyl named Almethea appears and offers to lead her 'into another, more perfect world where [she] can much better learn than in this one the things that are truly important'. Christine eagerly follows her to the top of a mountain, where a ladder drops down, allowing her to ascend into heaven. She is so enchanted by what she sees there that she wishes all her bodily parts could be transformed into eyes to help her take it all in. She describes the sweet smells, the heavenly music and the great learning and understanding that all its inhabitants possess. Her experience of a more perfect world makes the sorrows of her own even more acute, but it also fills her with hope. When she wakes up in her study again, she is newly armed with lessons to teach the nobility of France, confident that they can create something closer to heaven on earth.

Over the years many of Julian's readers have commented on how refreshing her theology is. Unlike her contemporaries, who tend to labour over the horrors of hell, she chooses to concentrate on heaven instead. She tells us that, while she initially desired to have a 'full view of hell and purgatory', so that she could learn more about her faith and 'live more to God's glory', she was denied such a vision.[37] Instead, Jesus drew her gaze to the wound in his side, a symbol of his suffering on earth, stretching it open to reveal 'a beautiful and delightful place large enough for all mankind that will be saved to rest there in peace and in love'.[38] By sharing what she has seen, Julian hopes to comfort and console her readers into living a good life, rather than frighten them into it. She tells us that she was 'much moved with love towards [her] fellow Christians, that they might see and know the same as I saw' because she wanted it to be a 'comfort' to them. Readers should be 'mindful that this life is short' and strive to 'love God better', not because they are afraid of hell or suffering but because they are confident that they will find eternal rest.[39]

Marie's vision of heaven is the end of a knight's quest, firmly situated in the world of love and chivalry that her stories so often inhabit. For the academic Christine, whom we are apt to find in her study, surrounded by books, heaven is a place of understanding. For Margery, who so often felt lonely and ostracized, it is a place of acceptance, community and validation. And for Julian, writing from a city still recovering from the plague, it is an end to suffering. The writings of these four women remind us that, whatever our beliefs, and whenever or wherever we were born, our hopes for the future will be shaped by the experience of our lives. Suffering, loss and death are inevitable but, if looked at from the right angle, they can be transformed into something far more enduring—hope.

Conclusion

AFTERLIFE

'Ayes cure de bonne renommée, car elle te demourra plus longue-
ment que quelconques autre tresor.'*

CHRISTINE DE PIZAN, *The Treasures of the City of Ladies*

If they travelled forward in time to pay us a visit, what would Marie,
Christine, Julian and Margery make of our world? Would everything feel
entirely unfamiliar? Or would they recognize more than we might think?
Would they be feminists? Or would they find the twenty-first century *too*
progressive? Would they delight in how many opportunities women have
available to them, how much freedom they enjoy and how much they have
achieved? Or would they be frustrated at the gender pay gap, the everyday
sexism, the discrimination against the LGBTQIA+ community and women
of colour? It's not hard to imagine that, if they decided to extend their stay,
they might wind up wondering exactly how far we've really come, and what
it's going to take for equality to finally be achieved.

It is far rarer for unmarried women to be criminalized for having sex, and
archaic assumptions that women who do get married will be obedient to
their husbands have eroded. Divorce is a much easier option than it once was,
and in many countries gay marriage is finally legal. But while many of the
medieval restrictions on wives have been shed, some continuities remain,
from the endurance of wedding vows ('till death us depart') to the pressure
many women still feel to get married. Feminists who want a wedding face a
conundrum when the ritual, by and large, is still based on the transference of
a woman from one man to another—even in secular ceremonies a bride is
likely to be walked down an aisle and 'given away' by her father.

---

* 'Have regard to thy name, for that shall continue longer than any treasure.'

Even though women today usually choose their marriage partner, that doesn't mean everyone ends up happily ever after. Many couples find themselves miserable, unfulfilled or just a bit bored and end up looking for an escape. Adultery is no longer a crime in much of the world, and certainly not one punishable by death; as of April 2022, new laws in the UK removed adultery as a basis for divorce entirely.[1] Yet people still cheat, and we remain fascinated by the idea of infidelity. Headlines about affairs in high-profile relationships make for endlessly popular clickbait. Just as medieval readers were entertained by tales of clandestine love in Marie's *lais*, Arthurian legend and the poetry of Chaucer, so we settle down the sofa to be entertained by tales of infidelity and marital discord.

The Wife of Bath may be a fictional character created hundreds of years ago, but her experience of violence within marriage is one that far too many women today can relate to. Although there is now much more support available for victims of domestic abuse, there are still many women trapped in abusive marriages or forced to take desperate measures to extricate themselves. And, worryingly, Christine's advice on how to navigate male violence rather than escape it is not nearly so distant as we might hope or expect. Following the tragic murder of Sarah Everard in March 2021, the Metropolitan Police flooded women with tips on how to stay out of harm's way, rather than making any discernible effort to tackle the real problem: male violence.[2] What women must do to survive men is a concern that has not been relegated to history.

Married or not, deciding whether to have children remains a significant preoccupation for women. Research has identified unmarried, childless women as the happiest subgroup in the UK, more likely to live longer than their child-rearing peers.[3] Yet there is still a pervasive ideology that all women should want children, that there is no love like of a mother for her child and that a woman's life is somehow empty without one. Even European governments express concerns about the decline in childbirth, but despite the persistent pressure (and for the first time in history) over 50 per cent of women over the age of 30 are now childless.[4] Sometimes, the delay or the decision not to have children is one that is taken out of the woman's hands, owing to external factors like infertility, not being able to find a partner at the right age, financial pressures, concerns that their partner will not be supportive or the extortionate price of childcare. However, there are plenty of other women who choose not to have children for their own reasons, prioritizing instead work, leisure, relationships or simply deciding that it doesn't feel right for them.

And what of pregnancy and childbirth itself? While the basic mechanics are the same, our knowledge, understanding and approach have moved on. The labour room is no longer a closed house, for women only—fathers can be in the room, should their partners wish them to be, and are often involved as a hands-on birth partner. Pain relief such as epidurals, gas and air and opiates are usually available to women, and the risks of childbirth have significantly reduced. We no longer rely on sermons from male priests to get information: there are reams of literature out there, written by those with first-hand experience, to help pregnant parents feel more informed as well as antenatal classes to help them prepare, at which partners are not only welcome but encouraged. Perhaps most significantly, women now talk about their birth experiences, sharing their stories to inform, empower or warn other expectant mothers. Margery's account of her first labour was unique at the time, but today she would be actively encouraged to talk about her traumatic experience.

There are, nevertheless, some surprising turns backwards, towards a more 'medieval' way of doing things that suggest there are things we can learn from older practices. Increasingly, the care of a mother during pregnancy and labour is placed in the hands of midwives, rather than doctors, with an emphasis on women knowing their rights and their options and, crucially, feeling like an informed participant in the process. Accompanying this move has been a trend towards 'natural' birth—which usually means labour with only natural pain relief, supported by techniques like hypnobirthing and reflexology, and even the encouragement of home births, when the time and situation lend themselves to doing so safely.

We need to tread carefully here. Evidence suggests that, based on these trends, women can feel pressured to strive for a 'beautiful' birth experience without medical intervention. Modern advice in this vein can leave the impression that, with the right meditative practice, breathing technique or mantra, a birth can be serene, even painless—not unlike the effortless experience of the Virgin Mary. This ideal is especially damaging when things don't go to plan, leaving women feeling like a failure for not managing to have the perfect birth. However, the increasing emphasis on freedom of choice, as well as an appreciation of midwifery and more natural remedies alongside medical pain relief, feels like a positive move, and one that is not so distant from a medieval birth, with its godsibs and its focus on the mother.

With regard to contraception and abortion there have, of course, been significant improvements—both ideologically and scientifically—but we are not nearly so far away from the medieval mentality as we might like to think. There is still no male contraceptive pill, no injections for men, no coil, no implant—all methods that are used on women even though they may well disrupt the hormonal balance of the female recipient or cause other side effects. And the Western landscape in terms of abortion and women's rights over their bodies is looking increasingly bleak. For almost 50 years, *Roe v. Wade* ensured that every woman living in the US had the right to an abortion in the first 12 weeks of pregnancy, until it was overturned by the Supreme Court in 2022. There are now 12 states in the US with a total ban on abortion, and others (like Georgia and Florida) that have reduced the window to six weeks and have either closed its clinics or are trying to bankrupt them with fines. As a result, clinics in states where abortion is still legal have been inundated, and women are having to travel over state lines to secure their terminations.

There has been some troubling talk accompanying an increased movement to the right, politically speaking, in the UK too. In November 2022 the senior Tory MP Jacob Rees-Mogg launched a verbal attack on abortion rights in the UK, labelling the procedure 'a cult of death' and the number of abortions in the country 'a modern tragedy'. When questioned, he refused to agree that the right to abortion should be protected, even in cases of rape and incest—even though it later came to light that his own investment company had profited from pills used to bring about early termination of pregnancy. While MPs and campaigners were quick to call such remarks 'dangerous' and 'grotesque', the fact that such a prominent member of the government felt able to espouse this opinion publicly is revealing.[5]

In the twenty-first century the world has opened up. Before the advent of technology, travel was laborious, expensive and dangerous; but now, all it takes is the swipe of a debit card to jump on a train, bus or tube. The roads are full of cars, and we can easily cross the ocean in a motorized boat or fly over it at superspeed. Women are not legally obliged to obtain the permission of a husband, partner, religious leader or landowner to venture abroad; no one today would find it odd to come across Margery out and about without her husband. However, women with wanderlust still face more risks than men do. Experts advise women who are planning to do more than a quick trip alone to make sure they've done their research, book onto tours, reach out to other travellers and ensure they don't overpack so they can get around safely and easily. They should make sure they don't stray too far from the beaten path, don't drink too much or do too many drugs. Even hundreds of years after Margery feared for her chastity, bereft and abandoned in

Constance, women still take measures to protect themselves when they travel alone.

It would also be naïve to suggest that all the inequalities that we see in the medieval workplace have now completely vanished. While there are far more corner offices reserved for women than there used to be, and very few professions that are closed to them, there is still a split between what might be deemed stereotypically 'male' and 'female' professions, or 'hard' and 'soft' skills. More women work in retail, nursing, midwifery and early-years childcare and teaching than any other occupation; in truck and bus driving, metalwork and machinery repair, on the other hand, men dominate. Just as Marie's popular tales were devalued as frivolous fodder, we still find less value (both monetary and ideological) placed on what is considered to be women's work. And, while it is slowly closing over time, the gender pay gap is still a very real problem in the modern world; at the current estimate, it will take a few lifetimes (257 years, to be exact) to close it.[6] Moreover, women still carry out a great deal of unseen and often uncompensated labour every day. A recent study showed that, even when women work full-time, they still bear responsibility for the bulk of the household tasks, prioritizing their partners' careers over their own.[7] Once you add race into the mix, the statistics become even bleaker. Women of colour are especially underrepresented in the corporate pipeline—at nearly every step their progress falls relative to white women and men of the same ethnicity, and an overwhelming majority experience racism in their working lives.[8]

Where female friendship is concerned, we can be much more optimistic. The twenty-first century is one which increasingly applauds and celebrates female friendship, something that our four medieval women would certainly appreciate. From TV dramas like *Big Little Lies* to books like the acclaimed Elena Ferrante series, arts and culture are making room for realistic explorations of the ties that bind between women. And for good reason. Scientific research has proven the importance of female friendship to health and well-being; a UCLA study by Laura Klein and Shelley Taylor showed that women are genetically wired to befriend and help people in times of stress, whereas men are far more likely to exhibit a fight-or-flight response.[9] The average female friendship lasts 16 years, six years longer than the average romantic relationship, and engaging with female friends can even reduce cortisol and increase serotonin levels—essentially, our female friends can lower our stress, give us a feeling of general well-being and even help us fight depression.[10] Research has even indicated that women with strong friendships have higher survival rates from breast cancer than those who are isolated.[11]

Testament not only to the power of female friendship but also to the amazing things that can be achieved when women work together and support one another are two of the biggest political movements of our current times. The phrase 'Me Too' was originally coined by activist Tarana Burke but exploded into the lexicon when Alyssa Milano tweeted it in 2017 and encouraged other women who had been sexually harassed or assaulted to do the same. Within 24 hours she had accrued 12 million responses on social media, with women sharing stories and offering support to one another.[12] And the Black Lives Matter movement, which continues to be one of the most powerful programmes of reform in political history, was created by three female friends: Patrisse Cullors, Alicia Garza and Ayo Tometi. Their ever-expanding global network leads protest marches, raises awareness and affects major change, working together to achieve a world where 'Black lives are no longer systematically targeted for demise'.[13] Women's friendship, it would seem, really does have the power to change the world.

Two women who made friends (and in doing so highlighted how far we still have to go in terms of women's influence and leadership) are the former prime ministers Jacinda Ardern (New Zealand) and Sanna Marin (Finland). In a now infamous interview they faced the kind of casual sexism that women in leadership are confronted with every day.[14] Their meeting was a historic occasion as it marked New Zealand's first ever visit from a Finnish PM; they used it to discuss such weighty topics as Russia's invasion of Ukraine and their concerns about a crackdown on protestors for women's rights in Iran. Afterwards they held a press conference, during which a male journalist asked: 'Are you two meeting just because you're similar in age and have got a lot of common stuff—or can Kiwis actually expect to see more deals between our countries down the line?' Ardern, visibly incredulous, responded by wondering aloud 'whether or not anyone ever asked Barack Obama and [former New Zealand prime minister] John Key if they met because they were of similar age'. She continued: 'We of course have a higher proportion of men in politics, it's reality. Because two women meet, it's not simply because of their gender.' In the Middle Ages it would have been rare for women to wield the kind of authority that a modern prime minister does. However, the misogyny that Ardern and Marin faced from the press is evidence of how much harder women must still work to be taken seriously.

Ardern was no stranger to everyday sexism during her term as prime minister. When she announced she was pregnant, three months after being sworn in, the global media went into frenzy, with many commentators wondering if she would be up to the task while also being a new mother. It's impossible to find any corresponding stories for male politicians with similar announcements, and the endless scrutiny caused Jacinda to comment in frustration: 'I'm pregnant, not incapacitated.'[15] And then, when she announced that she was stepping down from her position, the BBC ran the story with this headline: 'Can women have it all?' Such a choice of words inspired a swift and angry backlash. Readers compared the headline with parallel, ungendered coverage of the resignation of other politicians, such as Boris Johnson, and accused the BBC of 'staggering sexism' and 'misogyny'.[16]

The headline also exposed an enduring suspicion of women who try to 'have it all'. For most women, juggling different roles remains challenging. Nearly two-thirds of mothers feel driven to exhaustion by the pressure to be a 'supermum', and other studies have shown that women working part-time are far more likely to experience an increase in their home duties—from childcare to housework—than men.[17] The campaign Pregnant Then Screwed shows that, for women in the UK, a return to work may not be financially possible because childcare is so disproportionately expensive.[18] And although new policies to support women, such as paid maternity leave, annual leave, flexible working and working from home, have been introduced across the globe, women find a work–life balance much harder to achieve than men, because of the pressures from their employers and the media, as well as from the expectations they place on themselves. Christine—who found it so much easier to write when her husband died and her children left home—and Julian—who shut herself away from the world in order to think and write—would surely have been sympathetic.

Death is, of course, the great equalizer (or so they say) and is as inevitable today as it was hundreds of years ago. There are still wars, and terrible diseases we do not know the cause of and cannot cure; people still go hungry and thirsty; people still kill each other. The Middle Ages may have a reputation for violence, but they do not have a monopoly on death. However, for a myriad of different reasons, death was more visible and more anticipated for the average medieval person than it is for us today. And, for this reason, there is a lot that we can learn from them about how to cope with mortality. Naturally, many did crumple in despair at the loss of friends and family and found it hard to find ways to go on living without them. But they also found ways to navigate their grief, and to come out the other side in a new reality.

We all want a good death. Huge quantities of ink are still being spilled on self-help books that promise to help us face the end without fear, much in the vein of the medieval *Ars Moriendi*. For those of us left behind, writing can help process our grief, as it did for Christine. And imagining the lives of others enables us to become more empathetic and motivated to actively find ways of easing suffering, just as Margery and Julian strengthened their faith by inserting themselves into scenes from Christ's life and death, even forcing themselves to imagine what his pain and suffering must have felt like. These visions and meditations helped them to confront and come to terms with—even look forward to—the idea of their own death and virtual reality is now being wielded in a similar vein. In 2023 a new 'death simulator' was released that reportedly shows participants what it looks and feels like to die. The hope of Shaun Gladwell, the artist behind the platform, is that it will help ease the fears and anxieties surrounding death and dying.

As well as fears about death, we can see enduring preoccupations with how—or if—we will be remembered when we're gone. In different ways, our four women all hoped to make history. If they visited us today, how many traces of themselves would they find?

Marie de France signed her name in every book she wrote, an unusual practice for the time. Clearly, she wanted to be remembered. While the details of her own life are frustratingly elusive, her *lais* are memorably vivid and larger than life, including surprising representations of women and reversals of gender norms. Can we think of Marie as the mother to all the new retellings and queerings of timeless legends and folk tales? Authors from Angela Carter to Emma Donoghue and Karrie Fransman, who have turned fairy tales on their head for modern readers, surely owe a debt to the medieval writer who paved their way.

Though Christianity may be on the decline in Britain, Christians still look to Julian of Norwich for comfort and inspiration. During lockdown, her writings were re-popularized as people sought out coping mechanisms for dealing with isolation and boredom, and her most famous saying, 'All shall be well and all shall be well and all manner of thing shall be well', has become a mantra of comfort for many readers, secular as well as religious. Her words live on in the poetry of T. S. Eliot, W. B. Yeats and, more recently, in Maria Dahvana Headley's *The Mere Wife*, a feminist retelling of a medieval epic.

Anyone in the West who has written or engaged with feminist theory and literature, or who has written back to misogyny in any form, has Christine de Pizan to thank. 'Remember', she tells her female readers, 'how these men call you frail, unserious, and easily influenced but yet try hard, using all kinds of strange and deceptive tricks, to catch you, just as one lays traps for wild animals.' Her tool of the dream vision may have been set aside in favour of everything from comics (such as Emma's *The Mental Load*) to menstrual art (such as Sarah Levy's portrait of Donald Trump produced in response to his apparent disgust at women's monthly bleed), but the need to write back against sexism remains. It is women like Christine who paved the way for us to do so.

And what of Margery, the medieval misfit who, according to her contemporaries and twenty-first-century reviewers, is weird, irritating or 'crazy'? She teaches us that if the shoe doesn't fit, you shouldn't try and squeeze your foot into it. Forge your own path, make a new kind of shoe—or don't wear one at all. And don't pay any attention to what others have to say about it. For, as God says to Margery in one of her visions, 'You shall not take heed of their scorn, just let every person say as they wish.' Or, in other words: haters gonna hate.

The writing of these four extraordinary women continues to stand the test of time. We'll never know how many other medieval women hoped to craft a legacy by putting quill to parchment, only to have their words lost or their names forgotten. But, thanks to Marie, Julian, Christine and Margery, we know that they did exist. Undeterred by the obstacles in their path, or by the limitations placed on them by society, our poet, mystic, widow and wife all managed to make their voices heard. By listening to what they have to say, paying attention to what they have to tell us, we can learn more about their world, hundreds of years ago—and also, perhaps, our own.

ACKNOWLEDGEMENTS

Writing this book has been a dream come true. It has also been ever so slightly harder than I expected, due to my beautiful baby daughter arriving in the middle of the process. I learned very quickly that babies don't just smile beatifically in a bouncer next to you while you jiggle them with a casual foot and get your work done. And so there are a lot of people to thank, and I'll use baby brain as an excuse for the inevitable errors in this book. They're all my own, I'm sure.

Thanks first to my agent, Matt Turner, who heard me talking about Margery Kempe on the radio and got in touch to ask me if I'd ever thought about writing a book (the answer: only every day since I was old enough to know what a book was). *Poet, Mystic, Widow, Wife* wouldn't exist without his expertise and guiding hand. Thanks to everyone at Bloomsbury and University of California Press for being so flexible and kind when things got challenging. Especial thanks to Tomasz Hoskins, who always made the process feel like fun. I am grateful for his careful eye, his sensitive readings and his good humour. To Eric Schmidt for his belief in the project, and his enthusiasm. To Octavia Stocker, who immediately 'got' the book (and me!) and kept me inspired and energized while offering invaluable insight. To Sarah Jones for her careful project management. To the marketing and publicity teams (and especially Lizzy Ewer) for getting behind the book and creating so many exciting opportunities for me. And to the amazing designers for creating two book covers I love.

Thanks must also go to Patrick Brindle, Sarah Bowen, Robyn Read and Minna Vuohelainen for their mentorship. To Adrian Armstrong who kindly sourced various quotations for me when I couldn't get to the library with baby. To my supervisor, Julia Boffey, and her husband, Tony Edwards, for their endless support and kindness (and for fielding so many last-minute panicked questions as my deadline loomed closer). To my wonderful students at City, University of London—I learn something new from them every day. To my family and my husband's family, who were so quick to offer childcare to help me get the book finished. To James Watson and Louise

Roberts for taking such good care of me post-baby and for being such wonderful friends. To my grandparents, who are so strong and steadfast. To my exceptional mum and dad, Ruth and Nigel, who have always been my fiercest defenders and loudest cheerleaders, and who make me feel like I can achieve anything. To my incredible husband, Stuart, who put everything on hold to make sure I could get my writing done and whose positivity and enthusiasm have kept me going. I love you. And to all the extraordinary women in my life—Phoebe Bozeat, Helen Dalton, Vicki Grahame, Wendy Grahame, Lucy Holton, Andrea Koenker, Rosie Langridge, Jen Ridgway, Louise Roberts, Christie Scott, Georgia Smith, Emily Walsh and Rachel Waring, to name but a few. My supportive and generous-hearted NCT group. Taylor Swift, who provides the soundtrack to everything I write. My mother-in-law, Margaret, who I admire so much and who I'm lucky to call my friend. Clare, my lobster—you are brave and beautiful, and you make everything better. My creative and inspirational mum, who always encourages me to reach for the stars. And my baby girl, Alana, who changed my world. I hope I've made you proud!

NOTES

INTRODUCTION

The epigraph is taken from *The Writings of Julian of Norwich: 'A Vision Showed to a Devout Woman' and 'A Revelation of Love'*, ed. Nicholas Watson and Jacqueline Jenkins (Philadelphia, PA: University of Pennsylvania Press, 2006), 6.36–8.

1. *The Book of Margery Kempe*, trans. and ed. Barry Windeatt (London: Penguin, 1985), p. 127. The opening anecdote is taken from pp. 122–30.

2. E. Miller, 'Medieval York: The 12th and 13th Centuries', in *A History of Yorkshire: The City of York*, ed. P. M. Tillot (London: Victoria County History, 1961), p. 107.

3. *'Women's Secrets': A Translation of Pseudo-Albertus Magnus's 'De Secretus Mulierum', with Commentaries*, ed. Helen Rodnite Lemay (New York: SUNY Press, 1992), p. 48.

4. Aristotle, *Generation of Animals*, trans. A. L. Peck (Cambridge, MA: Harvard University Press, 1953), 729 A 25–34 and 727 B 10–25. For a useful summary of Aristotle's theory and how it pertains to conceptions of gender, see Ian Maclean, *The Renaissance Notion of Woman: A Study in the Fortunes of Scholasticism and Medical Science in European Intellectual Life* (Cambridge: Cambridge University Press, 1980), p. 8.

5. Isidorus Hispalensis, *Etymologiarum sive originum libri XX*, ed. W. M. Lindsay, 2 vols. (Oxford: Oxford University Press, 1911), Book VII, Chapter 1, p. 141.

6. *'Women's Secrets'*, p. 68.

7. Proverbs, 7.10–12, Holy Bible, Douay Rheims Version.

8. Largely translated in *Women in England, 1275–1525*, ed. P. J. P. Goldberg (Manchester: Manchester University Press, 1995), pp. 141–2.

9. Tertullian, 'On the Apparel of Women', in *The Ante-Nicene Fathers*, ed. Alexander Roberts and James Donaldson, vol. 4 (Buffalo, NY: Christian Literature Publishing Co., 1885), 4:14.

10. *The Book of Margery Kempe*, trans. and ed. Barry Windeatt, p. 27.

11. Marie de France, *The Lais of Marie de France*, ed. Keith Busby, trans. Glyn Burgess (London: Penguin, 1999).

12. Marie de France, 'The Fables' and 'Espurgatoire de Seint Patriz', in *Marie de France: Poetry*, ed. and trans. Dorothy Gilbert (London: W. W. Norton, 2015), pp. 175–240.

13. Marie de France, *Lais*, ed. Busby, trans. Burgess, p. 41.

14. Julian of Norwich, 'Short Text', in *The Writings of Julian of Norwich: A Vision Showed to a Devout Woman and A Revelation of Love*, ed. Nicholas Watson and Jacqueline Jenkins (Turnhout: Brepols, 2006), 6.36.

15. Julian of Norwich, 'Long Text', *Revelations of Divine Love*, ed. and trans. Barry Windeatt (Oxford: Oxford University Press, 2015), p. 74.

16. Christine de Pizan, *The Book of the City of Ladies*, ed. and trans. Rosalind Brown-Grant (London: Penguin, 1999).

17. *The Book of Margery Kempe*, ed. Lynn Staley (Kalamazoo, MI: Medieval Institute Publications, 1998), p. 290.

ONE: KNOCKED UP

The epigraph is from *The Book of Margery Kempe*, ed. Staley, p. 21.

1. *The Book of Margery Kempe*, ed. and trans. Windeatt, p. 11.

2. Tertullian, 'On the Apparel of Women', 4:14.

3. John Lydgate, 'A Balade in Commendation of Our Lady', in *Chaucerian and Other Pieces*, ed. Walter William Skeat (Oxford: Clarendon Press, 1897), pp. 275–80.

4. Emma Maggie Solberg, *Virgin Whore* (New York: Cornell University Press, 2018), p. 106.

5. Solberg, *Virgin Whore*, p. 38.

6. See Joan Cadden, *Meanings of Sex Difference in the Middle Ages: Medicine, Science, and Culture* (Cambridge: Cambridge University Press, 1993), particularly p. 184.

7. 'Women's Secrets', p. 65.

8. Christine de Pizan, *Book of the City of Ladies*, p. 21.

9. Solberg, *Virgin Whore*, p. 38.

10. 'Nativity', in *The N-Town Plays*, ed. Douglas Sugano (Kalamazoo, MI: Medieval Institute Publications, 2007), ll. 211–12 and 305–6, my translation.

11. 'Women's Secrets', p. 69, and John Trevisa, *On the Properties of Things*, ed. M. Seymour (Oxford: Clarendon Press, 1988), p. 296.

12. *The Trotula: An English Translation of the Medieval Compendium of Women's Medicine*, ed. and trans. Monica Green (Philadelphia, PA: University of Pennsylvania Press, 2002).

13. See Christine McCann, 'Fertility, Control and Society in Medieval Europe', *Comitatus*, 40 (2009), 45–62.

14. 'Women's Secrets', pp. 129–31.

15. See Kristen L. Geaman, 'Anne of Bohemia and Her Struggle to Conceive', *Social History of Medicine*, 29:2 (2016), 224–44.

16. 'Hali Meidhad', in *Medieval English Prose for Women*, ed. Bella Millett and Jocelyn Wogan–Browne (Oxford: Clarendon, 1990), pp. 31–3.

17. Christine de Pizan, *The Treasure of the City of Ladies*, ed. and trans. Sarah Lawson (London: Penguin, 2003), p. 137 and Chapter 2, n. 3.

18. Katherine French, 'The Material Culture of Childbirth in Late Medieval London and Its Suburbs', *Journal of Women's History*, 28:2 (2016), 126–48 (p. 131).

19. French, 'The Material Culture of Childbirth', p. 128.

20. Christine de Pizan, *Treasure of the City of Ladies*, pp. 137–8.

21. Rachel M. Delman, 'Gendered Viewing, Childbirth and Female Authority in the Residence of Alice Chaucer, Duchess of Suffolk, at Ewelme, Oxfordshire', *Journal of Medieval History*, 45:2 (2019), 181–203 (p. 184).

22. *Calendar of Inquisitions Post Mortem and Other Analogous Documents Preserved in the Public Record Office*, 20 vols. (London: HMSO, 1904–95), 7:485.

23. Heldris de Cornauille, *Le Roman de Silence*, ed. Lewis Thorpe (Cambridge: Heffer, 1972), ll. 2000–08. English translation by Peggy McCracken in *The Curse of Eve, the Wound of the Hero: Blood, Gender, and Medieval Literature* (Philadelphia, PA: University of Pennsylvania Press, 2003), p. 85.

24. 'Hali Meidhad', in *Medieval English Prose for Women*, ed. Millett and Wogan-Browne, pp. 31–3.

25. *The Trotula*, 102–3.

26. 'The Sickness of Women', in *Sex, Aging and Death in a Medieval Medical Compendium*, ed. M. T. Tavormina (Binghamton: SUNY Press, 2006), pp. 455–568 (p. 532). 'Tomida femina' is entered in the margin of an anonymous fifth-century *interpretatio* of the *Sententiae* of Iulius Paulus.

27. Cambridge University Library, MS Dd.V.53, fol. 107r–v. Translation from Peter Murray Jones and Lea T. Olsan, 'Performative Rituals for Conception and Childbirth in England 900–1500', *Bulletin of the History of Medicine*, 89:3 (2015), 406–33 (p. 421).

28. Wellcome Collection Western MS 632.

29. Thomas Cranmer, *Book of Common Prayer* (London, 1549), p. 9. For Sarum Rite, see Joanna M. Pierce, '"Green Women" and Blood Pollution: Some Medieval Rituals for the Churching of Women after Childbirth', *Studia Liturgica*, 29:2 (1999), 191–215 (p. 203).

30. *The Trotula*, p. 93.

31. Wellcome Collection, Western MS 632.

32. For a full account of Isabel's childbirth story, see Alice-Viktoria Dulmovits, 'Unseen Heirs: Written Traces of Pregnant Widows and Posthumous Children in Early Modern Spain, c.1490–1673', *Hipogrifo*, 6:1 (2018), 433–49.

33. 'Le Fresne', in Marie de France, *Lais*, ed. Busby, trans. Burgess, pp. 61–8.

34. *The Trotula*, p. 91.

35. Augustine of Hippo, *Treatises on Marriage and Other Subjects*, ed. and trans. Roy J. Defferari (Washington, DC: Catholic University of America Press), p. 13.

36. Geoffrey Chaucer, 'The Parson's Tale', in *The Canterbury Tales*, Harvard University Interlinear Translation, https://chaucer.fas.harvard.edu/pages

/parsons-prologue-and-tale [accessed 25 March 2024]. Caesarius of Arles, *Sermons*, trans. and ed. Mary Magdaleine Mueller (New York: Fathers of the Church, 1956–[1973]), p. 222.

37. *The Trotula*, pp. 76–7.

38. 'Hali Meidhad', in *Medieval English Prose for Women*, ed. Millett and Wogan-Browne, p. 23.

39. 'Single Women's Lament', in *Medieval Writings on Secular Women*, ed. Patricia Skinner and Elisabeth van Houts (London: Penguin, 2011), pp. 102–4.

40. William of Conches, *Dragmaticon Philosophiae* (Turnhout: Brepols, 1997), VI, 8.9.

TWO: TIED DOWN

The epigraph is from *The Book of Margery Kempe*, ed. Staley, p. 37.

1. Christine de Pizan, *Book of the City of Ladies*, pp. 4–7.

2. Christine de Pizan, *Book of the City of Ladies*, p. 9.

3. British Library, Harley MS 4431.

4. Christine de Pizan, *Book of the City of Ladies*, pp. 108–9.

5. Shannon McSheffrey, *Marriage, Sex, and Civil Culture in Late Medieval London* (Philadelphia, PA: University of Pennsylvania Press, 2006), p. 25.

6. Jean d'Arras, *Melusine, or The Noble History of Lusignan*, trans. and ed. Donald Maddox and Sara Sturm-Maddox (Philadelphia, PA: Pennsylvania University State Press, 2012), p. 43.

7. *Select Cases from the Ecclesiastical Courts of the Province of Canterbury*, ed. Norma Adams and Charles Donahue (London: Selden, 1981), no. D2, pp. 350–65.

8. Christine de Pizan, *Christine's Vision*, ed. and trans. Glenda K. McLeod (London: Routledge, 2018), p. 110.

9. Christine de Pizan, *Christine's Vision*, p. 110.

10. *The Paston Women: Selected Letters*, ed. and trans. Diane Watt (Woodbridge: D. S. Brewer, 2004), pp. 127–8.

11. *The Paston Women*, ed. and trans. Watt, pp. 122–3.

12. The following quotes are taken from 'Bisclavret', in Marie de France, *Lais*, ed. Busby, trans. Burgess, pp. 68–72.

13. Christine de Pizan, *Treasure of the City of Ladies*, p. 38.

14. *Select Cases of Trespass from the King's Courts 1307–1399*, vol. 1, ed. and trans. Morris S. Arnold, Selden Society, vol. 100 (1985), p. 80, no. 8.6.

15. *The Register of John Chandler Dean of Salisbury 1404–17*, ed. C. B. Timmins, vol. 39 (Devizes: Wiltshire Record Society, 1984), pp. 112–13, no. 315.

16. *Paston Letters and Papers of the Fifteenth Century*, ed. Norman Davis, 2 vols. (Oxford: Clarendon Press, 1971 and 1976), p. 861, ll. 3–19.

17. *The Paston Women*, ed. and trans. Watt, pp. 96–7.

18. *Paston Letters*, ed. Davis, p. 332, ll. 11–16.

19. Christine de Pizan, *Book of the City of Ladies*, p. 239.

20. The following quotations are taken from 'The Wife of Bath's Prologue', in Geoffrey Chaucer, *Canterbury Tales,* Harvard Interlinear Translation, https://chaucer.fas.harvard.edu/pages/wife-baths-prologue-and-tale-o [accessed 23 March 2024].

21. Jeffrey Richards, *Sex, Dissidence and Damnation: Minority Groups in the Middle Ages* (New York: Routledge, 1994), pp. 23–4, and James A. Brundage, *Law, Sex, and Christian Society in Medieval Europe* (Chicago, IL: The University of Chicago Press, 1987), p. 448.

22. *The Book of the Knight of the Tower,* trans. William Caxton (London: Oxford University Press, 1971), p. 35.

23. *Knight of the Tower*, p. 21.

24. Translated in *Women in England,* ed. Goldberg, pp. 141–2.

25. This and the following quotations are from 'Hali Meidhad', in *Medieval English Prose for Women*, ed. Millett and Wogan-Browne, pp. 27–9.

26. *The Life of Christina of Markyate*, trans. C.H. Talbot (Oxford: Oxford University Press, 2008), p. 9.

27. *The Life of Christina of Markyate*, p. 21.

28. *The Life of Christina of Markyate*, p. 16.

29. *Book of Margery Kempe*, ed. and trans. Windeatt, p. 27.

30. G. Geis, 'Lord Hale, Witches and Rape', *British Journal of Law and Society*, 5:1 (1978), 26–44 (p. 40).

31. *Book of Margery Kempe*, ed. and trans. Windeatt, pp. 16, 73 and 183.

32. *Book of Margery Kempe*, ed. and trans. Windeatt, p. 15.

33. *Book of Margery Kempe*, ed. and trans. Windeatt, p. 88.

THREE: BIT ON THE SIDE

The epigraph is from *The Lais of Marie de France: Text and Translation*, ed. and trans. Claire M. Waters (Ontario: Broadview Press, 2018), p. 276.

1. See *Annales Cambriae*, ed. John Williams (Cambridge: Cambridge University Press, 2012), and *Nennii Historia Brittonum,* ed. Joseph Stevenson (London, 1838).

2. Geoffrey of Monmouth, *The History of the Kings of Britain*, ed. and trans. Lewis Thorpe (London: Penguin, 1973).

3. 'The Knight of the Cart', in *Chrétien de Troyes: Arthurian Romances*, ed. and trans. William W. Kibler (London: Penguin, 2004).

4. Thomas Malory, *Le Morte d'Arthur*, ed. Stephen H.A. Shepherd (London: W.W. Norton, 2003).

5. Oxford English Dictionary online edn., 2023, 1a, https://www.oed.com/dictionary/adultery_n?tab = meaning_and_use#10027167 [accessed 19 March 2024].

6. 'Women's Secrets', p. 48.

7. *Lower Ecclesiastical Jurisdiction in Late-Medieval England: The Courts of the Dean and Chapter of Lincoln, 1336–1349, and the Deanery of Wisbech, 1458–1484,* ed. Lawrence Raymond Poos (Oxford: Oxford University Press, 2001), p. 219.

8. Andreas Capellanus, *The Art of Courtly Love*, ed. and trans. John Jay Parry (New York: Columbia University Press, 1960), pp. 177–86 and p. 149.

9. Christine de Pizan, *Treasure of the City of Ladies*, p. 51.

10. The following quotations are taken from 'Equitan', in Marie de France, *Lais*, ed. Busby, trans. Burgess, pp. 56–60.

11. Tracy Adams, 'Between History and Fiction: Revisiting the *Affaire de la Tour de Nesle*', *Viator*, 43:2 (2012), 165–92 (p. 192).

12. Elizabeth A. R. Brown, 'Philip the Fair of France and His Family's Disgrace: The Adultery Scandal of 1314 Revealed, Recounted, Reimagined, and Redated', *Mediaevistik*, 32 (2019), 71–103 (p. 81).

13. Adams, 'Between History and Fiction', p. 170.

14. Adams, 'Between History and Fiction', p. 170.

15. Brown, 'Philip the Fair and His Family's Disgrace', p. 73.

16. Adams, 'Between History and Fiction', p. 171.

17. Adams, 'Between History and Fiction', p. 180.

18. *'Women's Secrets'*, p. 129.

19. Heinrich Kramer and James Sprenger, *Malleus Maleficarum*, trans. and ed. Montague Summers (New York: Dover, 1971), p. 47.

20. Archivio Storico Diocesano di Lucca, Tribunale ecclesiastico, Cause criminali, vol. 13 (1359), fols 14r–15v.

21. *Book of Margery Kempe*, ed. and trans. Windeatt, p. 18.

22. The following quotations are from *The Book of Margery Kempe*, ed. and trans. Windeatt, pp. 17–18.

23. Guillaume de Lorris and Jean de Meun, *The Romance of the Rose*, ed. and trans. Charles Dahlberg, 3rd edn. (Princeton, NJ: Princeton University Press, 1995).

24. *The Romance of the Rose*, p. 323.

25. *The Romance of the Rose*, p. 165.

26. Christine de Pizan et al., *The Debate of the Romance of the Rose*, ed. and trans. David Hult (London: University of Chicago Press, 2010), pp. 18 and 20–21.

27. Christine de Pizan, *Book of the City of Ladies*, p. 172.

28. Christine de Pizan, *Book of the City of Ladies*, p. 110.

29. Christine de Pizan, *Book of the City of Ladies*, p. 126.

30. The following quotations are taken from Chaucer, 'The Miller's Tale', in *Canterbury Tales,* Harvard Interlinear Translation, https://chaucer.fas.harvard .edu/pages/millers-prologue-and-tale [accessed 25 March 2024].

31. Judith Bennett, '"Lesbian-Like" and the Social History of Lesbianisms', *Journal of the History of Sexuality*, 9:1/2 (2000), 1–24 (pp. 18–19).

32. Jean Gerson, 'Confessional ou directoire des confesseurs', in *Oeuvres complètes de Jean Gerson*, ed. Palémon Glorieux (Paris: Desclée, 1960), 1:85.

33. Hildegard of Bingen, *Scivias*, trans. Columba Hart and Jane Bishop (New York: Paulist Press, 1990), p. 279.

34. See Helen Rodnite Lemay, 'William of Saliceto on Human Sexuality', *Viator*, 12 (1981), 165–82 (pp. 177–8).

35. Étienne de Fougères, 'Le livre de manieres'. Translation by Robert L. A. Clark can be found in Jacqueline Murray, 'Twice Marginal and Twice Invisible: Lesbians in the Middle Ages', in *Handbook of Medieval Sexuality*, ed. Vern L. Bullough and James Brundage (London: Routledge, 1996), pp. 191–222 (p. 210).

36. Helmut Puff, 'Female Sodomy: The Trial of Katherina Hetzeldorfer', *Journal of Medieval and Early Modern Studies*, 30:1 (2000), 41–61.

37. Letters translated by Peter Dronke, *Medieval Latin and the Rise of the European Love Lyric*, vol. 2 (Oxford: Clarendon Press, 1968), pp. 479–80.

FOUR: WANDERLUST

The epigraph is from Geoffrey Chaucer, 'The Wife of Bath's Prologue and Tale'.

1. *Book of Margery Kempe*, ed. and trans. Windeatt, p. 64.

2. *Book of Margery Kempe,* ed. and trans. Windeatt, p. 68.

3. *Book of Margery Kempe*, ed. and trans. Windeatt, p. 64.

4. *Book of Margery Kempe*, ed. and trans. Windeatt, p. 29.

5. Felix Fabri, *The Book of the Wanderings of Brother Felix Fabri*, trans. and ed. Aubrey Stewart (London: Hanover, 1896), p. 3.

6. *Book of Margery Kempe*, ed. and trans. Windeatt, p. 101.

7. Fabri, *Book of Wanderings*, p. 10.

8. Anthony Bale, *A Travel Guide to the Middle Ages* (London: Viking, 2023), p. 136.

9. Fabri, *Book of Wanderings*, p. 8.

10. *Codex Calixtinus,* https://alumniacademy.yale.edu/sites/default/files/2020-07/Codex%20Calixtinus.pdf [accessed 19 March 2024].

11. H. P. Cholmeley, *John of Gaddesden and the Rosa Medicinae* (Oxford: Clarendon, 1912), p. 525.

12. William Wey, *The Itineraries of William Wey* (London: Nichols and Sons, 1857).

13. Matthew Paris, *Chronica Majora*, ed. H. R. Luard (London, 1872–3).

14. Fabri, *Book of Wanderings*, p. 124.

15. See Bale, *A Travel Guide to the Middle Ages*, pp. 127–30.

16. Bale, *A Travel Guide to the Middle Ages*, p. 100.

17. *Healing and Society in Medieval England: A Middle English Translation of the Pharmaceutical Writings of Gilbertus Anglicus*, ed. Faye M. Getz (Madison, WI: University of Wisconsin Press, 2010).

18. *Book of Margery Kempe*, ed. and trans. Windeatt, p. 236.

19. *Book of Margery Kempe*, ed. and trans. Windeatt, p. 245.

20. John Mandeville, *Book of Marvels and Travels* (London: Digireads, 2020).

21. Fabri, *Book of Wanderings*, p. 12.

22. Proverbs, 7:10–12, Holy Bible, Douay Rheims Version.

23. Chaucer, 'Wife of Bath's Prologue', *Canterbury Tales,* Harvard Interlinear Translation, https://chaucer.fas.harvard.edu/pages/millers-prologue-and-tale [accessed 24 March 2024].

24. *The Fifteen Joys of Marriage*, ed. and trans. Elisabeth Abbot (London: Orion, 1959).

25. Christine de Pizan, *Treasure of the City of Ladies*, pp. 135–6.

26. Christine de Pizan, *The Epistle of the Prison of Human Life*, trans. Josette A. Wisman (New York: Garland, 1984), pp. 94–5.

27. The following quotations are from 'Laustic', in Marie de France, *Lais*, ed. Busby, trans. Burgess, pp. 94–7.

28. David Carpenter, *The Struggle for Mastery* (London: Penguin, 2003), p. 192.

29. Fabri, *Book of Wanderings*, p. 207.

30. Fabri, *Book of Wanderings*, pp. 176–7.

31. Anne E. Bailey, 'Flights of Distance, Time and Fancy: Women Pilgrims and Their Journeys in English Medieval Miracle Narratives', *Gender and History*, 24:2 (2012), 292–309 (p. 303).

32. Fabri, *Book of Wanderings*, p. 12.

33. Leigh Ann Craig, *Wandering Women and Holy Matrons: Women as Pilgrims in the Later Middle Ages* (Leiden: Brill, 2009), p. 172.

34. Craig, *Wandering Women*, p. 172.

35. Margaret of Beverley's story can be read at https://www.umilta.net/jerusalem.html [accessed 19 March 2024].

36. Fabri, *Book of Wanderings*, pp. 166–7.

37. Fabri, *Book of Wanderings*, p. 190.

38. The following quotations are from *Book of Margery Kempe*, ed. and trans. Windeatt, pp. 66–7.

39. Fabri, *Book of Wanderings*, p. 250.

40. *Codex Calixtinus.*

41. Fabri, *Book of Wanderings*, p. 250.

42. *Airs, Waters, Places*, in *Hippocrates*, trans. W. H. S. Jones (London: Heinemann, 1923), p. 24.

43. Cadden, *The Meaning of Sex*, pp. 163–4.

44. Mandeville, *Book of Marvels and Travels*, p. 93, and Marco Polo, *The Travels*, trans. and ed. Nigel Cliff (London: Penguin, 2015), p. 87 (italics added).

45. Bale, *A Travel Guide to the Middle Ages*, p. 115.

46. This and the following quotations are from *Book of Margery Kempe*, ed. and trans. Windeatt, pp. 104–5.

FIVE: HUSTLING

The epigraph is from *The Lais of Marie de France*, ed. and trans. Waters, p. 50.

1. Christine de Pizan, *Christine's Vision*, pp. 111–12.

2. Boethius, *The Consolation of Philosophy of Boethius*, trans. H. R. James (London, 1897).

3. Christine de Pizan, *Christine's Vision*, pp. 111–12.

4. Deidre Jackson, 'Picturing Work', in *A Cultural History of Work in the Medieval Age*, ed. Valerie L. Garver (London: Bloomsbury, 2019), pp. 31–64 (p. 58).

5. Christine de Pizan, *Book of the City of Ladies*, p. 76.

6. *Book of Margery Kempe*, ed. and trans. Windeatt, p. 132.

7. Giovanni Boccaccio, *Concerning Famous Women*, trans. and ed. Guido Guarino (New Brunswick, NJ: Rutgers University Press, 1963), p. 220.

8. Boccaccio, *Concerning Famous Women*, p. 188.

9. Christine de Pizan, *Book of the City of Ladies*, p. 29.

10. Caroline M. Barron, 'The "Golden Age" of Women in Medieval London', in *Medieval London: Collected Papers of Caroline M. Barron* (Kalamazoo, MI: Medieval Institute Publications, 2017), pp. 361–84.

11. Boccaccio, *The Decameron*, trans. J. M. Rigg (London: Digireads, 2018), p. 1353.

12. 'The Ballad of the Tyrannical Husband', trans. P. J. P. Goldberg, https://www.york.ac.uk/teaching/history/pjpg/BALLAD.htm#[1] [accessed 20 March 2024].

13. Christine de Pizan, *Treasure of the City of Ladies*, pp. 112–14, 154.

14. *Book of Margery Kempe*, ed. and trans. Windeatt, p. 13.

15. *Book of Margery Kempe*, ed. and trans. Windeatt, p. 14.

16. For more on women and brewing in the Middle Ages, see Judith M. Bennett, *Ale, Beer and Brewsters in England* (Oxford: Oxford University Press, 1999).

17. This and the following quotations about brewing and milling are from *Book of Margery Kempe*, ed. and trans. Windeatt, p. 14.

18. *Book of Margery Kempe*, ed. and trans. Windeatt, p. 15.

19. 'Madame Eglentyne: Chaucer's Prioress in Real Life', in Eileen Power, *Medieval People* (London: Routledge, 1999), p. 110.

20. This and the following quotations are taken from Chaucer, 'General Prologue', *Canterbury Tales,* Harvard Interlinear Translation, https://chaucer.fas.harvard.edu/pages/general-prologue-0 [accessed 24 March 2024].

21. 'Madame Eglentyne', in Power, *Medieval People*, p. 109.

22. *Ancrene Wisse*, ed. Robert Hasenfratz (Kalamazoo, MI: Medieval Institute Publications, 2000), and 'De institutione inclusarum', in *Aelredi Rievallensis, Opera Omnia*, ed. A. Hoste and C. H. Talbot (Turnhout: Brepols, 1971).

23. Introduction to *Ancrene Wisse*, ed. Hasenfratz, n. 37.

24. Cambridge, Corpus Christi College, MS 402, fol. 69r/27–8, 20–21: *The English Text of the 'Ancrene Riwle': 'Ancrene Wisse', edited from MS Corpus Christi College Cambridge 402*, ed. J. R. R. Tolkien (London: Oxford University Press, 1962).

25. *Aelred of Rievaulx's 'De Institutione Inclusarum': Two English Versions*, ed. John Ayto and Alexandra Barratt (Oxford: Oxford University Press, 1984),

p. 8, my translation, and for *Speculum Inclusorum*, see E. A. Jones, *Hermits and Anchorites in England, 1200–1500* (Manchester: Manchester University Press, 2019), pp. 76–8.

26. *Ancrene Wisse, Guide for Anchoresses: A Translation*, ed. and trans. Bella Millett (Exeter: University of Exeter Press, 2009), p. 101.

27. *Ancrene Wisse,* ed. and trans. Millett, p. 56.

28. See John W. Baldwin, 'The Image of the Jongleur in Northern France around 1200', *Speculum*, 72:3 (1997), 635–63.

29. Marie de France, *Lais*, ed. Busby, trans. Burgess, p. 41 (my emphasis).

30. Marie de France, *Lais*, ed. Busby, trans. Burgess, p. 41.

31. Marie de France, *Lais*, ed. Busby, trans. Burgess, p. 43.

32. Denis Piramus, *La Vie Seint Edmund le Rei*, ed. H. Kjellman (Gothenburg, 1935), p. 42.

33. William S. Woods, 'Femininity in the "Lais" of Marie de France', *Studies in Philology*, 47:1 (1950), 1–19 (p. 1).

34. Kate Lister, 'The Bishop's Profitable Sex Workers', *Wellcome,* https://wellcomecollection.org/articles/WxEniCQAACQAvmUE [accessed 21 March 2024].

35. Lister, 'The Bishop's Profitable Sex Workers'.

36. Jamie Page, 'Inside the Medieval Brothel', *History Today*, 69:6 (2019), https://www.historytoday.com/archive/feature/inside-medieval-brothel [accessed 21 March 2024].

37. For this translation, see Marion Turner, *The Wife of Bath: A Biography* (Oxford: Oxford University Press, 2023), pp. 68–9.

SIX: MAKING FRIENDS . . .

The epigraph is from *The Book of Margery Kempe*, ed. Staley, p. 18.

1. The meeting of Julian of Norwich and Margery Kempe can be found in *Book of Margery Kempe*, ed. and trans. Windeatt, pp. 45–7.

2. *Book of Margery Kempe*, ed. and trans. Windeatt, p. 37.

3. Cicero, 'De amicitia', in *Cicero de senectute, de amicitia, de divinatione*, trans. William Armistead Falconer (Cambridge, MA: Harvard University Press, 2001), p. 133, 189.

4. 'A Medieval Guide to Friendship', Medievalists.net, https://www.medievalists.net/2014/02/medieval-guide-friendship/ [accessed 21 March 2024].

5. Aelred of Rievaulx, *'De institutione inclusarum': Two English Versions*, ed. Ayto and Barratt, pp. 1–2, my translation.

6. 'A Talk of Ten Wives on Their Husbands' Ware', in *The Trials and Joys of Marriage*, ed. Eve Salisbury (Kalamazoo, MI: Medieval Institute Publications, 2002).

7. William Dunbar, 'Two Married Women', in *The Trials and Joys of Marriage*, ed. Salisbury.

8. Christine de Pizan, *Book of the City of Ladies*, p. 8.

9. Christine de Pizan, *Book of the City of Ladies*, pp. 229–30.

10. Christine de Pizan, *Book of the City of Ladies*, p. 56.

11. Christine de Pizan, *Book of the City of Ladies*, p. 237.

12. The following quotations are from 'Eliduc', in Marie de France, *Lais*, ed. Busby, trans. Burgess, pp. 111–26.

13. Roxane Gay, *Bad Feminist* (London: Corsair, 2014).

14. Julian of Norwich, *Revelations*, ed. and trans. Windeatt, p. 1.

15. Robert Mills, 'Gender, Sodomy, Friendship, and the Medieval Anchorhold', *The Journal of Medieval Religious Cultures*, 36:1 (2010), pp. 1–27 (p. 7).

16. *Book of Margery Kempe*, ed. and trans. Windeatt, p. 40.

17. The anecdote of the three widows, *Book of Margery Kempe*, ed. and trans. Windeatt, pp. 47–50.

18. The worthy woman from Aachen, *Book of Margery Kempe*, ed. and trans. Windeatt, pp. 241–4.

19. *Book of Margery Kempe*, ed. and trans. Windeatt, p. 137.

20. *Book of Margery Kempe*, ed. and trans. Windeatt, pp. 17, 34 and 187.

21. The account of Margery in Hessle is from the *Book of Margery Kempe*, ed. and trans. Windeatt, pp. 131–3.

22. The account of Margery in Rome is from the *Book of Margery Kempe*, ed. and trans. Windeatt, pp. 94–6.

23. *A Tuscan Penitent: The Life and Legend of St Margaret of Cortona*, trans. and ed. Father Cuthbert (Omaha, NE: Patristic Publishing, 2020), p. 126.

24. *A Tuscan Penitent*, p. 74.

25. *A Tuscan Penitent*, p. 100.

26. *Paston Women*, ed. and trans. Watt, pp. 52–3.

27. *Paston Women*, ed. and trans. Watt, p. 116–17.

28. For more on Jeanne du Faut, see Tanya Stabler Miller, *The Beguines of Medieval Paris: Gender, Patronage, and Spiritual Authority* (Philadelphia, PA: University of Pennsylvania Press, 2014).

29. 'Emare', in *The Middle English Breton Lays*, ed. Anne Laskaya and Eve Salisbury (Kalamazoo, MI: Medieval Institute Publications, 1995).

30. Virginia Woolf, *A Room of One's Own*, ed. David Bradshaw and Stuart N. Clarke (New York: Wiley, 2015), p. 60.

SEVEN: . . . AND INFLUENCING PEOPLE

The epigraph is from *Lais of Marie de France*, ed. and trans. Waters, p. 79.

1. The following quotations are from 'Lanval', in Marie de France, *Lais*, ed. Busby, trans. Burgess, pp. 73–81.

2. 'Deuz Amanz', 'Bisclavret' and 'Milun', in Marie de France, *Lais*, ed. Busby, trans. Burgess, pp. 82–6, 68–72 and 97–105.

3. 'Hali Meidhad', in *Medieval English Prose for Women*, ed. Millett and Wogan-Browne, pp. 39–41.

4. This and the following quotations are taken from Eleanor Janega and Neil Max Emmanuel, *The Middle Ages: A Graphic History* (London: Bloomsbury, 2021), pp. 149–51.

5. Eustache Deschamps, 'Le Miroir de Mariage', in *Oeuvres complètes de Eustache Deschamps: Publiées d'après le manuscrit de la Bibliothèque Nationale*, ed. Gaston Raynaud (Paris: Firmin Didot, 1878–1903).

6. Christine de Pizan, *Book of the City of Ladies*, p. 31.

7. *The Commentaries of Pius II*, trans. Florence Alden Gragg (Northampton, MA: Department of History of Smith College, 1939–40), Book IX, p. 580.

8. William Shakespeare, *Richard III* (London: Arden, 2009), Act I, scene iii.

9. Christine de Pizan, *The Book of Deeds of Arms and of Chivalry*, trans. Sumner Willard, ed. Charity Cannon Willard (Philadelphia, PA: Pennsylvania State University Press, 1999).

10. Christine de Pizan, *Book of the City of Ladies*, p. 29.

11. Christine de Pizan, *Book of the City of Ladies*, pp. 195–6.

12. Christine de Pizan, *Treasure of the City of Ladies*, pp. 21–4.

13. Christine de Pizan, *Book of the City of Ladies*, p. 57.

14. Christine de Pizan, *Book of the City of Ladies*, p. 30.

15. Christine de Pizan, *Book of the City of Ladies*, pp. 35–6.

16. Christine de Pizan, *Book of the City of Ladies*, pp. 37–8.

17. Christine de Pizan, *Book of the City of Ladies*, p. 38.

18. Christine de Pizan, *Book of the City of Ladies*, p. 110.

19. Christine de Pizan, *Book of the City of Ladies*, pp. 134–6.

20. Christine de Pizan, *Christine's Vision*, p. 120.

21. Christine de Pizan, *Le livre des fais et bonnes meurs du sage roy Charles V*, ed. Suzanne Solente (Paris: Honoré Champion, 1936), Part 2, Chapter 21; 1:190.

22. Christine de Pizan, 'Les lamentacions sur les maux de la France', in *Oeuvres poétiques de Christine de Pizan*, 3 vols., ed. Maurice Roy (Paris, 1886–96).

23. 'The Tale of Joan of Arc', in *The Selected Writings of Christine de Pizan*, ed. Renate Blumenfeld-Kosinski (London: W. W. Norton, 1997).

24. For this account of Margery in Canterbury, see *Book of Margery Kempe*, ed. and trans. Windeatt, pp. 31–3.

25. *Book of Margery Kempe*, ed. and trans. Windeatt, p. 17.

26. *Book of Margery Kempe*, ed. and trans. Windeatt, p. 72.

27. For this account of the preaching friar, see *Book of Margery Kempe*, ed. and trans. Windeatt, pp. 150–55.

28. *Book of Margery Kempe*, ed. and trans. Windeatt, p. 155.

29. *Book of Margery Kempe*, ed. and trans. Windeatt, p. 97.

30. *Book of Margery Kempe*, ed. and trans. Windeatt, p. 249.

31. *Book of Margery Kempe*, ed. and trans. Windeatt, p. 51.

32. *Book of Margery Kempe*, ed. and trans. Windeatt, p. 43.

33. *Book of Margery Kempe*, ed. and trans. Windeatt, p. 127.

34. 1 Corinthians, 14.34, Holy Bible, Douay Rheims version.

35. *Book of Margery Kempe*, ed. and trans. Windeatt, p. 8.

36. *Book of Margery Kempe*, ed. and trans. Windeatt, pp. 56, 180, 165.

37. *The Book of Margery Kempe*, ed. Sanford B. Meech and Hope Emily Allen (London: Oxford University Press, 1940), p. lxiv.

38. This and the following quotations are from Julian of Norwich, 'Short Text', in *Revelations*, ed. and trans. Windeatt, pp. 9–10.

39. Julian of Norwich, 'Long Text', in *Revelations*, ed. and trans. Windeatt, p. 165.

40. *Life of Saint Audrey: A Text by Marie de France*, ed. and trans. June Hall McCash and Judith Clark Barban (Jefferson, NC: McFarland & Co., 2006), ll. 4624–5.

41. Christine de Pizan, *Treasure of the City of Ladies*, p. 168.

42. Stephen Scrope, *The Epistle of Othea Translated from the French Text of Christine de Pisan*, ed. C. F. Buhler (Oxford: Oxford University Press, 1970).

43. Simone de Beauvoir, *The Second Sex*, trans. H. M. Parshley (London: Jonathan Cape, 1997), p. 136.

EIGHT: HAVING IT ALL?

The epigraph is from Christine de Pizan, *L'Avision-Christine*, ed. Mary Louise Towner (Washington, DC: Catholic University of America, 1932), p. 163.

1. Aelred of Rievaulx, 'Rule of Life for a Recluse', in *Aelred of Rievaulx: Treatises and Pastoral Prayer*, ed. and trans. David Knowles (Kalamazoo, MI: Cistercian Publications, 1971), p. 46.

2. Woolf, 'A Room of One's Own', p. 3.

3. Julian of Norwich, 'Long Text', in *Revelations*, ed. and trans. Windeatt, p. 164.

4. Julian of Norwich, 'Long Text', in *Revelations*, ed. and trans. Windeatt, p. 161.

5. Julian of Norwich, 'Long Text', in *Revelations*, ed. and trans. Windeatt, p. 164.

6. Julian of Norwich, 'Short Text', in *Revelations*, ed. and trans. Windeatt, p. 15.

7. Julian of Norwich, 'Long Text', in *Revelations*, ed. and trans. Windeatt, p. 62.

8. The account of Margery's sick husband is from *Book of Margery Kempe*, ed. and trans. Windeatt, pp. 181–2.

9. See 'Schwester Katrei und Die Frau von ein-und-zwanzig Jahren / Sister Catherine and the Twenty-One-Year-Old Woman', in *Ladies, Whores, and Holy Women: A Sourcebook in Courtly, Religious, and Urban Cultures of Late Medieval Germany*, ed. and trans. Ann Marie Rasmussen and Sarah Westphal-Wihl (Kalamazoo, MI: Medieval Institute Publications, 2010), pp. 47–97.

10. 'How the Good Wife Taught Her Daughter', in *Codex Ashmole 61: A Compilation of Popular Middle English Verse*, ed. George Shuffelton (Kalamazoo, MI: Medieval Institute Publications, 2008).

11. 'How the Wise Man Taught His Son', in *Codex Ashmole 61*, ed. Shuffelton.

12. Christine de Pizan, *Treasure of the City of Ladies*, p. 42.

13. Christine de Pizan, *Treasure of the City of Ladies*, p. 129.

14. The translation is from P. P. A. Biller, 'Marriage Patterns of Women's Lives: A Sketch of a Pastoral Geography', in *Woman Is a Worthy Wight: Women in English Society, c. 1200–1500*, ed. P. J. P. Goldberg (Stroud: Alan Sutton, 1992), pp. 60–107 (p. 81).

15. María Elvira Mocholí Martínez, 'The Nursing Madonna in the Middle Ages: An Interdisciplinary Study', *Religions*, 14:568 (2023), 1–23 (p. 13).

16. 'How the Good Wife Taught Her Daughter', in *Codex Ashmole 61*, ed. Shuffelton.

17. *Medieval Writings on Secular Women*, ed. Skinner and van Houts, pp. 191–2.

18. 'Hali Meidhad', in *Medieval English Prose for Women*, ed. Millett and Wogan-Browne, pp. 33–5.

19. Christine de Pizan, *Christine's Vision*, pp. 120–21.

20. Christine de Pizan, *Christine's Vision*, p. 117.

21. Christine de Pizan, *Christine's Vision*, p. 129.

22. W. T. Waugh, 'Sir John Oldcastle (Continued)', *The English Historical Review*, 20:80 (1905), 637–58 (p. 656).

23. *Book of Margery Kempe*, ed. and trans. Windeatt, p. 127.

24. *Book of Margery Kempe*, ed. and trans. Windeatt, p. 136.

25. *Book of Margery Kempe*, ed. and trans. Windeatt, p. 118.

26. *Book of Margery Kempe*, ed. and trans. Windeatt, pp. 37–9.

27. *Book of Margery Kempe*, ed. and trans. Windeatt, p. 91.

28. Helen Gurley Brown, *Having It All: Love, Success, Sex, Money, Even If You're Starting with Nothing* (New York: Simon and Schuster, 1982).

NINE: DEATH

The epigraph is from *The Writings of Julian of Norwich*, ed. Watson and Jenkins, p. 131.

1. This account of Julian of Norwich's near-death experience is from 'Long Text', in *Revelations*, ed. Windeatt, pp. 41–3.

2. Translation from *Ancrene Wisse*, ed. and trans. Millett, p. 46.

3. See Rebecca Flynn, 'In Search of Isold de Heton: Biased Portrayals of the Medieval Anchoress and Their Continued Afterlife', *Magistra*, 26:1 (2020), 51–68.

4. Boccaccio, *Decameron*. Quoted in *Medieval Culture and Society*, ed. David Herlihy (New York: Harper and Row, 1968), pp. 351–8 (pp. 352–3).

5. Boccaccio, *Decameron*. Quoted in *Medieval Culture and Society*, ed. Herlihy, pp. 355–6.

6. Jean E. Jost, 'The Effects of the Black Death: The Plague in Fourteenth-Century Religion, Literature, and Art', in *Death in the Middle Ages and the Early Modern Times*, ed. Albrecht Classen and Marilyn Sandidge (Berlin: De Gruyter, 2016), pp. 193–238 (p. 193).

7. John of Reading, *The Black Death*, ed. and trans. Rosemary Horrox (Manchester: Manchester University Press, 1994), p. 87.

8. Boccaccio, *Decameron*. Quoted in *Medieval Culture and Society*, ed. Herlihy pp. 355–6.

9. 'The Sins of the Times', in *Political Poems and Songs I*, ed. Thomas Wright (Longman, Roberts and Green, 1859), pp. 279–81.

10. This and the following quotations are taken from Julian of Norwich, 'Long Text', in *Revelations*, ed. and trans. Windeatt, pp. 129–30.

11. This account of Margery's visit to Calvary is from *Book of Margery Kempe*, ed. and trans. Windeatt, pp. 71–4.

12. *Book of Margery Kempe*, ed. and trans. Windeatt, pp. 193–4.

13. *Book of Margery Kempe*, ed. and trans. Windeatt, p. 182.

14. *Book of Margery Kempe*, ed. and trans. Windeatt, p. 140.

15. *Book of Margery Kempe*, ed. and trans. Windeatt, p. 12.

16. *Book of Margery Kempe*, ed. and trans. Windeatt, p. 12.

17. 'A Rule of Life for a Recluse', in *Aelred of Rievaulx: Treatises and Pastoral Prayer*, ed. Knowles, p. 88.

18. Mary Frances Wack, *Lovesickness in the Middle Ages: The 'Viaticum' and Its Commentaries* (Philadelphia, PA: University of Pennsylvania Press, 1990), pp. 31–50.

19. *The Wooing of Our Lord and The Wooing Group Prayers*, ed. and trans. Catherine Innes Parker (London: Broadview Press, 2015), pp. 211–12.

20. *Book of Margery Kempe*, ed. and trans. Windeatt, pp. 24, 187.

21. 'Guigemar', in Marie de France, *Lais*, ed. Busby, trans. Burgess, p. 41.

22. 'Guigemar', in Marie de France, *Lais*, ed, Busby, trans. Burgess, pp. 43–55.

23. 'Equitan', in Marie de France, *Lais*, ed. Busby, trans. Burgess, pp. 56–60.

24. 'Prologue', in Marie de France, *Lais*, ed. Busby, trans. Burgess, pp. 41–2.

25. 'Chaitivel', in Marie de France, *Lais*, ed. Busby, trans. Burgess, pp. 105–8.

26. Christine de Pizan, *Cent Ballades*, trans. A.S. Kline (2020), https://www.poetryintranslation.com/PITBR/French/ChristineDePisanCentBallades.php [accessed 22 March 2024].

27. *Medieval Writings on Secular Women*, ed. Skinner and van Houts, pp. 264–7.

28. *The Ars Moriendi*, ed. and trans. Jeffrey Campbell (1995), https://ruor.uottawa.ca/server/api/core/bitstreams/58843413-d566-4425-a7a9-0ca2afd34432/content [accessed 22 March 2024].

29. 'Espurgatoire de Seint Patriz', in *Marie de France: Poetry*, ed. and trans. Gilbert, pp. 203–4.

30. 'Espurgatoire de Seint Patriz', in *Marie de France: Poetry*, ed. and trans. Gilbert, p. 209.

31. These torments and more can be found in 'Espurgatoire de Seint Patriz', in *Marie de France: Poetry*, ed. and trans. Gilbert, pp. 212–23.

32. *Book of Margery Kempe*, ed. and trans. Windeatt, p. 54.

33. *Book of Margery Kempe*, ed. and trans. Windeatt, p. 54.

34. 'Espurgatoire de Seint Patriz', in *Marie de France: Poetry*, ed. and trans. Gilbert, pp. 226–7.

35. *Book of Margery Kempe*, ed. and trans. Windeatt, p. 55.

36. Christine de Pizan, *Le chemin de longue étude*, trans. Andrea Tarnowski (Paris: Livre de Poche, 2020).

37. Julian of Norwich, 'Long Text', in *Revelations*, ed. and trans. Windeatt, p. 81.

38. Julian of Norwich, 'Long Text', in *Revelations*, ed. and trans. Windeatt, p. 72.

39. Julian of Norwich, 'Long Text', in *Revelations*, ed. and trans. Windeatt, p. 51.

CONCLUSION: AFTERLIFE

The epigraph is from Christine de Pizan, *Le livre de la cité des dames*, ed. and trans. Anne Paupert (Paris: Champion, 2023), p. 114.

1. 'Farewell Adultery: New Divorce Laws Come into Effect in April 2022', *Birkbeck Perspectives,* http://blogs.bbk.ac.uk/bbkcomments/2022/02/25/farewell-adultery-new-divorce-laws-come-into-effect-in-april-2022/ [accessed 24 March 2024].

2. Alexandra Topping, 'Sarah Everard Murder Sparked UK Reckoning with Male Violence', *The Guardian,* https://www.theguardian.com/uk-news/2022/mar/03/sarah-everard-sparked-uk-reckoning-with-male-violence-say-charities [accessed 24 March 2024].

3. Sian Cain, 'Women Are Happier without Children or a Spouse, Says Happiness Expert', *The Guardian,* https://www.theguardian.com/lifeandstyle/2019/may/25/women-happier-without-children-or-a-spouse-happiness-expert [accessed 24 March 2024].

4. Sophie Wingate, 'Half of Women Have Not Had a Child by Age of 30 for First Time Ever, Figures Show', https://www.independent.co.uk/news/uk/office-for-national-statistics-statistics-england-wales-b2002280.html [accessed 24 March 2024].

5. Adam Forrest, 'Jacob Rees-Mogg Attacks Abortion Rights as Cult of Death', *The Independent,* https://www.independent.co.uk/news/uk/politics/rees-mogg-abortion-death-cult-b2235286.html [accessed 24 March 2024].

6. Action Aid, 'Gender Pay Gap', https://www.actionaid.org.uk/our-work/womens-economic-rights/gender-pay-gap [accessed 24 March 2024].

7. Deloitte, 'Women @ Work 2023: A Global Outlook', https://www2.deloitte.com/content/dam/insights/articles/glob175810_global-women-at-work/Women_at_Work_2023.pdf [accessed 24 March 2024].

8. McKinsey & Company, 'Women in the Workplace 2023', https://www.mckinsey.com/featured-insights/diversity-and-inclusion/women-in-the-workplace [accessed 24 March 2024].

9. Shelley E. Taylor et al., 'Biobehavioural Responses to Stress in Females: Tend-and-Befriend, Not Fight-or-Flight', *Psychological Review*, 107:3 (2000), 411–29.

10. Natalie Morris, 'Women Have an Average of Six Best Friends in Their Life-time', *The Metro*, https://metro.co.uk/2019/02/18/women-average-six-best-friends-lifetime-8651367/ [accessed 24 March 2024].

11. 'Women with More Social Connections Have Better Survival', BreastCancer .org, https://www.breastcancer.org/research-news/social-connections-linked-to-better-survival [accessed 24 March 2024].

12. Amy Brittain, 'Me Too Movement', *Britannica,* https://www.britannica .com/topic/Me-Too-movement [accessed 24 March 2024].

13. Black Lives Matter, https://blacklivesmatter.com/about/ [accessed 24 March 2024].

14. Elsa Maishman, 'Jacinda Ardern and Sanna Marin Dismiss Claim They Met due to "Similar Age"', *BBC News,* https://www.bbc.co.uk/news/world-63803342 [24 March 2024].

15. Eleanor Ainge Roy, 'I'm Pregnant Not Incapacitated', *The Guardian,* https:// www.theguardian.com/world/2018/jan/26/jacinda-ardern-pregnant-new-zealand -baby-mania [accessed 24 March 2024].

16. 'BBC Apologises for Sexist Headline on Jacinda Ardern's Resignation', *NDTV World News,* https://www.ndtv.com/world-news/bbc-admits-error-over-jacinda-ardern-headline-after-sexism-backlash-3710000 [accessed 24 March 2024].

17. 'Pressure to Be a "Supermum" Affecting Women's Mental Health', BUPA, https://www.bupa.com/news/press-releases/2022/normal-mums [accessed 24 March 2024].

18. *Pregnant Then Screwed,* https://pregnantthenscrewed.com/ [accessed 24 March 2024].

SELECTED FURTHER READING

PRIMARY SOURCES

Ancrene Wisse, Guide for Anchoresses: A Translation, ed. and trans. Bella Millett (Exeter: University of Exeter Press, 2009).

The Book of Margery Kempe, trans. and ed. Barry Windeatt (London: Penguin, 1985).

Fabri, Felix, *The Book of the Wanderings of Brother Felix Fabri*, trans. and ed. Aubrey Stewart (London: Hanover, 1896).

The Fifteen Joys of Marriage, ed. and trans. Elisabeth Abbot (London: Orion, 1959).

France, Marie de, *The Lais of Marie de France*, ed. Keith Busby, trans. Glyn Burgess (London: Penguin, 1999).

'Hali Meidhad', in *Medieval English Prose for Women*, ed. Bella Millett and Jocelyn Wogan-Browne (Oxford: Clarendon Press, 1990), pp. 31–3.

'How the Good Wife Taught Her Daughter', in *Codex Ashmole 61: A Compilation of Popular Middle English Verse*, ed. George Shuffelton (Kalamazoo, MI: Medieval Institute Publications, 2008).

Julian of Norwich, *Revelations of Divine Love*, ed. and trans. Barry Windeatt (Oxford: Oxford University Press, 2015).

The Life of Christina of Markyate, trans. C. H. Talbot (Oxford: Oxford University Press, 2008).

Medieval Writings on Secular Women, ed. Patricia Skinner and Elisabeth van Houts (London: Penguin, 2011).

The Paston Women: Selected Letters, ed. and trans. Diane Watt (Woodbridge: D. S. Brewer, 2004).

Pizan, Christine de, *The Book of the City of Ladies*, ed. and trans. Rosalind Brown-Grant (London: Penguin, 1999).

———, *Christine's Vision*, ed. and trans. Glenda K. McLeod (London: Routledge, 2018).

———, *The Treasure of the City of Ladies*, ed. and trans. Sarah Lawson (London: Penguin, 2003).

The Trotula: An English Translation of the Medieval Compendium of Women's Medicine, ed. and trans. Monica Green (Philadelphia, PA: University of Pennsylvania Press, 2002).

A Tuscan Penitent: The Life and Legend of St Margaret of Cortona, trans. and ed. Father Cuthbert (Omaha, NE: Patristic Publishing, 2020).

'*Women's Secrets': A Translation of Pseudo-Albertus Magnus's 'De Secretus Mulierum', with Commentaries*, ed. Helen Rodnite Lemay (New York, SUNY Press, 1992).

SECONDARY SOURCES

Bale, Anthony, *A Travel Guide to the Middle Ages* (London: Viking, 2023).

Barron, Caroline, 'The 'Golden Age' of Women in Medieval London', *Medieval London: Collected Papers of Caroline M. Barron* (Kalamazoo, MI: Medieval Institute Publications, 2017), pp. 361–84.

Bennett, Judith, *Ale, Beer and Brewsters in England* (Oxford: Oxford University Press, 1999).

———, '"Lesbian-Like" and the Social History of Lesbianisms', *Journal of the History of Sexuality*, 9:1/2 (2000), 1–24.

Cadden, Joan, *Meanings of Sex Difference in the Middle Ages: Medicine, Science, and Culture* (Cambridge: Cambridge University Press, 1993).

Craig, Leigh Ann, *Wandering Women and Holy Matrons: Women as Pilgrims in the Later Middle Ages* (Leiden: Brill, 2009).

French, Katherine, 'The Material Culture of Childbirth in Late Medieval London and Its Suburbs', *Journal of Women's History*, 28:2 (2016), 126–48.

Goldberg, P. J. P., *Women in England, 1275–1525* (Manchester: Manchester University Press, 1995).

Janega, Eleanor, and Neil Max Emmanuel, *The Middle Ages: A Graphic History* (London: Bloomsbury, 2021).

Jones, E. A., *Hermits and Anchorites in England: 1200–1500* (Manchester: Manchester University Press, 2019).

McSheffrey, Shannon, *Marriage, Sex, and Civil Culture in Late Medieval London* (Philadelphia, PA: University of Pennsylvania Press, 2006).

Solberg, Emma Maggie, *Virgin Whore* (New York: Cornell University Press, 2018).

Turner, Marion, *The Wife of Bath: A Biography* (Oxford: Oxford University Press, 2023).

PLATE CREDITS

1. Marie de France, 1275–1300. Parchment. Collection of the Bibliothèque nationale de France, MS-3142, F. 256. Photo: History and Art Collection / Alamy Stock Photo.

2. *The Romance of the Rose,* by Guillaume de Lorris and Jean de Meun, fourteenth century. Parchment, leaves 255 × 188 mm. Bibliothèque nationale de France. Département des Manuscrits. Français 25526.

3. How Lancelot kissed Guinevere for the first time, from *Lancelot du Lac,* fifteenth century. Vellum. Bibliothèque nationale de France, Fr 118, F. 219v. Photo: Bibliotheque Nationale, Paris, France / Bridgeman Images.

4. Mother receiving her newly born baby in bed, from *Liber introductorium ad iudicia stellarum,* written by Guido Bonatti de Forlivio for Henry VII, c. 1490. Vellum. British Library, London, UK, Ar 66, F. 148. Photo: British Library, London, UK. From the British Library archive / Bridgeman.

5. Siware's lying-in at the birth of her son, Edmund, from John Lydgate's *Lives of Saints Edmund and Fremund,* c. 1434–44. British Library, London, UK, Harley MS 2278, F. 13v. Photo: British Library, London, UK. From the British Library archive / Bridgeman Images.

6. The Wife of Bath, illustration from Geoffrey Chaucer's *Canterbury Tales,* printed by William Caxton, c. 1422–91. Letterpress and woodcuts, book 9 $6\frac{1}{64}$ in. (25.3 × 18.1 cm). Yale Center for British Art, Paul Mellon Collection. Photo: Yale Center for British Art, Paul Mellon Collection, Bridgeman Images.

7. *Plate with Wife Beating Husband,* c. 1480. Copper alloy, wrought, 3 ⅞ × 20 ¼ in. (9.8 × 51.5 cm). Metropolitan Museum of Art, gift of Irwin Untermyer, 1964, 64.101.1499. Open Access.

8. Christine de Pizan writing at her desk, from *The Book of the Queen,* c. 1410–14. Vellum, gold leaf. British Library, London, UK, Harley MS 4431, F. 4r. Photo: British Library, London, UK. From the British Library archive / Bridgeman Images.

9. Christine de Pizan presenting her book to Queen Isabella of Bavaria, from *The Book of the Queen,* c. 1410–14. Vellum, gold leaf. British Library, London, UK, Harley 4431, F. 3r. Photo: British Library, London, UK. From the British Library archive / Bridgeman Images.

10. The wound of Christ, from *The Prayer Book of Bonne of Luxembourg, Duchess of Normandy.* Attributed to Jean Le Noir and Workshop, before 1349. Tempera, grisaille, ink, and gold on vellum, overall 5 ³⁄₁₆ × 3 ³⁄₁₆ × 1 ⅝ in. (13.2 × 9.7 × 4.2 cm). Metropolitan Museum of Art, the Cloisters Collection, 1969, 69.86. Open Access.

11. *Anchoress,* c. 1400–1410. Mixed material, book 400mm × 255 mm. The Parker Library, Corpus Christi College, Cambridge, CCCC MS 079, f. 95v. Photo: Images courtesy of the Parker Library, Corpus Christi College, Cambridge.

12. *Liber Trotile,* from *Book of Learned Medical Treatises with Some Additional Practical Texts* (Miscellanea Medica XVIII), early fourteenth century. Vellum and paper, book 9 ¹⁄₁₆ × 5 ⁴⁵⁄₆₅ in. (23 × 14.5 cm). Public Domain Mark. Source: Wellcome Collection. Pg 65. F. 33r.

13. Pilgrim badge in shape of female sexual organ surmounted by ithyphalli, c. 1375–1425. Lead, 1 ½ in. length. The British Museum, donated by Dr. George Witt, WITT.268. Photo: © The Trustees of the British Museum / Art Resource, NY.

14. Monsters from the land of the Merkites, from the *Livre des merveilles du monde,* c. 1410–12. Tempera on vellum. Bibliothèque Nationale, France, MS 2810, F. 29v. Photo: Bibliothèque Nationale, France / Bridgeman Images.

15. *Christ as the Man of Sorrows,* first quarter of the fifteenth century. Tempera with brown ink scribe lines, inscribed red ink, and gold and silver on parchment, 9 ¹¹⁄₁₆ × 6 ⁷⁄₁₆ in. (24.6 × 16.4 cm). The Barnes Foundation, Philadelphia, Pennsylvania. Photo: © Barnes Foundation / Bridgeman Images.

16. Purgatory, from the *Psalterium liturgicum,* thirteenth century. Vellum. Musée Condé, Chantilly, France, MS 10/1453. F. 110. Photo: © Musée Condé, Chantilly / Bridgeman Images.

17. *The Annunciation,* c. 1480–85. Jean Bourdichon. Tempera colors, gold, and ink, leaf: 6 ⁷⁄₁₆ × 4 ⁹⁄₁₆ in. (16.4 × 11.6 cm). The J. Paul Getty Museum, Los Angeles, MS. 6, 84.ML.746, F. 27.

18. St. Margaret or Marian of Antioch. Unknown artist. From the book of hours, possibly from Flanders, late fifteenth century. Bodleian Library collection, Oxford. Photo: The Print Collector / Alamy Stock Photo.

19. Joan of Arc, from Antoine Dufour's *Les vies des femmes célèbres,* c. 1505. Illuminated by Jean Pichore. Ink on vellum, 13 ²⁵⁄₆₄ × 8 ²¹⁄₃₂ × 1 ⅜ in. (34 × 22 × 3.5 cm). Musée Dobrée Nantes, France, MS 17, F. 76. Photo: Musée Dobrée Nantes, France / Bridgeman Images.

20. Miniatures from Boethius, *Consolation de philosophie,* about 1460–70. Coëtivy Master (Henri de Vulcop?), illuminator, Anicius Manlius Severinus Boëthius, author, Jean de Meun, translator, et al. Tempera colors, gold leaf, gold paint, and ink. The J. Paul Getty Museum, Los Angeles, MS. 42, 91. MS.11.

INDEX

childbirth, 12–14, 17, 21, 31, 34, 36, 41, 160,
    162, 186, 205–6
  birthing chambers, 19–27
  birthing girdles, 23–24
  Kempe, 9, 12–13, 196
childcare, 165–67
  breastfeeding, 165–66
  corporal punishment, 166
  motherhood, 165–66
Christina (Theodora) of Markyate,
    44–48, 50–51
Christine de Pizan, 15, 64, 93–98, 139,
    140–46, 156–57, 162, 187
  biographical details, 7–8, 93–96, 167–
    69, 172–73, 187
  biography of Charles V, 145
  and book production, 10, 95–96
  death, 190
  dreams, 120
  on extravagance, 20
  female friendship, 120–21
  and heaven, 193
  legacy, 156–57
  and marriage, 36–37, 38–41, 50–51,
    102–3, 141–42
  motherhood, 166–67
  patronage, 145
  on travel, 80–81
  visions, 192
  See also Book of the City of Ladies, The
    (Christine de Pizan)
Christine's Vision (Christine de Pizan), 93,
    167, 169
Clere, Elizabeth, 129
Codex Calixtinus, 75, 90
conduct poems, 163–64
contraception, 27–29, 48, 196–97
Cornificia (Roman poet), 98
courtly love, 5, 56–58, 64

Danse Macabre, 176–77
De Amore (On Love, Capellanus), 57
De institutione inclusarum (A Rule of Life
    for a Recluse, Aelred of Rievaulx),
    109–10, 118
  Passion Meditation, 182–83
'Deux Amanz, Les' (Marie de France), 136
divorce, 194–95

Edward III, King of England, 30, 60, 87
Edward IV, King of England, 61
Eleanor of Aquitaine, 5, 73, 83
Eliduc (Marie de France), 121–22
'Emaré' (poem), 131–32
Equitan (Marie de France), 57–58, 185
'Espurgatoire de Seint Patriz' (The Purga-
    tory of St Patrick, Marie de France), 191
Étienne du Castel, 7, 36–38, 93, 197

Fabri, Felix, 73–75, 78–79, 81, 85, 87,
    89–90
female friendship, 116–33, 198
  Christine de Pizan, 120–21
  Kempe, 124–25, 156–57
  Paston family, 128–29
  religion and, 123–27
  silk trade and, 129–31
femmes soles, 99–100

Galen, 15–6
gossip, 117–20
gossip songs (alehouse poems), 118–19, 123
  'A Talk of Ten Wives on Their Hus-
    bands' Ware', 118–19
'Guigemar' (Marie de France), 185
Guildeluec and Guilliadon (Marie de
    France), 121–23

hagiographies, 149–50, 153
Hali Meidhad (Holy Virginity), 19, 22,
    29–30, 44, 137, 167
Henry II, King of England, 5, 83
Henry IV, King of England, 61, 82,
    168–69
Henry V, King of England, 148, 169
Henry VI, King of Englan, 84, 139, 175
Hetzeldorfer, Katherina, 69
'How the Good Wife Taught Her Daugh-
    ter', 163–64, 166
'How the Wise Man Taught His Son',
    164
Hypsicratea, Queen, 64, 143

Isabeau of Bavaria, queen of France, 8, 33,
    141
Isabel de la Cavallería, 25–26
Isabella, Queen of England, 58, 60

Founded in 1893,
UNIVERSITY OF CALIFORNIA PRESS
publishes bold, progressive books and journals
on topics in the arts, humanities, social sciences,
and natural sciences—with a focus on social
justice issues—that inspire thought and action
among readers worldwide.

The UC PRESS FOUNDATION
raises funds to uphold the press's vital role
as an independent, nonprofit publisher, and
receives philanthropic support from a wide
range of individuals and institutions—and from
committed readers like you. To learn more, visit
ucpress.edu/supportus.